Notions of Violence and Ethnic Cleansing on the Eve of the First World War

South-East European History

Mihai Dragnea
Series Editor

Vol. 11

Panagiotis Delis

Notions of Violence and Ethnic Cleansing on the Eve of the First World War

The Balkan Wars of 1912-13

PETER LANG

Lausanne - Berlin - Bruxelles - Chennai - New York - Oxford

Library of Congress Cataloging-in-Publication Control Number: 2023039074

Bibliographic information published by the Deutsche Nationalbibliothek.
The German National Library lists this publication in the German
National Bibliography; detailed bibliographic data is available
on the Internet at http://dnb.d-nb.de.

Cover design by Peter Lang Group AG

ISSN 2768-7554 (print) ISSN 2768-7562 (online)
ISBN 9781636672267 (hardback)
ISBN 9781636672274 (ebook)
ISBN 9781636672281 (epub)
DOI 10.3726/b20638

© 2024 Peter Lang Group AG, Lausanne
Published by Peter Lang Publishing Inc., New York, USA
info@peterlang.com - www.peterlang.com

This publication has been peer reviewed.

CONTENTS

Acknowledgements   vii

Introduction   1

Chapter 1 A Longue Durée Borderland Crisis: 1804–1912   15

Chapter 2 Bekir Fikri of Grevena: Micro Dynamics of Violence in the
           Vilayet of Manastir   41

Chapter 3 An Undeclared War in the Sidelines: The Paramilitaries
           and the Locals   63

Chapter 4 An Undeclared War in the Sidelines: The Military
           Occupation   81

Chapter 5 Notions of Violence and Ethnic Cleansing in Thrace and
           the Pomak Christianization   107

Chapter 6 The Epirus Front: A Case of Counterinsurgency and the
           Albanian Factor   133

           Conclusions   163
           Bibliography   171

ACKNOWLEDGEMENTS

The journey for this book was long, challenging, and fulfilling. It started in Athens in 2011 and it continued in London, Budapest, and Vancouver. The final result is a revised version of my PhD thesis. The initial source of inspiration was Heather Jone's class "War Cultures" at the LSE. Along the way, I was lucky enough to meet great scholars and friends who gave me ideas and provoked me intellectually. First of all, I am heavily indebted to my supervisor Evdoxio Doxiadi who stepped in, in a very difficult situation and saved the day. He was always there to give his advice and he was genuinely interested in this project.

Simon Fraser University, my Alma matter proved to be a great place to do PhD work atop of the picturesque Burnaby Mountain. The History Department and the Hellenic studies program accommodated me institutionally while many great colleagues assisted me. Dimitris Krallis with his interesting ideas, Mark Leier with his unique insight about Canadian history, Thomas Kuehn with his intake and valuable feedback in Ottoman History. Special thanks are owned to my supervisory committee members, Megan MacKenzie and Theodora Dragostinova from Ohio State University, who gave wonderful ideas and helped to the revision of this thesis into a book. Ruth Anderson was always there to solve my administrative issues.

Needless to say, that the intellectual environment of Central European University shaped me as historian. The supervision of Tolga Esmer and Vladimir Petrovic built the foundations for this project. I also enjoyed the privilege to hear the thoughts of many prominent scholars for my work that were kind enough to invest time despite their heavy workload. Among them were: Isa Blumi, Ryan Gingeras, Nathalie Clayer, Cathie Carmichael, Eyal Ginio, John Paul Newman, Ramazan Hakki Oztan, Antonis Liakos, Vasilis Fouskas, Tetsuya Sahara, Stefan Papaioanou, Max Bergholz, Robert Gerwarth, Yura Konstantinova, Apostolos Papadimitriou, Othon Anastasakis, Hannes Grandits, and Stathis Kalyvas.

Special thanks also go to the wonderful archivists at the American School of Classical Studies and Historical and Ethnologic Society in Athens as well as the Military Archives in Veliko Tarnovo, Bulgaria. Vemund Aarbake deserves special mention. He believed and supported this idea from the very beginning as he was his own and for that I am grateful.

My best friend Chris Aliprantis was always there whenever needed. Our travels around the globe were very refreshing during the painful period of writing. Mihai Dragnea, the series editor, and Phil Dunshea kindly offered a home for my book, while Dimitar Tasic with his detailed comments contributed greatly to the final shaping. In this long journey my family was always by my side and helped me and believed in me as nobody else ever did. Christos my father, Dimitra my mother, and John my brother have a special place in my heart.

Last but certainly not least, my partner Maria. Since we have crossed our paths she has become a constant source of inspiration and made me believe in me at times when I was highly in doubt of myself. For that reason, and many more this book is devoted to her.

I take full responsibility for potential mistakes and I hope that my work will contribute somehow to the discussion for a very thorny topic which has created a lot of misconceptions about the Balkan region.

Athens, June 2023
To Maria…

INTRODUCTION

In February 2020 the Greek Government issued a decree ordering the immediate closure of the border with Turkey in the area of Evros in Western Thrace. This action took place in order to contain the constant influx of refugees coming from the war-ravaged countries of the Middle East. The timing of this decision came in a fragile moment in the midst of a humanitarian crisis that had started in 2015 and regenerated a fierce debate in the public sphere of Europe. While left-wing voices urged the EU to open borders and repeatedly cautioned their governments about the revival of the dark 1930s, growing conservative political movements across Europe have been pushing for stricter immigration policies and border protection along with their broader social agendas under the guise of abetting the national security threats these migrations have and will cause. Both sides have employed historical paradigms in order to prove the validity of their proposals, and the decade of the 1910s is at the center of attention once again. In Greece two narratives have prevailed in regard to this issue. The first one stresses that we must never forget that millions of Greeks who were in the same position when the Ottoman Empire collapsed and needed the assistance of the Greek nation, while the second counter argument warns that it was only because the refugees were ethnic Greeks (having the same language and religion) who escaped the wrath of Anatolian Muslims that the Greek nation mobilized to help them; hence, what is now expected of the Greeks is incomparable.

This discourse is not new for the Balkan Peninsula. Its roots could be traced back to the last years of the Ottoman era. More than a century ago, at the same spots which are closed now by the Greek Government, thousands of refugees were gathered from the European parts of the Ottoman Empire devastated by the Balkan Wars. This time, however, movement along the former imperial highways flowed east in the opposite direction: these Muslims wanted to reach the eastern provinces of the Ottoman Empire to find shelter. The 1912–3 Balkan Wars constituted a landmark in this process that informed state formation throughout the region and intensified a wave of trans-regional migration. This wave started in the eighteenth-century wars between the Ottoman and the Christian Empires, and accelerated in the Crimean (1853–6) and the Russo-Ottoman War of 1877–8. Although the 1912–3 conflicts did not have the duration of WWI they brought dramatic changes in the peninsula as well as in the wider Near East. This episode constituted a key turning point that opened the last chapter of the Ottoman Empire as a multi-ethnic entity and constituted a pivotal event for the trajectory of the Eastern Question.

In the current book I attempt to dig deeper into some specifics of this crucial transition in order to place the Balkan Wars into a broader context. In particular, the two main questions that I address are: what the Balkan wars can teach us about violence in war and how the local, ground level looks as opposed to overarching narratives of state violence and the role of governments. In this project, I aim to unveil and evaluate certain patterns of behaviour during an era of mass violence by offering a transnational study on the mechanisms of violence and ethnic cleansing during the Balkan Wars of 1912–3 in the regions that encompassed the former vilayets of Jannina (Epirus), Macedonia, and Thrace. The broader goal of this study is twofold. First, is to contribute to the better understanding of a crucial episode in modern Balkan history and the history of the Near East. Second, is to incorporate these wars into the literature about the "Greater War" (1912–1923) which challenges the Western Eurocentric hegemony of the historiography on WWI.[1]

---

1   Robert Gerwarth, *The Vanquished: Why the First World War Failed to End, 1917–1923* (London: Penguin, 2016); Tomas Balkelis, War, Revolution, and Nation-Making in Lithuania, 1914–1923 (Oxford University Press. Oxford 2018); Jay Winter, The Day the Great War Ended, 24 July 1923: The Civilianization of War (Oxford University Press: Oxford 2022); Jochen Böhler, Civil War in Central Europe, 1918–1921: The

One of the things that I pertain in this book is to see the Balkan Wars as a prelude for the Great War, but for different reasons from those that traditional literature has suggested.[2] This conflict, which was part and parcel of a story about imperial aftershocks, porous borderlands, rise of warlords, and the emergence of new states, has a line of continuity with WWI in East Central Europe. The way to show this continuity is by comparing similarities and differences of the Balkan conflicts and the First World War such as patterns associated with violence, social engineering techniques, and occupation regimes. This work builds in an already established tradition that analyzed how the Balkan states functioned as a testing ground for practices of ethnic homogenization that were followed by major European powers.[3]

My logic follows Norman Naimark's idea who argues that ethnic cleansing has two distinctive characteristics: it is a modern European phenomenon but it is also related with the social conditions of each territory.[4] For the particular case, the essential preconditions that informed the historical background before the wars were: the creation of new nation states competing for space, the fluidity of imperial borderlands, the ineffectiveness of the Ottoman authorities to patrol its fragile border zone, the mixed human geography, and the emergence of non-state actors.[5] Throughout the pages of this book I indent to show that ethnic cleansing is not a straightforward process and the intensity as well as quality of violence depended on a variety of factors such as: the affiliations of the locals, the pre-war symbiosis of neighbouring ethnic groups, the stance of the military authorities, and the goals of the belligerent states.

In terms of terminology: according to the United Nations (UN) there is no clear definition due to non-recognition of ethnic cleansing as an

Reconstruction of Poland (Oxford University Press: Oxford, 2018); Tomasz Pudłocki-Kamil Ruszała, eds., Postwar Continuity and New Challenges in Central Europe, 1918–1923: The War That Never Ended (London: Routledge, 2012).

2 Dominic Geppert and William Mulligan, eds., *The Wars Before the Great War* (Cambridge: Cambridge University Press, 2015); James Pettifer and Tom Buchanan, eds., *War in the Balkans: Conflict and Diplomacy before World War I* (London: IB Tauris, 2016); Richard C. Hall, *The Balkan Wars* (London: Routledge, 2000).

3 Michael Schwartz, *Ethnische „Säuberungen" in der Moderne* (Berlin, Boston: De Gruyter, 2013), 235–318.

4 Norman Naimark, *Fires of Hatred, Ethnic Cleansing in Twentieth-Century Europe* (Harvard: Harvard University Press, 2002).

5 Omer Bartov-Eric D. Weitz (eds.), *Shatterzone of Empires: Coexistence and Violence in the German, Habsburg, Russian and Ottoman Borderlands* (Bloominghton: Indiana University Press, 2013).

independent crime by International law. The UN commission that worked in Yugoslavia came out with the conclusions that ethnic cleansing could be described as: (...) (a policy) renders an area ethnically homogeneous by using force or intimidation to remove persons of given groups from the area. "(...) a purposeful policy designed by one ethnic or religious group to remove by violent and terror-inspiring means the civilian population of another ethnic or religious group from certain geographic areas."[6] Historian Mark Mazower defines it as: "a combination of massacre and expulsions, deliberate acts of terror, and looting, social humiliation, and mass rape".[7]

Admittedly, while these elements are inherent to this process, they are mainly connected to state sponsored violence. In this book, I would like additionally to point out that this complex phenomenon generates bottom up forms of violence that function as supplementary to state. For this reason, I think it is fruitful to examine these traditional forms in tandem with their by-products by investigating two dimensions: the dynamics of the military occupation and the various notions of inner communal violence.

The locals in the areas under study by no means remained passive and were involved directly or indirectly in numerous ways. In Epirus, Macedonia, and Thrace segments of the native population took part and assisted or even opposed new occupation regimes and ratified peace treaties. Two crucial components I believe greatly determined this outcome. The first was connected to prewar relations and the second to the opportunities and challenges of conflict. These relations, whether hostile or friendly, quite often were motivators determining certain behaviours during the war. Although these notions of violence cannot be described strictly as a civil war because it involved different ethno-religious groups, the assumption yet is not irrelevant. Hundreds of villages in Rumeli inhabited by Muslims and Christians of various doctrines had developed intimate relations. These tendencies were augmented by the new element that the Balkan Wars brought regarding to the conduct of war. It was in these crucial conflicts that regular armies assisted by irregulars, were mobilized for an expansive campaign and systematically waged a war to "hostile" local populations. While the usage of irregulars was certainly not something new for the Ottoman Empire, it was the first time that this type of warfare was combined with modern technology and the effectiveness of the

---

6 https://www.un.org/en/genocideprevention/ethnic-cleansing.shtml, date accessed 27/11/2020.

7 Mark Mazower, Review Essay *Violence and the State* in the Twentieth Century, *The American Historical Review* 107, no. 4, (2002), 1162.

state machinery and created a fertile ground for practices that could not have been exercised in peacetime. This laboratory in turn created new "technologies of violence" and a knowhow that would be applied in the interwar period against "foreigners". These practices additionally reflected the way that the Balkan states tried to exploit the locals' divisions through a policy of divide et impera.

Greece and Bulgaria are selected as main pillars for this study. The main reasons for this selection were two: (i) the existence of a long lasting rivalry over Macedonia in the wake of the twentieth century. This rivalry which was regenerated in the sidelines in the early stages of the Balkan war is one of the keys to understand deeper the mechanisms of ethnic cleansing and wartime violence, (ii) these countries were allies in the First Balkan War and enemies in the second. The Serbian and Montenegrin cases are not discussed here something that I invite scholars to do so in future researches in order to incorporate an essential dimension of the war. The main reasons that led to this exclusion are primarily linguistic and the fact that Serbia and Greece seemed to play a similar role in juxtaposition to Bulgaria, while Montenegro had a more limited scope in the wars.

$$***$$

The task to analyze wartime violence is very challenging. As Sinisa Malecevic argues, war constitutes a product of social development and it is dependent on the complex relations of human beings. One of its profound impacts is that it could be a catalyst for social transformation.[8] Michael Mann in his classical study tried to understand ethnic cleansing by classifying nine categories of perpetrators: ideological, bigoted, violent, fearful, careerist, materialist, disciplined, comradely, and bureaucratic.[9] This multiplicity of actors is systematized also in the edited work Question of Genocide which categorizes three levels of historical subjects: the very top (state level), the meso (regional officers, police, military), and the basic which represents the lower strata of the society.[10] The interconnection among the three levels shows the different sets

---

8 Sinisa Malecevic, *The Rise of Organized Brutality: A Historical Sociology of Violence* (Cambridge: Cambridge University Press, 2017), 142.

9 Michael Mann, *The Dark Side of Democracy: Explaining Ethnic Cleansing* (Cambridge: Cambridge University Press, 2005), 27–30.

10 Ronald Grigor Suny, Fatma Müge Göçek, Norman M. Naimark, eds., A *Question of Genocide: Armenians and Turks at the End of the Ottoman Empire* (Oxford: Oxford University Press, 2011).

of agencies and how actions from the top level influence the lower and vice versa. Benjamin Lieberman expanded this problematic by discussing the role of bystanders and how the war compelled individuals to switch roles being both victims and perpetrators.[11]

On another level, Christian Gerlach's pioneer concept of the"extremely violent societies" offered a useful tool to theorize the complexity of violent dynamics in periods of war. In order to be considered a society as violent it needs to adhere to the following premise: various groups become victims of mass physical violence in a process where state organs and a diversity of actors partake with multiple motivations.[12] This idea broadened the scope of analysis including a problematic about the different nature of perpetrators as well as their various incentives to commit violent acts. Philip Therr, on the other hand, made a crucial remark on this issue maintaining that when we analyze ethnic cleansing we should always be aware that perpetrators and victims cannot be divided in a binary way. In many occasions refugees exercised and endured physical violence because the war forced them to take sides.[13]

Another perspective to look at these dynamics is offered by works that examine the recent historical background and the role of intimacy in local communities. Studies from civil wars are particularly helpful and show that although military necessities are a factor that influences the levels of violence, it is by no means the only one.[14] Prewar cleavages should be considered too.[15] Victimization before the war rendered civilians in promoting violence against their co-patriots because they identify the latter as the ones that perpetrated violence in the previous period.[16] Moreover, the role of primary groups (family members, neighbours, and friends) is essential for the understanding of what is often referred to as "intimate violence" that shows how personal relations

---

11 Benjamin Lieberman, *Terrible Fate: Ethnic Cleansing in the Making of Modern Europe* (Maryland: Rowman and Littlefield, 2013).

12 Christian Gerlach, Extremely Violent Societies: An Alternative to the Concept of Genocide, *Journal of Genocide Research* 8, no. 4 (2006): 460.

13 Philipp Ther, *The Dark Side of Nation State: Ethnic Cleansing in Modern Europe* (New York and Oxford: Berghahn Books, 2014), 8.

14 Stathis Kalyvas, *The Logic of Violence in Civil War* (Cambridge: Cambridge University Press, 2007), 330–363.

15 Domenech Herreros, Pre-war Grievances and Violence Against Civilians in Civil Wars. Evidence from the Spanish Civil War in Catalonia, 2018, *International Journal of Conflict and Violence*, 12 (2018): 1–20.

16 Laia Balcells, "Rivalry and Revenge: Violence against Civilians in Conventional Civil Wars", *International Studies Quarterly* 54 (2010): 307.

affect people's violent behaviour by mingling private incentives with political.[17] The level of politicization of the locals and the role of intimacy are key analytical tools that I make use in order to examine the different nuances of ethnic cleansing and inner communal violence.

Relevant literature in a Balkan/Ottoman framework has made significant advances the past decades placing violence within a wider political, economic, and social context. Ipek Yosmaoglu's micro study of the kaza of Serres in the first decade of the twentieth century explained how local violence functioned as a qualitative factor for the hardening of ethnic boundaries and challenged traditional views that perceived violence in Ottoman Macedonia as a product solely of ethnic tensions.[18] A similar approach is offered by historian Max Berghotz in another micro study that concerns an incident that took place in the small community in Bosnia during WW2. Specifically, the author shows how an event in the micro level triggered violent dynamics that the meso and macro levels did not pursue shaping identities in many ways.[19] Theodora Dragostinova one the other hand dealt with strategies of survival of populations that were caught amidst the Greco-Bulgarian conflict in the first half of the twentieth century by illustrating how survival and wellbeing navigated these people to twist between different nationalities depending on the circumstances.[20] Janet Klein offered a fresh perspective to socio-economic aspects of the late Ottoman Empire by investigating the role of the Kurdish chieftains of the Hamidiye Cavarly Regiment who became important brokers and opted for a complex set of historical contingencies that do not comply with linear national identities.[21] On another level, Hannes Grandits and Nathalie Clayer outlined how the term loyalty instead of ethnicity might be a more suitable analytical category in describing certain attitudes in wartime. During this period, people are forced to take sides and many times initiatives coming

---

17 Joce Marco-Mercedes Rodrigo, Irregular War. Local Community and Intimate Violence in Spain (1939–1952), *European History Quarterly* 49, no. 2 (2019): 231–232.

18 Ipek Yosmaoğlu, Blood Ties: Religion, *Violence and the Politics of Nationhood in Ottoman Macedonia* (Ithaca, NY: Cornell University Press, 2014), 5.

19 Max Bergholz, *Violence as a Generative Force: Identity, Nationalism, and Memory in a Balkan Community* (Ithaca, NY: Cornell University Press, 2016), 6, 311.

20 Theodora Dragostinova, *Between Two Motherlands. Nationality and Emigration among-the Greeks of Bulgaria, 1900–1949* (Ithaca, NY: Cornell University Press, 2011), 3.

21 Janet Klein, *The Margins of Empire. Kurdish Militias in the Ottoman Tribal Zone* (Stanford: Stanford University Press, 2011), 10–13.

from the lower level shape policy decision making.[22] Mark Biondich underlined another dimension arguing that the popular violence in the Balkans was rooted in religious and social grievances and the outbreak of war could not have left local communities neutral.[23] Cathie Carmichael finally underlined the significance of the historical background arguing that, although the ideas that inspired violent practices originated from Europe, they also entailed an inherent dimension with a symbolical meaning.[24]

The centennial for the Balkan Wars marked also a renewed interest and several conferences, edited volumes, and journal articles added new knowledge to the existing literature.[25] Still, some crucial aspects remain underresearched. One of the most important in my opinion has to do with the absence of a transnational and comparative study that inspects the mechanisms of violence and ethnic cleansing in the main war theatres. Although some works analyze the violence that erupted they have the main drawback that they sometimes treat the locals as passive objects without attributing them proper agency.[26] On another level, some recent works have a politicized

22 Nathalie Clayer, Hannes Grandits, Robert Pichler, eds., *Conflicting Loyalties in the Balkans. The Great Powers, the Ottoman Empire and Nation Building* (London: IB Tauris, 2011), 6, 11.

23 Mark Biondich, *The Balkans: Revolution, War, and Political Violence Since 1878* (Oxford: Oxford University Press, 2011), 42.

24 Cathie Carmichael, *Ethnic Cleansing in the Balkans. Nationalism and the Destruction of Tradition* (London: Routledge, 2003), 109.

25 Hakan Yavuz-Isa Blumi, eds., *War and Nationalism. The Balkan Wars, 1912–1913, and Their Sociopolitical* Implications, (US: University of Utah Press 2013); Sabine Rutar-Katrin Boeckh, eds., *The Balkan Wars from Contemporary Perception to Historic Memory* (London: Palgrave, 2017); *The Wars of Yesterday. The Balkan Wars and the Emergence of Modern Military Conflict, 1912–1913. Experience, Perception, Remembrance* (New York: Bergham Books, 2018); Dimitris Stamatopoulos, ed., *Balkan Nationalism(s) and the Ottoman Empire* (Istanbul: ISIS Press, 2015) II; Eyal Ginio, *The Ottoman Culture of Defeat* (Oxford: Oxford University Press, 2016); Dogan Cetinkaya, "Atrocity, Propaganda and the Nationalization of the Masses in the Ottoman Empire during the Balkan Wars (1912–13)", *International Journal of Middle East Studies* 46 (2014): 759–778; Eugene Michail, "Western Attitudes to War in the Balkans and the Shifting Meanings of Violence, 1912–91", *Journal of Contemporary History*, 47 (2012): 219; Enika Abazi, and Albert Doja, "Time and Narrative: Temporality, Memory, and Instant History of Balkan Wars", *Time and Society* 27, no. 2 (2018): 239–272; Ramazan H. Öztan, "Point of No Return? Prospects of Empire after the Ottoman Defeat in the Balkan Wars (1912–13)". *International Journal of Middle East Studies*, 50 (1), 65–84.

26 Stefan Papaioanou, *Balkan Wars between the Lines: Violence and Civilians in Macedonia, 1912–1918* (PhD Thesis: University of Maryland, 2012).

inclination following the logic of who was the initial perpetrator.[27] Others recycle old stereotypes outdated in recent literature.[28]

On the contrary, traditional literature of the Balkan states has not developed in the same degree. Ethnocentric interpretations that based their assumptions on a deeper historical continuum were problematic because they mainly served pre-constructed narratives of the uninterrupted existence of nations in the longue durée and failed to grasp the mechanisms of transition from empires to nation states.[29] Greek historiography has made some timid steps adopting novel approaches such as recent trends on the study of ethnicity, but still the social aspects of the war have not attracted great attention. Serbian historiography, by contrast remained more nation state oriented recycling older interpretations.[30] In the Bulgarian case the richness of the production is not necessarily reflected by analytical vigour or innovation.[31] The central point of a number of Bulgarian historians is that during the Balkan wars the Serbian and the Greek state waged an undeclared war against the Bulgarian element in their zones of occupation.[32] The main problem of this view is that by considering all locals as ethnic Bulgarians it does not take into consideration the different nuances of ethnic affiliation and makes it almost impossible to discern the dynamics from the bottom up and the interaction of the military with the locals. However, there is a level of validity in this assertion. Indeed, Greece and Serbia waged a war to the locals mobilizing different

27 Hakan Yavuz, and Hakan Erdagöz, "The Tragedy of the Ottomans: Muslims in the Balkans and Armenians in Anatolia", *Journal of Muslim Minority Affairs*, 39 (2019): 3.
28 Paul Mojzes, *Balkan Genocides: Holocaust and Ethnic Cleansing in the Twentieth Century* (Maryland: Rowman & Littlefield Publishers, 2015).
29 See for example the history of the Balkan Wars written by an institution related to the Army in the Balkan statis (Amy History Directorate, GES/DIS, *Epitomi Istoria ton Valkanikon Polemon*) and for the Bulgarian Side: Bozhidar Dimitrov, *Istinskata Istoriya na Valkanskata Voyna* (Sofia: 168 Tsasa, 2007).
30 Naoum Kauchev, Notis on Some Trends in Serbian and Greek Historiography of the First Balkan War, *Etudes Balkaniques*, 2 (2013): 37–43; Dalibor Jovanovski, "Greek Historiography and the Balkan Wars", in *On Macedonian Matters: From the Partition and Annexation of Macedonia in 1913 to the Present. A Collection of Essays on Language, Culture and History,* ed. Jim Hlavac-Victor Friedman (Munchen: Verlag Otto Sagner, 2015), 31–46.
31 For an analytical overview of Bulgarian literature see: Bisser Petrov and Svetlozar Eldarov, "Institutionalizing Memory: 100 Years Balkan War Studies in Bulgaria", *Etudes Balkaniques*, 2 (2013): 7–36.
32 The most representative example: Georgi Genov, *Sa Protivata na Balgarite ot Belomorska Makedonija Srešáu Grackoto Igo 1912–1916* (Sofia: Veritas et Pneuma, 1998).

techniques in an attempt to homogenize places that were not homogenous. In this demographic "Hobbesian war" Bulgaria participated in the same extend and precisely here lies one of the key explanatory frameworks that this book uses to explore the dynamics of violence: that an undeclared war took place behind the front lines. This war, was as important as in the battlefields, and determined the intensity and quality of violence. By shedding new light to this "invisible war in the sidelines" it is possible to contribute to the better understanding of the mechanisms of violence and ethnic cleansing in general and the historical circumstances that generated it in the Balkans in particular.

The current book belongs to the tradition developed by scholars working on a Balkan/Ottoman regional framework. The main lacuna that I aspire to cover is that relevant works have either a micro or a wider geographical focus covering more extended time periods. Instead, the focus here is regional examining thoroughly the nine-month experience of war. In a living space that spanned from the Dardanelles Straits to the Ionian Sea and from the Rhodopes to the mountainous range of Pindos, I explore different responses to the challenges of conflict by using case studies from various places within the same imperial territory. In this way, I try to grasp further the qualitative premises for violence and ethnic cleansing by showing the intertwining web that connects the war havoc and the pre-existing climate.

The methodological approach that I adopt entails a combination of transnational and the so called new military history. Transnational history has been defined according to some scholars as a "realm of interdependence that supersedes national sovereignty and boundaries".[33] German historian Ute Frevert described warfare as "inter- and transnational events par excellence" because no other phenomenon, apart from migration, brings so many people in such close contact.[34] Historian Jürgen Osterhammel argued that: "Transnationalism" refers to a special category of social relations that unfold in tension with and in contradiction to the assertion of "national sovereignties".[35] For this case, the special category of tenuous social relations is

---

33 Deborah Cohen, Maura O'Connor, eds., *Comparison and History: Europe in Cross-National Perspective* (New York–London: Routledge, 2004).

34 Ute Frevert, *Europeanizing German History. Eighteenth Annual Lecture of the GHI, November 18, 2004*, 12. https://www.paris-iea.fr/en/events/la-guerre-comme-zone-de-contact-au-xixe-siecle-2.

35 Jürgen Osterhammel, "Transnational, 'History of Society: Continuity or New Departure?'", in *Comparative and Transnational History*, Central European Approaches and New Perspectives, ed. Heinz-Gerhard Haupt and Jürgen Kocka (New York, Oxford: Berghahn Books 2009), 46.

the interaction of the civil and military spheres that materialized within the Greek and Bulgarian sovereignties which were on the making in a period of wartime.

In regard to new military history, I follow the ideas developed by Peter Karsten who argues that the purpose of new military history is the study of the internal dynamics of military and civil relations with a focus on the relationship between military systems and the greater society.[36] By analyzing in a transnational context the social and cultural conditions I aim to present a more nuanced picture of the fluidity of what occurred in the local level, in rural as well as urban areas. In contrast to an existing literature on the political, diplomatic, and military history of the Balkan Wars, this story deals with the people that fought in these wars, officers, soldiers, and irregulars along with the vast groups of civilians who were caught in the cross fires.[37] The examination of the entangled experiences of the various actors, I believe, is a more suitable way to comprehend local complexities and to articulate how these loyalties were shaped by conflict.

To illustrate this I utilize numerous sources from a number of institutions and archives. I discovered these important historical documents during a series of very productive archival trips in Greece, Bulgaria, Austria, and the United Kingdom while the research languages include: Greek, Bulgarian German and English. The sources are: consular reports, foreign correspondences, state, and military archives, private collections, and the foreign press. The Greek Ministry of Foreign Affairs, the Army History Directorate, and the Central State Archives, located in Athens provided precious information for the Greek side. For the Bulgarian administration, material from the Central State Archives, the Bulgarian Academy of Sciences in Sofia, and the Central Military Archive at the city of Veliko Tarnovo were utilized. Very important material also existed at the British National Archives (Kew) and at the National Archives of Austria. Last but not least, the Hellenic Literature Archive, the Historical and Ethnological Society, the Gennadius Library, and

---

36 Cited in: Johana Bourke New Military History, in *Palgrave Advances in Modern Military History*, ed. Hughes M., and Philpott W. J. (London: Palgrave Macmillan, 2006).

37 Richard C. Hall, "The Next War: The Influence of the Russo-Japanese War in Southeastern Europe and the Balkan Wars of 1912–1913", *The Journal of Slavic Military Studies*, 17, no. 3 (2004): 563–577; Edward J. Erickson "From Kirkilisse to the Great Offensive Turkish Operational Encirclement Planning, 1912–22", *Middle Eastern Studies* 40, no. 1 (2004): 45–64; Ernst Christian Helmreich, *The Diplomacy of the Balkan Wars, 1912–1913* (Harvard University Press, 1938).

the Benaki Archive in Athens contained valuable collections of letters and memoirs from combatants who fought during the Balkan Wars. These sources (published and unpublished) are representative of a variety of categories and range from ordinary soldiers who fought in the Epirus front during the First Balkan War, to state officials who ended up in Thrace in the Second. These individuals came not only from the Greek and the Bulgarian state but also from other parts of the Ottoman Empire and abroad. Although I am aware that documents of that nature contain retrospective elements and they twist sometimes between the historical and the literary genre they still deserve scholarly attention. A cross-examination of official and unofficial sources maybe used to better synthesize a multi-dimensional approach.

**

Regarding the structure. This book is consisted of six chapters. The first is introductory and provides necessary background information by analyzing main developments in the peninsula since 1804 with a particular focus on the Macedonian issue after 1878 in order to facilitate readers who are not familiarized with the history of the Balkans.

The second chapter focuses on the persona of Bekir Fikri of Grevena in order to show how a pre-existing local strife could intensify violent dynamics involving a plethora of actors. Bekir Aga was a trained military officer who participated in the war in Yemen in 1911. A year before the Balkan wars he was involved in the political assassination of the local Greek metropolitan which triggered a series of events. During the wars he served as military commander in the kaza of Grevena and led an irregular corps who fought against a heterogeneous group of forces, paramilitaries, and the army alike. This case study I hope may help us trace the origins and modus operandi of the infamous Special Organization (SO) and to realize how challenging is in warfare to identify the incentives for violence when the lines are blurred between the local, the national, and the personal.[38]

Chapter 3 follows the process of how numerous groups of civilians took up arms, supported, resisted or became bystanders to the advancing armies of the Balkan states. Particular focus is given to the analysis of paramilitary formations such as the Internal Macedonian Revolutionary Organization (IMRO),

---

38 The SO was the Special Service of the Ottoman Empire that was created by Enver Eby to organize subversive movements within enemy territory and was linked to the Armenian genocide. See: Polat Safi, "History in the Trench: The Ottoman Special Organization – Teşkilat-ı Mahsusa", *Middle Eastern Studies*, 48 (2012): 89–106.

the Greek "Scouts", and the Bulgarian Comitadji which acted as auxiliaries units, and were comprised by old irregular fighters. The analysis of the interaction of the IMRO, the Scouts, and the comitadjis with the locals and military authorities, as well as their ambiguous role during the First Balkan War, aims to revisit the origins of the Second Balkan War which regional historiography has solely approached it as the outcome of decision making in high politics.

Chapter 4 addresses the military administration of the captured areas by Greece and Bulgaria. From the city of Florina in the West to the city of Drama in the East I closely examine occupation patterns and the natives' responses. In particular, the areas that the armies of Greece and Bulgaria contacted each other became shatter zones[39] and generated an undeclared war in the sidelines which contributed to the radicalization of violent practices in the Second Balkan War. The most central aspect of this chapter is to highlight regional variations of violence and the differences between the rural mainland and the urban centers.

The fifth chapter examines Thrace a place has not attracted comparable attention to that of Macedonia. Although ethnic cleansing and Pomak Christianization are topics that have been somehow discussed in literature, they have not yet been properly contextualized.[40] Similar to Macedonia, Thrace was populated by a mixed synthesis. The Bulgarian advance and treatment of locals in the First Balkan War opened a spiral of violence which led to reprisals. One of my aims is to substantiate the approach of Eyal Ginio who argued that the changing discourse during the First Balkan War that gradually targeted Christian groups as traitors paved the way for ethnic cleansing. On another level, I attempt to place the Pomak Christianization and the short lived political experiment of the "Republic of Giumiurdzhina" within the context of the Balkan Wars.[41]

The last chapter on the Janina vilayet discusses one of the most overlooked territories of the Ottoman Empire. The Epirus front was among others a battleground between irregular forces and resembled to a counter insurgency

39 Contisted territories not clearly controlled by any power, that were about to face the most catastrophic consequences of nation state formation.
40 Fatme Myuhtar-May, *Identity, Nationalism, and Cultural Heritage under Siege* (Leiden: Brill, 2014).
41 Eyal Ginio, "Paving the Way for Athnic Cleansing. Eastern Thrace during the Balkan Wars", in *Shatterzone of Empires, Coexistence and Violence in the German, Habsburg, Russian and Ottoman Borderlands*, ed. Omer Bartov and Eric Weitz (Bloominghton: Indiana University Press, 2013), 283–297.

type of warfare (one of the regional differences with Macedonia).[42] The battle-mosaic of Epirus that included bands, local notables, and the regular army not only shaped the trajectory of the Albanian question but also defined relations between Greece and Albania. Hence, in this in this chapter apart from the dynamics of violence, I make an effort to add a new piece to the historical background that led to the ethno genesis of Albania by outlining the main premises that gave birth to the so called "Northern Epirus/Southern Albanian question".

***

A note on terms: The Ottoman administrative division refers to the term *vilayet* as a larger administrative area which is equal to a province. A *vilayet* is sub divided to *sancaks*, which were composed of *kazas*. *Rumeli* refers to the European parts of the Ottoman Empire. Comitadji is an irregular associated with Bulgaria and the IMRO. *Armed villagers* describe locally formed militias. For cities and villages I use the name from the Ottoman period and in parenthesis the contemporary that corresponds to the nation that belongs now, and the last name thereafter.

---

42 Hall, *The Balkan Wars*; Edward Erickson, *Defeat in Detail. The Ottoman Army in the Balkan Wars* (Praeger 2003).

· 1 ·

A LONGUE DURÉE BORDERLAND
CRISIS: 1804–1912

Spyros Melas (1882–1966) was a journalist and influential intellectual affiliated with the most prominent statesman of Modern Greece, Prime Minister
Eleftherio Venizelo. Immediately after the Young Turk Revolt, in July 1908,
he was assigned the duty by the Greek Government to go to Salonika as cor-
respondent and record impressions about the ongoing atmosphere. During
his visit Melas met with prominent members of the Committee of Union
and Progress (CUP), local politicians, and people that participated in the
irregular war that had destabilized the region for over a decade. Perhaps, his
most pivotal meetings occurred with two men: Enver Bey the future leader of
the CUP and Jane Sandanski the person that headed the "left wing" of the
IMRO. While the first meeting with the CUP cadre went smoothly and the
two men discussed the future of the Empire, in the second an event transpired
that deserves further attention. When Melas arrived to "Hotel England" in
which Sandanski resided, his bodyguards did not grant him entrance claiming that the later was preoccupied with some important matters. While the
journalist was ready to leave, one of his men asked him if he was a relative
with Pavlos Melas, since they had the same surname. Suddenly Spyros realized
why he did not get permission and decided to play the game of the bodyguard

denouncing any relation with the latter. Eventually Melas met with Sandanski and exchanged reluctantly some views.[1]

This episode depicts quite vividly the enmity that had been culminated in the previous decades between different factions in Ottoman Macedonia. Pavlos Melas was a persona non grata for persons associated with the IMRO as he was considered as the first Greek Macedonian guerrilla whose death mobilized a whole mechanism against the organization. This resentment, as I present in the following chapters, was one of the driving factors that was eventually transformed in intense violence in the local level in the wars of 1912–3. Yet, in order to understand the complex process of ethnic violence in the Balkans we need to establish a necessary background focusing on three crucial dimensions: the conduct of war, the irredentist projects of the Balkan States, and the Macedonian Question.

The nineteenth century constituted an era of nation state formation in the Balkan Peninsula. There is a long standing debate regarding to the initial motivations of the Balkan Revolutionary groups to take up arms against the Sublime Porte.[2] Maria Todorova argued that the Balkan struggles for emancipation essentially constituted a negation of the past and complete detachment from the Ottoman legacy.[3] Paschalis Kitromilides maintained that it was the state that forged the nation and not vice versa.[4] Mark Mazower in his attempt to refute stereotypical perceptions articulated by western onlookers underlined how the ideology of nationalism and the importation of western ideas generated violent dynamics in the region.[5] Frederick Anscombe lastly adopted a broader view trying to place these movements in a framework of European revolutions motivated by responses to the reformation attempts in the reign of Sultan Selim III (1789–1807).[6]

An alternative way to reflect on the complex process of the Balkan national awakening is to think of the period of 1804–1912 as a longue durée borderland crisis. More specifically, if we take into consideration the prolonged instability,

1 Spyros Melas, I Epanastasi tou 1909 (Athens: To Vima Vivliothiki, 2009), 75–78.
2 Dimitrije Djordjevic, Stephen Fischer-Galati, The Balkan Revolutionary Tradition (New York: Columbia University Press, 1981).
3 Maria Todorova, Imagining the Balkans (Oxford: Oxford University Press, 2009), 164.
4 Paschalis M. Kitromilides, "'Imagined Communities' and the Origins of the National Question in the Balkans", European History Quarterly 19, no. 2 (1989): 149–192.
5 Mark Mazower, The Balkans. A Short History (New York: Modern Library, 2000).
6 Frederick Anscombe, "The Balkan Revolutionary Age." The Journal of Modern History 84, no. 3 (2012): 572–606.

the resilience of the local movements, the intervention of the Great Powers, and the vital role of mobile transnational revolutionary groups it is possible to have a view to the larger picture uniting more properly the different fragments that national historiographies decomposed. A suitable example to reconsider this framework is the Greek War of Independence, 1821–7. A scrappy coalition among a group of merchants from Odessa[7], local chieftains, and notables from Morea, as well as members from the Greek educated elite of Istanbul (Phanariots) managed to wage a decade of revolutionary upheaval leading to the intervention of the Great Powers and the creation of the first nation state, in European soil, from the secession of an imperial territory. During this painful period characterized by fratricidal war, pillaging, and massacres many actors partook shaping local and regional dynamics. Chieftains disputed with the Phanariots about the organization of the state in the day after tomorrow costing blood and drawbacks.[8] The Porte, in response, mobilized the semi-autonomous Egyptian province offering to its indisputable leader Mohamed Ali a piece of land for his son Ibrahim Pasha in case of successful suppression. The arrival of the reformed, by French officers, Egyptian army caused the most intense existential threat that almost brought the revolutionary movement to its knees and the day was saved by a last minute intervention of the Great Powers in the battle of Navarino in 1827.[9]

The Greek case fits perfectly in many ways to the borderland crisis paradigm. Lose state control, local power brokers, trans-imperial elites, wandering revolutionaries, foreign intervention, and a fragile geostrategic position were combined and spawned a crisis with profound impact. The Serbian revolt, albeit not identical, entailed many similar elements. The 1804 uprising at first was not an endeavour to create a new political entity but rather a reaction to the suppressive regime of the Janissaries, the former elite corps of the Ottoman army. However, according to some historians, the endurance of the revolt within the framework of the Napoleonic Wars and the dynamics which were created in the battlefield gradually altered the nature of the rebellion to a war of national liberation.[10] The Serbian example functioned as a precursor

---

7 They founded the underground network "Friends Society" in Odessa in 1814.

8 For more information on the Phanariotis and their transformation in the nineteenth century see: Christine Philliou, *Biography of an Empire. Governing Ottomans in an Age of Revolution* (Berkeley: University of California Press, 2011).

9 For more see: Khaled Fahmy, *All the Pasha's Men. Mehmed Ali, His Army and the Making of Modern Egypt* (Cambridge: Cambridge University Press, 1997).

10 Dušan T. Bataković, *A Balkan-Style French Revolution? The Serbian Uprising in European Perspective, Balkanica*, XXXVI (2005): 113–129.

embodying a new notion of resistance with an ethno religious dimension. The main difference with the Greek case was that the Serbs did not enjoy the sympathy of an intellectual movement such as the Philhellenic, which mobilized segments of western public sphere, and did not have the geopolitical significance for the Great Powers, aside Tsarist Russia. Serbian rebels later on were mobilized to assist the Greeks while Balkan capitals such as Belgrade and Bucharest became nests that accommodated networks destined to instigate revolts. The legendary Bulgarian revolutionary Georgi Rakovski operated in Belgrade in the 1840s, whereas prominent figures of the April uprising (1876) in Bulgarian lands such as Vasil Levski and Hristo Botev were connected with the Romanian based Bulgarian Revolutionary Central Committee (BRCC).[11]

In fact, the agency of important individuals and major diplomatic aspects of the Balkan Revolutionary movements have attracted attention, particularly in the context of the post Napoleonic Concert of Europe.[12] A missing link in this story constitutes the ways that the masses were mobilized for these long lasting wars, and at this point comes the first remark: the conduct of war. In contrast to Western Europe, where sovereign kingdoms emerged after the Treaty of Westphalia (1648) and gradually incorporated the private contractors of the early modern period into standing armies, in the Ottoman Empire a different trajectory was followed. Five hundred years of Ottoman rule in Rumeli prevented the creation of an organized military. This had two implications. First, the Christians relied to the Porte for military protection and during the nineteenth century the former enjoyed the prerogative to skip military service by paying a certain fee (*cizye tax*). The second was that any kind of military activity by Christian groups was created vis a vis the state in the form of banditry.[13] The Balkan outlaws that were celebrated by national narratives such as the Serbian hadjuks, the Greek klephtes, and the bandits of Bulgaria were the only form of Christian armed activity developed during the Ottoman era. The ambiguous role of those groups had led some historians in the past to wrongly attribute them elements of proto-national agents.[14]

---

11 Something similar to the Greek Friends Society. Richard J. Crampton, *A Concise History of Bulgaria* (Cambridge: Cambridge University Press, 2005), 45–84.

12 Barbara Jelavich, *History of the Balkans* (Cambridge: Cambridge University Press, 1983); Miroslav Šedivý, *Crisis among the Great Powers: The Concert of Europe and the Eastern Question* (London: Tauris, 2016).

13 It was the opposite for the navy since Greeks sailors served in the Ottoman navy.

14 Erik Hobsbawm, *Bandits* (New York: Pantheon Books, 1981).

The political agency of irregulars is one of the themes that need to be carefully articulated. While it is true that the motivation of a person to become an outlaw derived from personal reasons such as to avoid taxation, enjoy prestige or to live a life in impunity, in the late Ottoman era the bandits became the steam engine of the revolutions.[15] Recent works have shown how the literature in the past has misinterpreted their role. By looking beyond the state and not taking for granted the center-periphery paradigm scholars reassessed them within the concept of the study of borderlands. By overemphasizing the anti-state activities of these individuals it is often neglected that banditry brought together a diverse group of people which shared a common culture of violence crucial for the strategies of the Sublime Porte. The incorporation of these groups into the state machinery functioned many times as safety valve.[16] It was quite common in inaccessible territories with low economic interest to assign duties to bandits so that to patrol commercial passages, the so called "armatole."[17] Financial bargaining in the Ottoman era was a common practice and the wars of Liberation constituted no exception. In several occasions during the Greek War of Independence chieftains that fought for the revolutionary cause shifted camps and sided with the enemy, in an agreement called "kapakia" (u-turn).[18]

One of the main reasons that led to this misconception was that historians utilized the weberian paradigm of the monopolization of legitimate force as an analytical framework. Liberal intellectuals in the nineteenth century utilized the term banditry to encapsulate all forms of non-state violence especially in Latin America where this phenomenon flourished but in a rather different context.[19] In that sense, the Ottoman Empire appeared as a state incapable of implementing the rule of law thereby an underdeveloped and failed entity. Still, this view neglects vital elements of the Ottoman way of governance. Dichotomous understandings on modernization viewed in an anachronistic way the Ottoman state not taking into consideration how the Porte tried to govern. Geopolitical and economic developments at the turn of the nineteenth century tremendously impacted the European provinces of the

---

15 For more see the classical study: John S. Koliopoulos, "*Brigands with a Cause: Brigandage and Irredentism in Modern Greece 1821–1912*" (Oxford: Oxford University Press, 1987).

16 Tolga U. Esmer, "Economies of violence. Banditry and Governance in the Ottoman Empire around 1800", *Past and Present*, no. 224 (2014), 163–199.

17 Encyclopædia Britannica. Inc. 2014. Retrieved 27/5/2020.

18 Kostis Papageorgis, *Ta Kapakia* (Athens: Kastaniotis, 2009).

19 Juan Pablo Dabove, Paramilitarism and Banditry, *The Global South* 12, no. 2 (2018): 33.

Empire. The Tanzimat reforms, initiated in the 1840s, apart from granting for the first time equality and civil liberties to non-Muslim subjects, they limited centralization to a provincial level. Throughout this period the Ottoman state ceded control to the "periphery" by taking into account "local customs and dispositions", and forming a dense web of interconnected networks among the imperial capital and the provinces.[20] The decentralized governing of the Porte allowed paramilitarism to flourish making violence fundamental bringing together a variety of groups that operated on the borders: bandits, paramilitaries, and revolutionaries.[21] All the ambiguous relations that had been cultivated by Istanbul converted eventually these groups into agents of the states that became its successors and rendered paramilitarism as legitimate means of political brokerage.

Not unexpectedly, banditry remained a thorny social issue for the Balkan states that dominated the political agenda way after their formation. Unlike professional military men who had received training in national institutions that instilled a sense of duty, irregular groups were somehow as agents in between motivated simultaneously by personal interests and political ideals. The incorporation of these ill-disciplined fighters who had obtained social capital and local networks to new regular armies was fully attained only in the interwar years.[22]

A more competent way to scrutinize this issue is to rethink it in terms of who were the vectors of violence. As Antonis Liakos argues, the violence in the warfare of the Balkans was a combination of two interconnected structures: the modern state and the traditional society. While the first was able

---

20 Uğur Bayraktar, "Reconsidering Local versus Central: Empire, Notables, and Employment in Ottoman Albania and Kurdistan, 1835–1878", *International Journal of Middle East Studies* (2020): 6–7.

21 This aspect belongs to a wider debate about state formation and monopolization of violence in Southeastern Europe. The most classical example is IMRO and its relation with the Bulgarian state after the Balkan Wars, see: John Gledhill and Charles King, "Institutions, Violence, and Captive Statis in Balkan History", in *Ottomans into Europeans: State and Institution building in Southeastern Europe*, eds. Alina Mungiu Pippidi and Van Meurs (Hurst, London 2010). In general about this issue: Umit U. "Ungor, Rethinking the Violence of Pacification: State Formation and Bandits in Turkey, 1914–1937", *Comparative Studies in Society and History* 54, no. 4 (2012): 746–769; Gerwarth, Robert, and John Horne. "Vectors of Violence: Paramilitarism in Europe after the Great War, 1917–1923." *The Journal of Modern History* 83, no. 3 (2011): 489–512.

22 Gledhill and King, "Institutions, Violence, and Captive Statis in Balkan History", 245–276.

to mobilize national armies, the second had a deeply embedded tradition in which the bearers were local chieftains and their men who offered to their leader unquestioned loyalty. For these outlaws the sense of belonging to a group was of crucial importance. In that sense, there is one the one hand organized state violence and on the other a more diffused and local. These two forms, as I present in the following chapters, intermingled in an unpreceded intensity during the Balkan wars of 1912–3.[23]

Yet, even more challenging is the task to discern the role and motivations of the non-usual suspects. While significant actors and the role of the state have attracted scholarly attention this does not go for the "masses".[24] Thousands of peasants that formed the backbone of the Balkan revolutionary armies had a more ambivalent role in wartime violence. Whether bystanders or participants, their agency due to their mass numbers was always crucial and determined the tide of battle. Particularly for the Serbian and Greek example, the participation of thousands of peasants and mountainous people gave impetus and made them doable. The bloodshed of the unknown villager that belonged to the lower strata of the society rendered possible the creation of the states in the peninsula. Unfortunately this category due to scarcity of sources has attracted hitherto little attention. This omission represents a lacuna that has left many questions unexplained related to the structural history of the rural Balkan societies. For that reason, it is difficult to assess the agency of the "ordinary" peasants in the early nineteenth century because of their ambiguous relations with the military and the absence of organized institutions and conscription. The loyalty was fluid, at the very least, and depended on the series of factors such as: family ties, locality, personal interests, and the disruption of everyday life.

The second point that needs further discussion is the national agendas of the Balkan states, particularly for the Greco-Bulgarian case. The centrality

23 Antonis Liakos, O Ellinikos Eikostos Aionas (Athens: Polis, 2019), 55.

24 Rositsa Gradeva "Secession and Revolution in the Ottoman Empire: Osman Pazvantoğlu and Rhigas Velestinlis," in Ottoman Rule and the Balkans, 1760–1850, Conflict, Transformation, Adaptation, ed. A. Anastasopoulos and E. Kolovos, Proceedings of an International Conference Held in Rethymno, Greece, 13–14 December 2003 (Rethymno: University of Crete, Department of History and Archaeology, 2007), 73–94; Katherine E. Fleming, The Muslim Bonaparte. Diplomacy and Orientalism in Ali Pasha's Greece (Princeton, New Jersey: PUP, 1999); Sükrü Ilicak, A Radical Rethinking of Empire. Ottoman State and Society during the Greek War of Independence, 1821–1826 (Unpublished Doctoral Thesis, Harvard University, 2011); Lucien J. Frary, Russia and the Making of Modern Greek Identity, 1821–1844 (Oxford: Oxford University Press, 2015).

of irredentism and the integration of Greek populations that lived scattered across the Ottoman Empire, the so called *eterocthones* (non-residents), dictated the foreign policy of Athens for over a century. This project that was better known as the "The Great Idea" (Megali Idea) envisaged the reinvigoration of a new Hellenic Empire that "spanned in two continents and five seas". This expansionist plan obviously collided with the geopolitical reality because it envisioned the annexation of Ottoman territories. These kinds of visions however were not a Greek exceptionalism and the other Balkan states articulated their own. Serbian irredentism had historical claims deriving from the battle of Kosovo of 1389 while the project of the Greater Serbia (Načertanije) which was first drafted by Ilija Garašanin a very prominent statesman in 1844 foresaw a Balkan expansion.[25]

The Bulgarian "rebirth" (*Vazrazhdane*)[26], on the contrary arrived, relatively late for a number of reasons such as: the political dominance of the Greek Patriarchate, the role of the Greek language as lingua franca, the proximity of the Bulgarian lands to the imperial center, and the absence of an educated elite in the Diaspora which would bear the principles of Enlightenment.[27] One of the key elements that distinguished the Greco-Bulgarian antagonism is that the Bulgarian National Movement was created primarily against Hellenic influence and particularly the influence of Greeks over the Ottoman Orthodox Church. The abolition of the Ohrid Archbishopric in 1767 and the usage of Greek in Ottoman territories had cultivated a climate of suspicion to early Bulgarian national apostles. This anti-Hellenic climate found for the first time fertile soil in the Danubian principalities due to an extremely unpopular regime imposed by the Phanariotes in the eighteenth century. Influential figures of the Bulgarian movement such as the cleric Ilarion Makariopolski, one of the pioneers for the creation of an independent Bulgarian Church,

---

25 Ilija Garasanin, The Draft, in : *National Romanticism: The Formation of National Movements : Discourses of Collective Identity in Central and Southeast Europe 1770–1945, Volume II* [en ligne]. (Budapest: Central European University Press, 2007) (généré le 06 janvier 2023).

26 For a general discussion see: Roumen Daskalov, *The Making of a Nation in the Balkans: Historiography of the Bulgarian Revival* (Budapest and New York: Central European University Press, 2005).

27 For more information see: Christo Gandev, *Problemi na Bălgarsko vǎzrazhdane* (Sofia: BAN, 1976).

collaborated with Georgi Rakovski in his dispute with the Patriarchate of Constantinople.[28]

On the contrary, early notions of Bulgarian nationalism were perceived by pundits in the Hellenic Kingdom as Russian fabrications and hybrids of Panslavism.[29] That was one of the main bones of contention that intoxicated relations between Greece and Bulgaria in the long nineteenth century. The non-recognition of a Bulgarian independency movement by Greece, and the creation of a movement with anti-Greek orientation, in response, set a dangerous precedent with detrimental effects. Any attempt for political partisanship in Bulgarian speaking lands was seen in Athens as the outcome of machinations of agents working for St. Petersburg. In contrast, the efforts of Bulgarian revolutionaries, particularly the clergy were concentrated in the 1860s to detach the Slavic speaking flock from the Patriarchate.[30]

The Greek state and the Patriarchate had a tenuous relation too in regard to the Great Idea, despite ostensibly similar agendas. Already there was a dispute between Athens and the Ecumenical Patriarchate due to the creation of an independent Greek Church during the reign of the Bavarian King Otto in 1833. Likewise, the two sides did not share same views about the handling of irredentist affairs. This did not come as a surprise since the Patriarchate was an official Ottoman institution that pursuit to manoeuvre within the current-system of governance, not necessarily embracing notions of the Great Idea as perceived in the Greek Kingdom. The unstable relation of the Patriarch Joachim III (1834–1912) with Athens at the beginning of the twentieth century was the most indicative example of this troubled affair.[31]

---

28 Daniela Kalkandjieva, "The Bulgarian Orthodox Church", in *Orthodox Christianity and Nationalism in Nineteenth-Century Southeastern Europe*, ed. Lucian N. Leustean (Fordham University Press: New York, 2014).

29 This is not to claim that the influence of the Great Powers was limited. Recent studies have refuted the argument about the involvement of Russia into Bulgarian affairs as a vehicle to set foot on the Balkans through the creation of a clientele state in the Black sea, showing how the former tried to navigate the complex relation between Christians and Muslims and reconcile ethnic differences within the existing Ottoman structures. See Chapter 2 of: Denis Vovchenko, *Containing Balkan Nationalism*: Imperial Russia and Ottoman Christians, 1856–1914 (New York: Oxford University Press, 2016).

30 Elli Skopetea, *To Protypo Vasileio kai i Megali Idea. Opseis tou Ethnikou Provlimatos stin Ellada* (Athens: Politypo, 1988), 325–331.

31 See more on: Paschalis M. Kitromilides, *Religion and Politics in the Orthodox World: The Ecumenical Patriarchate and the Challenges of Modernity* (London: Routledge, 2019).

Ultimately, the imperial firman of Sultan Abdul-Aziz (1830–76) in 1870 that authorized the creation of an independent Bulgarian church, the Exarchate, and the creation of an autonomous Bulgarian principality after the Russo-Ottoman war of 1877–8 (Treaty of Berlin), broadly defined the trajectory of the relations of the Balkan countries. The condemnation of the Exarchate for ethno-nationalism by the Ecumenical Patriarchate and the territorial aspirations of Bulgaria and Serbia crystallized a competition in multiple levels. Athens, Sofia, and Belgrade were soon engaged in parallel dialogues with the Great powers in a quest to acclaim the sympathy of the West. The Great Powers' support was crucial given the experience of the Greek War of Independence and the role of the British Prime Minister William Gladstone during the crisis of the Eastern Question (1875–8) which ended up in the autonomy of Bulgaria.[32] In contrast, direct channels of communication among the Balkan capitals barely existed.[33] A failed attempt to create an alliance between Greece and Serbia in 1867 and a short war between Serbia and Bulgaria in 1885 due the annexation of Eastern Rumelia only increased distances.[34]

Eventually, the apple of discord became the three administrative units (vilayets) that composed Ottoman Macedonia.[35] The population of this eth-nically mixed area that was comprised of Turks, Slavs, Greeks, Albanians, Jews, Roma, Vlachs, and other ethnic-groups became the locus of Balkan irredentism. Nearly all the nation-states of the peninsula had claims on the territories of the three vilayets of Salonika, Manastir, and Kosovo.[36] Ottoman Macedonia represented a typical example of an imperial borderland that became a contested territory. In the late Ottoman era the effort of the Balkan states to shape national identities was concentrated on the creation of ethnic distinctions that informed relations and fragmented local communities.[37] In

32 Alexis Heraclides and Ada Dialla, *Humanitarian Intervention in the Long Nineteenth Century: Setting the Precedent* (Manchester: Manchester University Press, 2016), 148–168.

33 For the propaganda of the Balkan states, see the very important book of: Ivan Hohev, *My Country-Right or Wrong! The Propaganda of the Balkan Countries in Europe and the US in 1821–1923* [in Greek] (Thessaloniki: Epikentro Publications, 2011).

34 Nikolaos Roussos, Charilaos Trikoupis and the Serbo-Greek Alliance of 1867, *Balkan Studies* 12, no. 1 (1971): 81–101.

35 See for example: Georgi N. Georgiev, The *Bulgarian National Liberation Movement in Macedonia* (1893–1912), *Macedonian Review* 2, no. 17: 21–34 (in Bulgarian).

36 Richard Hall, *The Modern Balkans: A History* (London: Reaktion Books, 2011), 71–73.

37 Svetlana Stamenova, "The Specifics of Balkan Ethnic Identity Construction: Ethnicisation of Localities", *National Identities* 19, no. 3 (2017): 320, 325; Harris Mylonas, "Nation

this rivalry intellectuals were the first to be mobilized. Linguistic and ethno religious maps were circulated in many languages so that to prove the historical, religious, and cultural rights that legitimized the irredentist projects of the respective states.[38]

Sofia was the first to be activated in this arena by trying to revise the Treaty of Berlin which annulled the Russian backed Treaty of San Stefano (1878) shrinking significantly the agreed size of the country. The decree of 1870 provided for villages whereby, when two-thirds of the population were followers of the Exarchy, to choose the jurisdiction of the Bulgarian church.[39] This further allowed the establishment of schools closely tied to the Bulgarian cause, all of which provided an opportunity to Sofia to consolidate claims in the region. Athens and Belgrade attempted to counterbalance the Bulgarian threat through the establishment of their own educational networks which functioned under the umbrella of irredentist organizations such as the Serbian Society of Saint Sava (1886) and the Greek National Society (Ethniki Etaireia).[40] Naturally, the fact that these educational centers were not funded by local communities, but by the Balkan states had certain ramifications. The teachers quite often came directly from those countries to propagate nationalist rhetoric while consulars controlled the appointments of the former and checked on a regular basis whether they fulfilled "properly" their duties. This strategy generated widespread polarization in the region, enhanced the alienation of the local population and cultivated a nostalgia for a distant fatherland that convinced many youngsters that the Empire was a prison in which they were trapped.[41]

Yet, educational activities were not only a matter that engaged the nation states. The reforms of Sultan Abdülhamid II (r. 1876–1909) in the late nineteenth century had also had implications on the educational network. The founding of schools which aimed at first to train military officers, gradually expanded to cover the needs for bureaucrats and people from a wealthy

Building Policies in the Balkans: An Ottoman or Manufactured Legacy", *Nations and Nationalism* 25, no. 3 (2019): 874.

38 Henry Robert Wilkinson, Maps and Politics: A Review of the Ethnographic Cartography of Macedonia (Liverpool: Liverpool University Press, 1951).

39 Dragostinova, *Between Two Motherlands*, 23–34.

40 Biondich, *The Balkans*, 67–68.

41 Bernard Lory, "Schools for the Destruction of Society: School Propaganda in Bitola 1860–1912", in *Conflicting Loyalties in the Balkans*, ed. Grandits, Clayer, Pichler, 53–59.

background.[42] In many cases the schooling network was employed by provincial elites as a vessel for negotiation. In some areas the locals asked pressures to Istanbul to allocate funds for educational purposes. This initiative was closely associated with the concept of Ottomanism, which was an ideological platform that envisaged the reform, modernization, and decentralization of the empire. The basic premises of Ottomanism opposed notions of the other two ideologies of Islamism and Pan-Turanism.[43] People that advocated Ottomanism perceived the orientation of identity strictly in religious terms (Islamism) as incompetent to cope with the challenges of a changing geopolitical environment. The same applied for any kind of ideas oriented to race (Pan-Turanism). Ottomanism was a project that encompassed, at least in name, all ethno-religious groups of the empire (millets) regardless of language and religion. The forging of a supra-national/imperial identity was the glue that would tie together the different communities and render diversity to an asset.[44] Many non-Turkish groups found this idea tempting and made an attempt to be integrated into the new imperial polity. For instance, in the Western Balkans Albanian notables requested resources to build their own schools in order to instil a civic sense of nationhood and to contain the allure of the educational networks controlled by the Balkan states.[45]

Still, educational and intellectual struggles were only the first stages in this multi faced rivalry. The engagement of army officers and irredentist societies altered the equation adding a military dimension. Yet, in order to understand the articulation of the foreign policy of the states of the Peninsula we need to be aware of the central role that these networks possessed. As Christopher Clark shows in his study about the origins of WWI, the foreign policy of the Serbian Kingdom was not solely exercised by the state. Instead,

42 Selçuk A. Somel, *The Modernization of Public Education in the Ottoman Empire, 1839–1908: Islamization, Autocracy, and Discipline* (Leiden: Brill, 2001); Benjamin J. Fortna, *Imperial Classroom: Islam, the State, and Education in the Late Ottoman Empire* (Oxford: Oxford University Press, 2002).

43 See more on: Kemal Karpat, *The Politicization of Islam: Reconstructing Identity, State, Faith, and Community in the Late Ottoman State* (Oxford: Oxford University Press, 2002).

44 For a discussion on that see: Michelle U. Campos, *Ottoman Brothers. Muslims, Christians, and Jews in Early Twentieth-Century Palestine* (Stanford: Stanford University Press, 2010); Julia Phillips Cohen, *Becoming Ottomans: Sephardi Jews and Imperial Citizenship in the Modern Era* (Oxford: Oxford University Press, 2014).

45 Isa Blumi "Teaching Loyalty in the Late Ottoman Balkans: Educational Reform in the Vilayets of Manastir and Yanya, 1878–1912." *Comparative Studies of South Asia, Africa and the Middle East* 21, no. 1 (2001): 15–23.

two levels of policy implementation existed that fought for the same goals but sometimes with different means. In the first level belonged the official state which included the embassies, consulates, emissaries, and attaches that were reporting back to Belgrade. The second level was more shady and was composed of unofficial channels such as: spies, paramilitaries, local patrons, and people that belonged to the criminal underworld. The second level coordinated ostensibly with the first but only loosely. Colonel Dragutin Dimitrijević alias "Apis" represented the most notorious example. He was the man that machinated the assassination of King Alexandar and his wife in 1903 and headed the secret society of the "Black Hand" that killed Archduke Franz Ferdinand that sparked WWI.[46] The agency of the second level because of the local leverage was so firm that in many cases defied the official state, acting independently. At the turn of the twentieth century these two levels of policy generated discrepancies between the decision makers and the situation on the lower lever with profound impact.

The Greek National Society was another representative example. Founded in 1894 by military officers, a year after the bankruptcy of the Greek state, the society had as declared goal to function as a pressure group for the reformation of the army and the materialization of the Great Idea. Its most infamous involvement took place in 1897 when demands of Greeks on the island of Crete for union, were combined with pressures of the society and the public opinion and led the Greek government to declare war to the Porte. This conflict lasted only for a month but the defeat was a huge blow to the prestige of the Greek officer corps and the Monarchy.[47]

However, the landmark event that shaped the trajectory of the Macedonian Question constituted the founding of a local revolutionary network in the city of Salonika in 1893, namely the Internal Macedonian Revolutionary Organization. The IMRO constituted a regional response to the rise of nationalism and to pressing socio economic concerns, especially the land issue. The ideological platform of the IMRO is a very complicated topic because regional historiographies tried to appropriate the organization into their own national narratives. North-Macedonian historians claim that the IMRO had set as ultimate priority the independence of Ottoman Macedonia.[48] Bulgarian

---

46 Christopher Clark, *The Sleepwalkers: How Europe Went to War in 1914* (London: Penguin, 2013), 3–13.

47 Giannis Giannoulopoulos, *I Eugenis mas Typhlosis. Exoteriki Politiki kai Ethnika Themata apo tin Itta tou 1897 eos ti Mikrasiatiki Katastrophi* (Athens: Vivliorama, 2003), 33–47.

48 Blazhe Ristovski. *Istoriya na Makedosnkata Natziya* (Skopje: MANU, 1999).

historians, on the other hand, assert that the organization was essentially a vessel preparing the annexation of Ottoman Macedonia to Bulgaria.[49] Greek and Serbian historiography share similar views with Bulgarian perceiving the IMRO as a vehicle serving the Bulgarian expansionist agenda.[50] Apparently, these interpretations neglect one of the most important components of the IMRO: its grassroots support. The initial appeal of the organization was closely related to a supra-national message. Instead of using the language of nation the IMRO favoured, at the beginning at least, a more socialist agenda since its leaders had foreseen the importance of peasants and tried to forge allegiances.[51]

An immediate by-product of the formation of the IMRO was the founding in 1895 in Sofia of the Supreme Macedonian-Adrianople Committee (SMAC).[52] The so-called supremists (Varhovniyat Makedono-Odrinski Komitet) faction originated approximately from 100,000 to 200,000 Slavic speaking refugees who due to failed revolts in the 1890s resettled to Bulgarian territories. These people founded clubs that essentially functioned as pressure groups for the promotion of an expansionist agenda to official state policy. The Bulgarian military was also closely associated with the SMAC and the first leader of the committee was the Bulgarian general Ivan Tsonchev, a veteran of the Serbo-Bulgarian war of 1885.[53]

The assassination of Prime Minister Stefan Stambolov (1895), a politician who followed an anti-Russian policy by trying to suppress subversive activities and appease the Sublime Porte, signalled a major shift toward a more active presence in Macedonia and control of the IMRO. The ambivalent relations between the two organizations had become a matter of endless

---

49 Dimitar Gotzev, *Ideyata za avtonomiya kato taktika v programite na natzionalnoosvoboditel-noto dvizhenie v Makedoniya i Odrinsko (1893–1941)* (Sofia: Universitetsko izdatelstvo "Sv. Kliment Ohridski", 1983).

50 See an overview on: Martin Valkov, *The Internal Macedonian-Adrianople. Revolutionary Organization and the Idea for Autonomy for Macedonia, Adrianople and Thrace, 1893–1912* (Budapest: Masters' Thesis, Central European University, 2010).

51 The vast majority of arable lands in Ottoman Macedonia were owned by Muslim, Jews, and Greeks and cultivated by Slavic Speaking peasants. Tasos Kostopoulos, "Land to the Tiller. On the Neglected Agrarian Component of the Macedonian Revolutionary Movement, 1893–1912", *Turkish Historical Review*, 7 (2016): 13–16.

52 See more on: Svetlozar Eldarov, *Varhovniyat makedono-odrinski komitet i makedono-odrinskata organizatciya v Balgariya* (Sofia: Ivray, 2003).

53 Duncan M. Perry, *The Politics of Terror: The Macedonian Liberation Movements: 1893–1903* (Durham, N.C: Duke University Press, 1988), 35.

debates among Bulgarian and North Macedonian historians.[54] As a matter of fact, the interaction among the IMRO and the SMAC was ambiguous at the very least. Gotse Delchev and Damian Gruev, the indisputable leaders of the Macedonian movement attended congresses of Bulgarian clubs in Sofia to engage in a dialogue that aimed to a common agenda. However, this relation was not straightforward and was characterized by many twists and turns.[55]

The most important challenge to the IMRO constituted the first and last major uprising that took place in Rumeli in the beginning of the twentieth century. Both organizations had created armed units that had been conducting guerrilla operations in Ottoman Macedonia since the late 1890s, the so called comitadji: a term deriving from the word committee. These bands that were also called chettas (Serbian) recruited experienced native bandit leaders and villagers who vowed obedience and support to the organization's goals. Treason was brutally punished while the bands quite often spent winter months in Bulgaria to regroup. Other chettas that belonged to the SMAC were controlled by Macedonian migrants and Bulgarian army officers.[56]

On August 2, 1903 after years of underground activities the leadership of the IMRO decided to instigate a full scale revolt. Nearly 20,000 men were mobilized and set ablaze the European parts of the Ottoman Empire. The revolt was not contained in Macedonia but spread throughout the Janina and Edirne vilayets. In the city of Kruševo, in the Manastir vilayet, the revolutionaries proclaimed a ten days Republic and manifested openly the goals of the organization demanding autonomy and agrarian reforms. The response of the Sublime Porte was severe. 200,000 reserves moved swiftly to brutally suppress the revolt. The final outcome numbered 4,500 dead, 3,000 rapes and more than 200 villages destroyed while approximately 100,000 people were left homeless.[57] The public outcry from the Ottoman reprisals resulted to the intervention of the Great Powers. The Dual Monarchy and Tsarist Russia imposed the implementation of the so called Mürzsteg program in October

---

54   See for example: Slavko Dimevski, *Makedonskoto Nacionalno Osvoboditelno Dvizhenie i Egzarhiyata (1893–1912)* (Skopje: Kultura, 1963).

55   Tchavdar Marinov, "We, the Macedonians: The Path of Macedonian Supra-Nationalism (1878–1912)", in *We, the People: Politics of National Peculiarity in Southeastern Europe*, ed. Diana Mishkova (New York: Central European University Press, 2009): 107–138.

56   Dmitar-Tasić, *Paramilitarism in the Balkans: Yugoslavia, Bulgaria, and Albania, 1917–1924* (Oxford: Oxford University Press, 2020), 68.

57   Keith Brown, *Loyal Unto Death: Trust and Terror in Revolutionary Macedonia* (Bloomington: Indiana University Press, 2013), 4–5.

1903 which was an attempt to supervise the reform of the Ottoman gendar-merie and security forces.[58]

The so called Ilinden-Preobrazhenie uprising (St. Elias day) was the most pivotal event that shifted the balance of power in the Balkan region. Until then, Greece had participated into Macedonian affairs more loosely but this was about to change. Athens realized for the first time the magnitude of the IMRO's appeal. Intellectual and irredentist circles in the capital were imme-diately mobilized to convey the message about the imminent danger of losing permanently Macedonia. The director of the Athenian newspaper "Empros" Dimitrios Kalapothakis founded the Macedonian Committee. The Committee was essentially a nongovernmental organization that aimed to prepare the ground for insurgency in Ottoman Macedonia. In its ranks were recruited a wide strata of people including army officers, intellectuals, bandits, and poli-ticians.[59] The period 1904–8 which is more widely known in Greek literature as the "Macedonian Struggle", the Balkan states and primarily Greece and Bulgaria clashed over the fates of Macedonia.[60]

The Macedonian conflict constituted the first proxy war of the twentieth century. In no other place in the globe took place an undeclared war funded by nation states for an imperial territory. This sophisticated way of interven-tion made its presence for the first time in Rumeli transforming the underlying rivalry of the Balkan states into something more concrete. The conflict was ultimately militarized with armed bands as protagonists. The agents of the Balkan states united forces with local patrons and systematized a culture of violence that cultivated dangerous local dynamics. In this new chapter Greece and Bulgaria became the main players. Serbia kept some distances until 1908 because Belgrade was preoccupied with, the Austrian administrated, Bosnia-Herzegovina. The first Serbian secret association of "self-defence" was founded in 1905 in Macedonia. Although political in nature at first, it soon changed character embracing guerrilla tactics. The annexation of Bosnia-Herzegovina

58 Julian Brooks, Managing Macedonia: British Statecraft, Intervention, and "Proto-peacekeeping" in Ottoman Macedonia, 1902–1905 (Unpublished PhD Thesis, Simon Fraser University, 2014).

59 Basil Gounaris, "Social Gathering and Macedonian Lobbying. Symbols of Irredentism and Living Legends in Early Twentieth Century Athens," in *Greek Society in the Making, 1863–1913: Realities, Symbols and Visions*, ed. Philip Carabott (Brookfield, Vt.: Variorum, 1997), 100–112.

60 The most classic study from a Greek perspective: Douglas Dakin, *The Greek Struggle in Macedonia, 1897–1913* (Thessaloniki: Institute for Balkan Studies, 1966).

(1908) pushed the Serbian Government to become more actively engaged by setting up plans to send officers to organize bands in Kosovo and Macedonia.[61]

The Greeks inaugurated their penetration by articulating an economic plan and mobilizing the Hellenic Diaspora to purchase estates in Ottoman Macedonia in an attempt to nationalize the lands.[62] Athens also dispatched officers and volunteers from the Kingdom, as well as from other parts of the Ottoman Empire such as experienced fighters from the island of Crete. The first national martyr, the aforementioned Pavlos Melas, was an officer of the army, member of the National Society, and offspring of a prominent family. The premature killing of Melas in 1904 was idealized by contemporary press that depicted him as the embodiment of virtue: the man who gave up his reputation, promising career, and family to fight for the Great Idea. Mela's sacrifice was not in vain. Shortly after his death a wave of sympathy mobilized segments of the society and the political spectrum.[63] The Greek foreign policy also promoted a short term tactical allegiance with the Sublime Porte following the logic of the lesser evil. The same applied to the Ottomans who had been shocked by the magnitude of the IMRO after the Ilinden uprising.

The peasants had to deal with an endemic climate of violence which blurred the lines amongst national agitators, bandits, and bystanders. The key for this battle, over the hearts and souls, was the control of villages through extortions and alliances since the loyalty of a village to the Exarchy or the Patriarchate denoted ethnic affiliation.[64] Switching from the one church to the other, whether forceful or not, constituted a standard practice in villages in Ottoman Macedonia. Marauders terrorized local inhabitants whenever needed, and checked out their reliability. Teachers and priests became central figures. Closing down of schools and political assassinations was the main means to afflict a mental shock to the locals. The conduct of war was quite similar with the early Balkan revolutionary era. The bands utilized hit and run

61 Biljana Vučetić, "Some Considerations on the Emergence of the Serbian Chetnik Movement in Macedonia during the Last Period of Ottoman Rule", *Istorijski zapisi*, godina LXXXVIII, no. 3–4 (2015): 125–127.

62 Yura Konstantinova, *Balgari i Gartsi v Borba za Osmanskoto Nasledstvo* (Sofia: Faber, 2014), 152–153.

63 Anastasia Karakasidou, "Affections of a Greek Hero: Pavlos Melas and Heroic Representations in Greece", in *Balkan Identities: Nation and Memory*, ed. Maria Todorova (New York: NYU Press, 2004).

64 See more on: Anastasia Karakasidou, *Fields of Wheat, Hills of Blood: Passages to Nationhood in Greek Macedonia, 1870–1990* (University of Chicago Press, 1997).

tactics in order to instigate a reign of terror and substituted the power vacuum that the Ottoman state was not able to fulfill. The logistical coordination of the proxy war for the Greek side included two centers. The first was the Macedonian Committee that controlled the vilayet of Manastir. The second was the Greek Consulate in Salonika that controlled the respective vilayet. The Salonika Consul, Lampros Koromilas was the man that connected his name the most with the Macedonian Struggle. The Consulate functioned as the top of a pyramid organization which dictated the policy to the vice consulates and the so-called national centers. The national centers were in fact local village or town committees composed by notables who had aligned themselves with the Greek cause.[65]

The next category of actors included irregular bands the so called Macedonian fighters which belonged mainly to two types. The first were a mixture of volunteers coming from abroad and officers of the Greek army. The second were native bandits who were recruited after agreements which were reached with the national centers, and it was not a surprise to see chieftains during the Macedonian proxy war to change sides. Perhaps, the most well-known example is the case of captain Vangeli Kotta (Kote Hristov), from the village of Roulia (Kotta), near the city of Lerin (Florina). Captain Kottas was a prominent member of the IMRO in the wider area until an internal dispute in 1902 forced him to change sides. Kottas, albeit Slavic speaking he has been celebrated by Greek historiography as a glorious Macedonian fighter who served the cause by repelling the actions of the Exarchists. For his actions he was hanged by the Ottoman authorities in Manastir in 1905.[66]

The man who recruited Kotta for the Greek cause reflects another type of agents that operated in the proxy war: the priests. In the wake of the Macedonian proxy war the Greek Patriarchate mobilized its network in order to deter the expansion of the Exarchy. The role of priests that attached themselves to the Macedonian affair went way beyond ecclesiastical matters as they somehow functioned as intelligence officers.[67] Germanos Karavangelis was a very representative example of a clergyman that was involved in the Macedonian issue. He was born in the Ottoman Empire in the island of Lesvos in 1866 and followed a successful career in the Orthodox Church.

65   Dimitris Livanios, "Conquering the Souls: Nationalism and Greek Guerrilla Warfare in Ottoman Macedonia, 1904–1908", *Byzantine and Modern Greek Studies* 23: 195–221, 199.9.

66   Iakovos Michailidis-Konstantinos Papanikolaou, *Aphanois Gigeneis Makedonomachoi* (Thessaloniki: Etaireia Makedonikon Spoydon, 2008), 170.

67   Henry Noël Brailsford, *Macedonia: Its Races and Their Future* (Metheun, 1906), 192–194.

Karavangelis was the Metropolitan of Kostur (Kastoria) and his work significantly contained the IMRO and reinstated the Patriarchate influence. From his base he coordinated an intelligence network that supervised the situation in the countryside and organized visits in order to boost the morale of the peasants.

Yet, the actions of priests and national agitators cannot alone provide an adequate explanation about the culture of violence that was generated in the wake of the Balkan Wars. In the end of the day, the locals, whether they wanted or not they became involved. This especially concerned the most contested religious and linguistic group: Slavic speaking Christians. Athens and Sofia had adopted an identically different view regarding the ethnic affiliation of these populations. Athens claimed that every person that declared loyalty to the Greek Patriarchate should be considered as Greek regardless of vernacular language. Sofia, on the other hand, based its claims on language and considered Slavic speaking populations as Bulgarians per se. Consequently, those that chose to remain under the jurisdiction of the Patriarchate were ascribed the derogatory connotation of Grecomans (Greek-fanatics).[68] This dynamic had put in the eye of the storm the clergy generating conditions of a civil strife. The role of intimacy made this rivalry personal in the local level as it included many times the assassination of people that were acquainted with each other.[69] As Ipek Yosmaoğlu argues in her study on the kaza of Serres, violence in the region was a catalyst for the politicization of communal differences in two ways. First, it made impossible to remain a bystander, and second it unified people around a wider community tied by blood.[70]

The ordinary people that became participants directly or indirectly represents the category which is the largest and most complicated to analyze. Spies, informers, villagers who provided shelter and individuals who lived a double life were some of the roles distributed. This is a crucial remark that needs to be further articulated. When the rivalry between Greece and Bulgaria was formulated on a state level, it was simultaneously diffused in the micro and the meso politicizing local frictions. Numerous duties required a plethora of persons. This participation shaped loyalties and familiarized people with a

68 Yura Konstantinova. "'Followers of the Patriarchate and 'Slavic Speakings at the End of the Nineteenth and the Beginning of 20th Century", *Études Balkaniques*, 3: 137–147.

69 Basil Gounaris, "Preachers of God and Martyrs of the Nation. The Politics of Murder in Ottoman Macedonia in the early 20th century", *Balkanologie* IX, no. 1–2 (Decembre 2005/31): 31–43.

70 Yosmaoğlu, *Blood Ties*, 217.

culture of violence and insurgency. Obviously not all villages were involved in the same degree. Yet, the ongoing climate and the gradual lack of trust to the official state turned civilians in some cases to seek for alternative ways to survive. It was in this crucial period that local and personal rivalries in the micro level were intermingled with broader political agendas and generated a dangerous precedent.[71]

Nevertheless, ethnic-groups of this period should not be perceived as something concrete. More sophisticated approaches have shown that the locals were not mere victims of national agitation and had their own agency.[72] Family ties, economic incentives, kinship, and security concerns played sometimes a more significant role. Anthropological studies described this phenomenon as "national mobility"; a process where the individual decision to adopt a nationality was driven by political motivations not cultural. This choice was not entirely free, but rather dictated by pragmatic needs.[73] This fluidity of loyalties was something that the agents of national propaganda were well aware and systematically employed.

Eventually Athens was on the winning side of the Macedonian imbroglio as the alliance with the Ottomans paid off. The IMRO on the eve of the Young Turk Revolt had lost its momentum and did not represent an important threat. However, there was another reason that played an equally central role for the withdrawal of the organization. The Ilinden uprising did not only alarm Athens but also had generated a fratricidal war between the IMRO and the SMAC. Relations between the two organizations were very tense on the eve of Ilinden. Leading members of the IMRO have not yet been convinced about the readiness of the organization to wage a full scale insurgency but a serious incident accelerated the events. An uprising that took place in the area around Gorna Dzhumayav (Blagoevgrad), today south western Bulgaria in late 1902 that was brutally repressed by the Ottomans ultimately

---

71 A good study on that is: Persephoni Karampati, "Opla kai Sphragides. Ethniki Drasi kai Koinotikoi Dichasmoi stin Periodo tou Makedonikou Agona", in *Anorthodoxoi Polemoi. Makedonia, Emphylios, Kypros* ed. Ioannis Stefanides, Stathis Kalyvas, Vasilis Gounaris (Athens: Patakis, 2013).

72 See for example: Isa Blumi, "Contisting the Edges of the Ottoman Empire: Rethinking Ethnic and Sectarian Boundaries in the Malësore, 1878–1912," *International Journal of Middle East Studies*, 35 (2003): 237–256.

73 Georgios Agelopoulos, Perceptions, Construction, and Definition of Greek National Identity in Late Nineteenth–Early Twentieth Century Macedonia', *Balkan Studies* 36, no. 2: 256–257.

compelled the IMRO to adopt a radical revolutionary solution.[74] Some historians claim that this revolt was machinated by General Tsonchev and a small fraction that collaborated with the SMAC and had infiltrated the IMRO: the Salonika based "Bulgarian Secret Revolutionary Brotherhood" led by the Bulgarian teacher Ivan Garvanov. The logic behind this suicidal move was to employ the bloodshed in order to provoke the IMRO leadership and generate a wave of sympathy in western public opinion. The failure of Ilinden signalled a temporary breakdown in the relations of the two irredentist networks.[75] In 1905 and 1908 the Rila and Kyustendil congresses of the IMRO only officialised this new reality creating fractions.[76] The first one the Federalists, led by Jane Sandanski the head of the Serres branch of the IMRO advocated the creation of an autonomous Macedonia within the Ottoman Empire. The second, the Centralists constituted essentially the continuation of the SMAC after it dissolution by the Bulgarian Government in 1903, and the third led by Boris Sarafov an influential Bulgarian officer was somewhere in between. During the crucial years of the Macedonian proxy war these factions not only failed to coordinate activities against the Porte and Greece but they resorted in killing each other. The tip of the iceberg was the assassination of Sarafov by Santanski's right hand man Todor Panitsa in 1907.[77]

The Young Turk revolt terminated, at least in name, the Macedonian proxy war. The CUP, the Ottoman Empire's most prominent clandestine political movement that strove to end the autocratic regime of Abdülhamid and to reinstate the constitution that the sultan had suspended in 1878 led a successful revolt in the summer of 1908. The Young Turks' revolution can be definitely considered as a transnational event. Its implications surpassed the limits of the Ottoman Empire instigating a series of events that detonated a regional crisis with profound impact. This revolt was also linked with a wider wave of revolutionary upheavals across the globe which spanned from the Portuguese Empire to China and from Iran to Tsarist Russia.[78]

74 Vemund Aarbake, *Ethnic Rivalry and the Quest for Macedonia, 1870–1913* (Boulder: Eastern European Monographs, 2003), 104–107.
75 Fikret Adanir, Die Makedonische Frage. Ihre Entstehung und Entwicklung bis 1908 (Wiesbaden: Franz Steiner Verlag, 1979), 139–170.
76 Valkov, *The Internal Macedonian-Adrianople*, 58–64.
77 Dimitar Bechev, *Historical Dictionary of the Republic of Macedonia* (Maryland: Scarecrow Press, 2009), 82.
78 Erik Jan Zürcher, "The Young Turk Revolution: Comparisons and Connections", *Middle Eastern Studies* 55, no. 4 (2019): 481–498.

Most importantly, it shaped decisively the nature of Turkish nationalism. The CUP began as a series of revolutionary cells based in Paris and as a movement it was born from the army's medical schools of the late Hamidian era. Main figures of the Unionists had roots from the borderlands. These activists were actively engaged in political affairs because they had been witnessing the increasing gap among Christians and Muslims in terms of economic and social status.[79] The Committee gained momentum in 1906 due to a series of internal crises and revolts in the empire and political agitation by Christian groups in the Balkans. This was the moment that the leaders realized the need to expand their networks to non-Muslims. The merger of the CUP with the, Salonika based, "Ottoman Freedom Society" founded by the future leading figure Mehmed Talaat allowed the Young Turks to obtain a centralized base concentrated in a particular region. The ideological platform of the CUP was not clearly articulated and traversed among the three mainstream ideologies. Its policy could be described as: centralist, anti-European, and anti-interventionist. Sukru Hanioglu's study supports that the Committee never articulated a coherent ideological agenda and it was not until 1902 in the first congress that the members discussed substantial issues regarding ideological directives. Nonetheless, the CUP never acquired the characteristics of a popular movement and its ideas were confined in intellectual circles. The lack of coherent ideology had a major ramification. Even though it managed to destroy the Hamidian regime it did not replace it with a new political framework.[80]

One of the debates that have concerned historians in regard to the outbreak of the Balkan Wars has to do with the role of the Young Turk policy toward Christian populations. Balkan historians argue that it was the suppressive nature of the CUP and the constant violation of the Treaty of Berlin which left no alternative but to declare war to the new regime.[81] In contrast, Turkish historians support that the policy of the Committee in Rumeli was a response to constant provocations by irredentist organizations and their patron states. According to this viewpoint, the Balkan alliance employed a

79 Erik Zürcher, "The Young Turks – Children of the Borderlands?", *International Journal of Turkish Studies* 9, no. 1–2 (2003): 275–286.
80 Şükrü Hanioğlu, *Preparation for a Revolution: The Young Turks, 1902–1908* (New York: Oxford University Press, 2001).
81 Article 23 in particular which guaranteed some basic rights for the Christian populations. Feroz Ahmad, *The Young Turks: The Committee of Union and Progress in Turkish Politics, 1908–1914* (Oxford: Clarendon Press, 1969).

turbulent situation as justification for a war that had already been decided and its purpose was twofold: the partition of the Ottoman Empire and the attainment of aggressive nationalistic agendas.[82]

In fact, both explanations have valid points. Undoubtedly, the most thorny issue in the political agenda was the firm willingness of the Young Turks to centralize the empire which faced enormous difficulties in the provinces who pursuit regional autonomy and had supported the CUP on this premise. The committee took a series of extremely unpopular measures toward Christians. One of the moves that showed this radicalization was a boycott of Greek commercial activities which was accompanied by a series of legislations that favoured Turkification.[83] Among them belonged, the mandatory military conscription, the ban of political organizations of national orientation, the reformation of the education system, and the settlement of Muslim refugees from Bosnia Herzegovina. The Association Law of 1909 that restricted every organized party based on ethnicity generated further resentment because it violated the principle of equality which was one of the main pillars that attracted Christian followers to the agenda of the CUP.[84] The decision of the Young Turks to equip and organize Muslim armed bands in Macedonia was the final act that denoted that the ideology of Ottomanism was a dead letter from the new regime.[85]

Victimization of Christians yet represented the one side of the coin. Many comitadji leaders participated in celebrations in Salonika and on several occasions they delivered weaponry immediately dissolving their formations. Nevertheless, this was just only a façade. The vast majority of Greek bands were transferred to the southern border in Thessaly, while the members of 55 IMRO bands that surrendered were peasants that belonged to local militias and not to experienced units. The confiscated equipment was almost obsolete and all the valuable machine guns and armaments were hidden in the

---

82 More information about the historiography on this issue see: Mehmet Hasicalihoglu, "The Young Turk Policy in Macedonia. Cause of the Balkan Wars?", in *War and Nationalism* and same author: *Die Jungtürken und die Mazedonische Frage (1890–1918)*, ed. Yavuz- Blumi (Munich: R. Oldenbourg. 2003), 100–102.

83 Konstantinos Svolopoulos, *Elliniki Exoteriki Politiki, 1900–45* (Athens: Estia, 2008), 57–58.

84 Christopher Psilos, *The Young Turk Revolution and the Macedonian Question* (Leeds University: Unpublished PhD Thesis 2000), 168–180.

85 Ryan Gingeras, "Beyond Istanbul's 'Laz Underworld': Ottoman Paramilitarism and the Rise of Turkish Organized Crime, 1908–1950", *Contemporary European History* 19, no. 3 (2010): 218.

countryside for future purposes.[86] Another challenge represented the issue of political partisanship. In the early stages of their rule the Young Turks made an attempt to reconcile relations between different groups in Macedonia by trying to establish a supranational "Ottoman Club" as an umbrella to the organizations that were willing to cooperate with the CUP, regardless of ethnicity and religion. However, some Christian clubs during a failed counter coup instigated by lower *ulemas* (Muslims trained in Islamic law) old Hamidian bureaucrats, and highly ranked officers in the summer of 1909 supported the counterrevolutionaries.[87]

Most importantly, the reason that led to the breakdown between the members of the different ethno religious groups and the CUP was a misreading of the initial aims of the revolution. The Young Turks envisioned from the very beginning the consolidation of a modern centralized state which would replace the old imperial polity. This was diametrically different for Christian populations which considered the July declarations of equality, fraternity, and freedom as a golden opportunity for self-government.[88] Ultimately, the actions of the CUP that targeted the special status of the millets were perceived as an attempt to create a Turkish consciousness paving the way for the emergence of a Christian opposition based on national characteristics.[89]

While it is true that both explanations contributed to our knowledge they still miss the most important link which is one of the central points that I intend to underline in this book. During the crucial years of 1908–1912, while we have a rapprochement on a state level and a series of bilateral treaties gradually crystallized the Balkan alliance, this never diffused to the local level.[90] The dynamics of the Macedonian proxy war, fed by a circle of blood, remained almost intact and followed distinct paths as vividly described in the article of the Turkish speaking newspaper Yeni Gazete in early 1909: "Bulgarians and Greeks slaughter each other everywhere in Macedonia and the Mohamedans

86 Douglas Dakin, *The Unification of Greece*, 1770–1923, trans. Xanthopoulos Athanasios (Athens: Morfotiko Idryma Ethnikis Trapezis, 2012), 267.
87 Mehmet Hasicalihoglu, "The Young Turk Policy in Macedonia", 112.
88 Erik Jan Zürcher "Macedonians in Anatolia: The Importance of the Macedonian Roots of the Unionists for their Policies in Anatolia after 1914", *Middle Eastern Studies* 50, no. 6 (2014): 968.
89 Vangelis Kechriotis, "The Modernization of the Empire and Community Privileges. Greek Orthodox Responses to Young Turk Policies", in *The State and the Subaltern*, ed. Touraj Atabaki (London: IB Tauris, 2007), 69–70.
90 Igor Despot, *The Balkan Wars in the Eyes of the Warring Parties: Perceptions* and Interpretations (Bloomingtthon: IUniverse, 2012), 37–48.

are being forced to participate to this killing".[91] The Greek newspaper Pharos, published in Salonika, circulated an article with a similar tone: "After a short term armistice caused by the proclamation of the Constitution, the situation in the hinterland is again threatening and soon will surpass the {violent}levels before the constitutional period".[92]

These two abstracts encapsulate the main change of the 1908 revolt: the militarization and deeper engagement of Muslim populations to the proxy war. Muslim refugees coming from other parts of the empire staffed new armed bands that operated against Christians. Nevertheless, this did not go hand in hand with a Christian reconciliation. Apart from some sporadic flashes that constituted the exception, the rivalry between Greek and Bulgarian factions never ended. Greeks consulates throughout Macedonia constantly reported the activities of IMRO and Supremist bands as the most important threat, even during the summer of 1912.[93] Aside from a short thaw that lasted a couple of months in 1908, the insurgency rapidly resumed. The formation of the league was not able to reverse this tide. The involvement of the Balkan states in the proxy war intensified local frictions in some occasions to a point of no return. These dynamics of violence in the micro level were deeply embedded and not entirely controlled by high decision politics. This is the one of the pillars that explains the quality and quantity of violence in 1912–3. The others were the brutality of the battlefield and the military occupation.

The Italian attack in Tripoli, the last Ottoman possession in North Africa in 1911, showed with the most emphatic way the vulnerability of the Ottoman state. The Great Powers' lack of uniform response in Rome's aggression provided a unique opportunity for a military intervention by the Balkan League. On October 8, 1912 Montenegro declared war to the Porte. Within weeks Serbia, Bulgaria, and Greece followed suit.[94] The declaration caught the Great Powers off guard and constituted the first and the last time that the Eastern Question was defied by peripheral powers.

---

91 Cited in: Vasilis Tzanakaris, *O Kokkinos Soultanos. O Avdoul Chamit kai i Agnosti Thessaloniki* (Thessaloniki: Metaixmio, 2011), 431.

92 Ibid., 430.

93 See for instance Istoriko Archeio Ypourgeiou Exoterikon (IAYE), 152.1.1912; IAYE, 126.4.1912; IAYE, 125.2.1912.

94 Michael A. Reynolds, *Shattering Empires. The Clash and Collapse of the Ottoman and Russian Empires* (Cambridge: Cambridge University Press, 2011), 32–34.

· 2 ·

BEKIR FIKRI OF GREVENA: MICRO DYNAMICS OF VIOLENCE IN THE VILAYET OF MANASTIR

Theodoros Chrysanthakopoulos was one of the many men that enlisted in the Greek army to participate in the Balkan Wars. Athenian by birth, Chrysanthakopoulos had the privilege not to fight in the front line serving as finance officer in a hospital in the town of Servia, in today Greek Western Macedonia. His correspondence was very rich and almost daily he was sending letters communicating every day matters with his family. One day, however, he sent a letter to his brother with a rather different context. There he expressed his deep concerns about the appearance of a certain Bekir with 2,000 Albanians irregulars in the outskirts of the town.[1] The eye of the careful observer might wonder why Chrysanthakopoulos refers to a specific individual and not to a regular unit of the Ottoman army. As mentioned above, he was from old Greece[2] and did not have any familiarity with the area. Thus, this meant that Bekir was somehow notorious in order to be so widely known. And indeed that was the case.

Yüzbasi Bekir Fikri was born in 1882 in the mixed village of Tsourchli (Agios Georgios) near the city of Grevena. He was from a humble background

---

1 Elliniko Istoriko kai Logotechniko Archeio (ELIA), Archeio Theodorou Chrysan-thakopoulou, 08/11/1912.

2 As it was called the Kingdom of Greece before 1912.

as his father Mourtos was a servant in the estates of a rich Greek family named Gagali. Mourtos enlisted in the army as a reserve soldier (redif), and offered a proper education to his son. The mother tongue of Bekir was Greek since his village was inhabited entirely by Greek speaking Christians and Muslims (Vallahades).[3] Most sources attribute Albanian origins to the Fikri family. After his basic training Bekir moved to Manastir in order to attend the Military High School which he completed in 1903. His baptism of fire took place in 1907 when his unit was dispatched to Yemen for counter insurgency operations. This was an experience that shaped decisively the mental world of the Ottoman captain. Bekir became a close witness of the process of forging connections with local Yemeni networks and the way that the Ottomans governed this remote province.[4] After his return in 1907 he joined the CUP and received the honorary award as captain of the gendarmerie of Grevena.[5]

Bekir Fikri represented the category of cadres who even though of Albanian origin, he fought until the very end for the cause of the Young Turks and the survival of the Empire.[6] Most importantly, he was the only officer of the Ottoman Army that utilized effectively his counter insurgency knowledge from the war in Yemen by mobilizing all the available forces at his disposal: border guards, redifs, gendarmes, and the civilian population. In this way, he managed to wage a six months long guerilla war to the Greek army that spanned almost in an area of 100km.[7] In this chapter, by using the example of Bekir, I present in what way local strife could enhance violent dynamics and unveil some patterns that were later on adopted by the Ottoman security apparatus and particularly the Special Organization.

A Different Macedonian Question: The Kaza of Grevena

In the south western part of the Manastir vilayet the kaza of Grevena was located. The kaza was in a very fragile geostrategic position. It bordered in

3 Efimerida Empros: 17/01/1914.
4 Thomas Kuehn, *Empire, Islam, and Politics of Difference. Ottoman Rule in Yemen, 1849–1919* (Leiden: Brill, 2011).
5 Elsie Robert, *Historical Dictionary of Albanian History* (London: Tauris, 2012), 179–180.
6 Isa Blumi, *Reinstating the Ottomans* (London: Palgrave, 2011).
7 Edward J. Erickson-Mesut Uyar, *A Military History of the Ottomans: From Osman to Ataturk* (Praeger, 2009), 230, 233.

the West with the vilayet of Janina and in the South with the Kingdom of Greece. During the Macedonian proxy war Greek paramilitary units utilized it as a passage. Pavlos Melas, the national Martyr of the Macedonian affair was one of the first that went through this area in 1904. This small administrative district presented some differentiations in its composition. Ethnic antagonism existed but in a rather different form due to absence of concrete Slavic speaking enclaves. Contemporary censuses indicate an ongoing struggle among the Greeks and the Vlachs regarding this particular area. According to a Greek census of the early twentieth century the kaza was inhabited by: 25,530 Orthodox Greeks, 4,702 Muslims (mainly Greek speaking Vallahades), and 685 Vlachs (roumanizontes). Vlachs were considered by Greek circles people that did not identify as Greeks and affiliated themselves closer to Romania.[8] On the other hand, Vasil Kantsev in his ethnographic study presents a rather different reality. While he almost agrees with the total number 29,000 of the population and the number of Muslims 4,871, he counts as Vlachs 9,220 and as Orthodox Greeks 13,717.[9] The discrepancy here derives from the fact that Greek authorities recognized the Vlach speaking people as Greeks and only a few as propagandists of Romanian interests.

The Vlach issue lied in the heart of ethnic tensions in the kaza. As with most groups that comprised the *millets*, similarly Vlachs cannot be regarded as a monolithic and uniform body (the Vlach language is an idiom without written form). Recent studies have shown that even within the millet structures a lot of tensions existed depending on the socio-economic stratification.[10] Therefore, prosperous Vlach communities in the cities of Manastir and Moschopoli, served as "guardians of hellenism", while many Vlachs were successfully integrated in the nation states of the Balkans.[11] One the other hand, populations that inhabited the mountainous regions were mainly pastoral and characterized by semi nomadic activity. These two worlds were the

---

8   Genika Archeia tou Kratous (GAK): Archeio Tsondou Varda, Folder no. 30, 1910, 285.

9   Vasil Kanchov (1862–1902) was an ethnographer, teacher and politician who served as the general inspector of the Bulgarian schooling network in Ottoman Macedonia. *Macedonia. Ethnografia I Statistika* (1900), 283.

10 Varak Ketsemanian, The Hunchakian Revolutionary Party *and the* Assassination Attempts Against Patriarch Khoren Ashekian and Maksudzade Simon Bey in 1894", *International Journal of Middle East Studies*, no. 4 (2018): 50.

11 Giuseppe Motta, "The Fight for Balkan Latinity. The Vlachs until WWI", *Mediteranean Journal Social Sciences*, 2 (3 Sept. 2011): 254–256.

basic poles that shaped the economic and political realities that Vlachs had to deal with.[12]

The 1848 European revolutions and the spirit of romantic nationalism led Romanian intellectuals to orient their attention to the Vlachs of the Ottoman Empire. The first traveller that recorded impressions was the poet Dimitrie Bolintineanu in 1854. In 1860 the Macedono-Romanian Committee was founded in Bucharest which was an organization that promoted the creation of schools and churches in Ottoman Macedonia by promoting a Vlach identity closer to Romania. One of the pioneers of Romanian efforts in Ottoman Macedonia, the monk Averkios, was born in the Vlach village of Avdella in the kaza of Grevena. After living in the Danubian Principalities he returned and tried to recruit young men to receive Romanian education.[13] Another crucial representative was Apostol Margarit from the same village who built a career as a teacher of Romanian language. His actions attracted the attention of the Greek Patriarchate that declared him persona non grata and forced him to relocate to Romania where he joined the Macedono-Romanian Committee. After his repatriation he continued setting up schools in the late 1860s, and eventually became Inspector General of the Romanian educational network in 1877. Before his death he attempted without success to orient the Vlach church to the Catholic by opening channels of communication with the Austro-Hungarian and French authorities.[14]

This multifaceted antagonism prompted violent dynamics in the kaza of Grevena.[15] The Vlachs as semi-nomads were very reluctant to the idea of a territorial expansion of the Greek Kingdom because the annexation of Thessaly in 1881 had deprived them from winter grazing areas and made the passage very difficult due to requirement of travel documents. This was probably explains the decision of many Vlachs from Grevena to side with

---

12 Vasilis Nitsiakos, "Oi Vlachoi tis Elladas. Ethniki entaxi kai politismiki aphomiosi", in O
     Ellinikos Kosmos Anamesa stin Epochi toy diaphotismou kai ton Eikosto aiona, ed. Konstantinos
     Dimadis (Athens: Ellinika Grammata, 2007), 485–494; For more see: Nickolas Balamaci,
     Can the Vlachs Write Their Own History? Journal of Hellenic Diaspora 17, no. 1
     (1991): 9–36.

13 In 1879 it was renamed as: Society of Macedono-Romanian Culture. Spiridon Sphetas,
     "To istoriko plaisio ton ellinoroumanikon scheseon", Makedonika 33, no. 1 (2002): 29–30.

14 Tom Winnifrith, The Vlachs. The History of a Balkan People (New York: St. Martin's.
     1987), 141.

15 Ali Arslan, Greek-Vlach Conflict in Macedonia, Études balkaniques 2, 84.

the Ottomans as auxiliaries in the short Greco-Ottoman War of 1897.[16] The Hellenizing efforts of the Patriarchate and the encouragement of irregular activities at the turn of the century led the Romanian government in November 1905 to allocate funds for the creation of armed bands adopting at the same time a harder stance toward the Greek population in the country.[17] The same year, a Sultanic edict (*irade*) recognized the Vlachs as a distinct and in part self-governing ethno-religious group (*millet*) under the umbrella of Ottoman rule.[18] This strife among Greeks and Vlachs was soon employed by the Bulgarian side and the IMRO. Already an informal cooperation existed because of the participation of Vlachs for arms smuggling in Western Macedonia which strengthened after 1906 when IMRO bands started operating in Vlach settlements.[19]

The Young Turk revolution profoundly impacted the region and actors under study. Already after the Ilinden uprising and the unsuccessful attempt to establish the rule of law, the Ottomans needed to rely to non-official channels.[20] The Vlachs were a group that they could count on because of the non-territorial interest of Romania.[21] The proclamations of the CUP promising equality to the ethno-religious groups in the Empire caused concerns to Greek circles. Athens advised consuls not to support the Young Turks and this line was also adopted by the Patriarchate. The reasoning behind this move was that the agenda of the CUP was harmful to Greek interests and threatened to undermine the role of the Patriarch.[22]

The next group that needs further elaboration is the Greek speaking Muslims of Western Macedonia, the so called Vallahades. French Physician Francois Pouqueville was one of the first travelers writing about this religious group in the early nineteenth century. The Vallahades were concentrated

16 John Koliopoulos, "Brigandage and Irredentism in Modern Greece", *European History Quarterly* 19, no. 2 (1989): 216.

17 Sphetas, "To istoriko plaisio ton ellinoroumanikon scheseon", 43.

18 Lena Divani, *Ellada kai Meionotites: to systima Diethnous Prostasias tis Koinonias ton Ethnon* (Athens: Kastaniotis, 1999), 97.

19 Nikola Minov, "The Vlachs and the IMRO", *Macedonian Historical Review*, YDK, 94, 497.7:135.1, 189–190, 195–197.

20 Nadir Özbek, "Policing the Countryside. Gendarmes of the late Nineteenth Century Ottoman Empire", *International Journal of Middle East Studies* 40, no. 1 (2008): 47–67.

21 Ali Arslan, "The Vlach Issue during the Late Ottoman Period and the Emergence of the Vlach Community (millet)", *Études balkaniques* 4: 122.

22 Mehmed Hacisalihoglu, "The Young Turk Revolution and the Negotiaton for the Solution of the Macedonian Question", in *Turcica*, Vol. 36, no. 4 (2004): 168–170.

between the cities of Kastoria, Grevena, and Siatista, today's Greek Western Macedonia. They took their name from the Muslim vow *wallahi* (By God) and they were Greek speaking. They resided in mixed or Muslim villages and were scattered across the kazas of Grevena and Anaselitsa (Voio).[23] In the kaza of Grevena ten Muslim and seven mixed villages existed. Their occupation was mainly farmers and stock rearers. According to some studies the Vallahades were Greek speaking populations that were Islamized at the beginning of the second half of the seventeenth century. One theory suggests that this conversion process was voluntary and initiated by the brothers Lioufi, who were probably devsirmes trained in Istanbul. After their return to Macedonia the brothers with their Islamic names Sinan Cavus and Husseyin Cavus conveyed the message of the Koran.[24] Another theory suggests that security and economic concerns drove their decision to convert due to unrest in the late eighteenth century by the Orlov uprising[25] and land privileges.[26] Some historians correlate the Vallahades with the *ciftlik* institution because the holders of this title were remarkably concentrated in this area.[27] According to historian Elizabeth Kontogiorgi, the Vallahades possessed the most fertile lands in Western Macedonia and a significant number of them had obtained the title of Bey.[28]

Despite being Muslims, they retained elements from Christianity. Religious syncretism in the Ottoman era was not uncommon, and the Vallahades constituted one of the most representative examples. Close relations between Christians and Muslims and religious superstition resulted often in the deviation from orthodox doctrines because the locals were seeking a more practical religion to provide answers for their concerns about the supernatural,

---

23 Konstantinos Tsourkas-Stilpon Kyriakidis, Tragoudia Vallahadon. *Makedonika,* 2 (2017): 461–465.

24 Phokion Kotzagiorgis, "Conversion to Islam in Ottoman Rural Societies: The cases of Vallahades and Pomaks, 133–135", in *Ottoman Rural Societies and Economies*, ed. Elias Kolovos (Crete University Press: Rethymno, 2015).

25 An unsuccessful rebellion that took place in 1770 machinated by Tsarist Russia during the war against the Ottoman Empire in 1768–1774. It started in the Peloponnese after the arrival of the Russian admiral Alexei Orlov and was brutally repressed.

26 Apostolos Vakalopoulos, *Istoria tis Makedonias, 1354–1833* (Institute for Balkan Studies: Thessaloniki, 1973), 348, 356.

27 Kotzagiorgis, *Conversion to Islam*, 143.

28 Elizabeth Kontogiorgi, *Population Exchange in Greek Macedonia: The Rural Settlement of Refugees 1922–1930* (Oxford Historical Monographs, Clarendon Press—Oxford, 2006), 198–200.

the death, and the evil.[29] The Vallahades kept a lot of Christian traditions and some scholars have even claimed that the phenomenon entailed some elements of Crypto-Christianity.[30] Recent scholarship that offers a more sub-stantiated approach to Islam in the Balkans perceives the creation of these communities as the result of a two way cross fertilization known as the "indig-enization of Islam", the by-product of a cultural osmosis in which pre Ottoman cultural elements were integrated to Islam and became inherent parts of a long term process of acceptance to conversion.[31]

Another crucial distinctive characteristic of the Vallahades was that in their vast majority they followed the Bektashi order and not Sunni Islam. Geographer Frederick Hasluck who conducted a very well detailed ethno-graphic research in the area provided useful information. The first major Bektashi tekke which was serving the Muslims of Anaselitsa was connected to Eminen Baba who is considered an early preacher.[32] The rise of national-ist agitation in the late hamidian era, labelled groups that were associated with the Bektashi order as "imperfect Muslims that needed correction" and instigated a campaign to shut down *tekkes* and dispatch ulama preachers for re-education.[33]

The Assassination of the Metropolitan

On October 8, 1911 the Ottoman authorities officially announced the assas-sination of the Greek metropolitan of Grevena, Aimilianos. The priest who had gone missing for four days was found brutally murdered. Alongside with

---

29 Nicholas Doumanis, *Before the Nation: Muslim Christian Coexistence and Its Destruction in late Ottoman Anatolia* (Oxford: Oxford University Press, 2013), 108.

30 Stavro Skendi, Crypto-Christianity in the Balkan Area under the Ottomans, *Slavic Review* 26, no. 2 (Jun., 1967): 245–246; One of them was the tradition of the cutting of the Basil cake so that to celebrate New Years Eve. Margaret M. Hasluck, "The Basil-Cake of the Greek New Year", *Folklore* 38, no. 2 (Jun. 30, 1927), 148.

31 Nikolay Antov, "Emergence and Historical Development of Muslim Communities in the Ottoman Balkans: Historical and Historiographical Remarks", in *Beyond the Mosque, Church the State. Alternative Narratives of the Nation in the Balkans*, ed. Thedora Dragostinova-Yana Hashamova (Budapest: CEU Press, 2016), 42.

32 Frederick W. Hasluck, *Christianity and Islam under the Sultans*, Vol 2 (Oxford, 1929), 526–530.

33 Nathalie Clayer, "Religious Pluralism in the Balkans in the Late Ottoman Era, 105–107", in *Imperial Lineage and legacies in the Eastern Mediterranean*, ed. Rhoads Murphey (London: Routledge, 2017).

Aimilianos, his companions were killed too, the priest Dimitrios Anagnostou, and their guide Athanasios Phasoulas. According to the Greek consulate of Manastir the perpetrators were Vlachs that collaborated with the Young Turks while this action signalled the beginning of an extermination campaign that targeted the higher Greek clergy.[34]

The assassination of Aimilianos arrived as a bomb and literally opened the Pandora's Box in the society of Grevena. The local Christians lamented his death and a big ceremony was organized for his burial. The Ottoman police took precautionary measures in order to prevent violent incidents while the Serbian and Russian Consuls attended the funeral. Commemorations were organized throughout the Greek communities in the Ottoman Empire and the Kingdom of Greece and the pioneer cinematographers from the Vlach village of Avdella, the Manakia brothers filmed the event.[35]

After few days, news regarding the identity of the perpetrators arrived. According to reports, the infamous Skoubraioi, a gang of "Vlachs" Vlachs executed the priest with the wholehearted support of Mitro Tsiakama, the so called "Prince of Krania".[36] Later on new information were added by involving this time the CUP head in the branch of Grevena, Captain Bekir Fikri, an alleged sworn enemy of the priest.[37] Circulating rumours mentioned that two days before the assassination Aimilianos paid a visit to the Governor of Grevena (kaimakam) after an urgent request of the latter. This meeting was attended by Bekir and the two men had a very intense conversation. The metropolitan expressed deep concerns about the hardship of Christian populations and the unacceptable behaviour of Fikri while Bekir responded by threatening the priest.[38]

Greek authorities were immediately mobilized to conduct an investigation and blamed the Ottomans for obstructing the process in order to cover the participation of Bekir.[39] Ottoman MP Georgios Bousios alongside with other Greek representatives severely protested in the parliament characterizing this event as the tip of the iceberg of the hardening of the stance of the Young Turk authorities toward Christians.[40] This protest resulted in the

---

34   IAYE, 122, 7, apo Mavroudi pros Kendriki Ypiresia, 8/10/1911.
35   IAYE, 62, 1, 17/11/1911.
36   IAYE, 122, 7, apo, Phoresti pros Kendriki Ypiresia, 8/10/1911.
37   IAYE, 122, 7, apo, Ntasso pros Kendriki Ypiresia, 13/10/1911.
38   IAYE, 122, 7, Synomilia tou Mitropoliti Aimilianou.
39   IAYE, 122, 7, apo Grevena pros Bousio, 14/10/1911, pp. 1–6.
40   IAYE, 122, 7, apo Peran pros Kendriki Ypiresia, 15/10/1911.

replacement of the kaimakam but not the removal of Bekir. However, the situation got complicated again. New information this time named as assailants
two Greeks bandits, Zikos and Ramos.[41] Indeed, a few days later the aforementioned were arrested in the city of Larissa in the Greek Kingdom and
confessed their crime.[42] The arrival of the news not only failed to de-escalate
the crisis, but instigated a new round of accusations' exchange. Greek consular authorities sent a new report providing a different narrative. According
to that, the assassination was a plot organized by the CUP, the Vallahades,
and the Vlachs after a chain of events: the governor of Grevena a short period
before the assasination had held responsible the Metropolitan for the death
of three gendarmes, after an ambush by a Greek band. This band belonged
to the Tsioukantama brothers from the Vlach settlement of Perivoli. Bekir
after the event gathered the Greek notables of Grevena and after blaming
them for the murder of the gendarmes threatened with imminent retribution.
This warning resulted in the death of Aimilianos by the collaboration of some
Muslim villagers and some Vlachs during his tour in Christian villages. The
ultimate proof that this action was political in nature was that the valuables
of the victim were found in the crime scene.[43]

This is the official story according to Greek diplomatic documents. As it
seems, Aimilianos was the target of an execution that which was highly politicized and involved individuals that were key players in the kaza. As historian
Max Bergholz argues, there are some certain events in the micro level that
may cause mental schemas of collective categorization that radically trans-
form social relations crystallizing an antagonistic sense of "us" and "them".[44]
The assassination of Aimilianos could be inscribed as such an event and the
outcome as I show played a key role in inter-communal relations a year before
the outbreak of the Balkan Wars.

Still, it was more than that. The role of the key participants in this murderous act may unravel the mechanisms of the Young Turks security apparatus
in a crucial period were state control was in defiance in Ottoman Macedonia.

41 IAYE, 122, 7, apo Konstantinoupoli pros Kendriki Ypiresia, 4/1/1911.
42 IAYE, 122, 7, apo Monastiri pros Kendriki Ypiresia, 16/11/1911; according to this inves-
    tigation this was the outcome of the score settling within the organization for financial
    reasons, Ilay Ileri, *A Page from the History of the Balkans*, 193–195.
43 IAYE, 122, 7, apo Ioannina pros Kendriki Ypiresia, 29/11/1911.
44 Max Bergholz, "Sudden Nationhood: The Microdynamics of Intercommunal Relations in
    Bosnia Herzegovina after World War II", *The American Historical Review* 118, no. 3 (June
    2013): 680–681.

The CUP after the proclamation of the constitution in 1908 adopted radical practices expressing military might though subterfuge and targeted assassinations in an attempt to keep the empire together.[45] Bekir did not possess any official position in the kaza as he was the head of the Young Turk's branch in Grevena. However, he was well aware of the assassinations that were taking place. This indicates that his role was something between intelligence officer and paramilitary. Recent studies on the Special Organization argue that the SO was a combination of intelligence gathering and irregular activities. Its modus operandi was heavily informed by the experience of officers that waged guerrilla warfare in the Balkans. In that sense it is possible to reassess his role as a representative example of the predecessors of the SO on the eve of its formation.[46]

Since 1908 Bekir had proven his ability in clandestine operations when on the eve of the Young Turks revolt he managed to form an armed band within a couple of hours by mobilizing local Muslims of Grevena.[47] As typical officer of the CUP he was working to prevent the disintegration of the Empire and naturally opposed any kind of irredentist activities.[48] Political agitators became primary targets for operatives such as Bekir. Since the authorities were not able to be openly involved in an assassination of a priest, this was a task that needed to be done by a non-official actor. Bekir had the knowledge to operate underground and to mobilize alternative channels in order to cover up any state exposure. Targeting the elites was a certain practice used in the late Ottoman era to decapitate and cause a mental shock to populations that many times had a blurred sense of ethnicity and were tied to their local notables and religious leaders.[49]

Metropolitan Aimilianos Lazaridis, one the other hand, was a representative example of a clergyman of the late Ottoman era who was involved in the Macedonian affair. He was born in Permata, a small city in Ikonio (Konya) in

---

45   Ryan Gingeras, *The Fall of the Sultanate: The Great War and the end of the Ottoman Empire* 1908–1922 (Oxford: Oxford University Press, 2016), 38.

46   Yücel Yiğit, "The Teşkilat-ı-Mahsusa and World War I", *Middle East Critique* 23, no. 2 (2014): 157–174.

47   Hanioglu, *Preparation for Revolution*, 228.

48   Ebru Boyar, *Ottomans, Turks and the Balkans: Empire Lost, Relations Altered* (London: I.B. Tauris, 2007), 100.

49   The predecessor of Aimilianos, Metropolitan Agathagkelos during his appointment had created a special fund which allocated money to the bands Riki Van Buschoten, *Anapoda Chronia: Syllogiki Mnimi kai Istoria sto Ziaka Grevenon* (Athens: Prethron, 1997), 37.

Asia Minor by a Christian, Turkish speaking family (Karamanlis). After his graduation from the Theological school of Chalki he was appointed in the Sacred Mitropoli of Salonika where he first met Lampro Koromila, the consul that coordinated irregular activities of Greek bands in the vilayet. Koromilas introduced him to a very influential Macedonian fighter namely, Athanasio Soulioti Nikolaidi, the founder of the "Thessaloniki Organization" an underground network tasked to repel the attempts of the Exarchists to penetrate into the city by employing economic boycott and targeted assassinations.[50]

Georgios Bousios, the Ottoman MP, was a man well acquainted with Aimiliano and together played a central role to the guerrilla warfare that took place in Macedonia.[51] Bousios was early involved in the Macedonian affair by enlisting to the national committee of Grevena and he assisted by smuggling weapons through Thessaly. For his actions he was imprisoned in 1906 in Manastir. Bousios had conflicting interests with Bekir, because the latter had been promoting the election of a Muslim representative for the kaza jeopardizing his seat.[52] Most importantly the Ottoman MP was a fierce anti-unionist and he has been involved in intense parliamentary debates about the conscription of Christians in the Ottoman army.[53]

The proclamation of the constitution in 1908 and the renewal of tensions in the kaza had alarmed Bekir. Muslims in the area were outnumbered and the need to forge new alliances was imperative.[54] Bekir in his memoirs was particularly critical to Greek irregulars underlying the urgency to promote a tactical convergence between Vlachs and Muslims.[55] The inability of the official authorities to safeguard the life and properties of locals had created a power vacuum leading many people to resort to violent or illicit practices substituting the state.[56]

50 Ioannis Papadimitriou, *O Ethnomartis Mitropolitis Aimilianos* (Athens, 2011), 17–20.

51 Pammakedonikos Syllogos, *Makedoniko Imerologio* (Athens: 1909), 308–309; Apostolos Papadimitriou, *Selides Istorias ton Grevenon* (Tsiartsianis: Grevena, 2016) 246.

52 IAYE, 122, 7, Antapokrisi ek Trikalon peri tis stygeras dolofonias tou aeimnistoy Mitropoliti Aimilianou kai syn ayto.

53 Ugur Peçe, "The Conscription of Greek Ottomans into the Sultan's Army, 1908–1912", *International Journal of Middle East Studies* 52, no, 3: 445.

54 Something similar but from the opposite direction happened during the Greco-Turkish was when the Greek army collaborated in the Southern Marmara with Kirkassian bands. See Ryan *Gingeras, Sorrowful Sorrows* (Oxford: Oxford University Press, 2009).

55 Nathalie Clayer, *Oi Aparches toy Alvanikou Ethnikismou*, trans. Andreas Sideris (Ioannina: Isnaphi, 2009).

56 Argyropoulos, *Mnimes apo to Makedoniko Agona*, 72.

The most representative example perhaps was the abovementioned Mitros Tsiakamas (Tsikma), a sworn enemy of Greek irredentism in the Vlach villages of Grevena. Tsiakamas was probably the most ardent supporter of Romanian influence in the kaza. He was involved from the very early stages in ethnic antagonism when in 1884 set up the first Romanian school in Krania. In the 1897 war he supported the Ottoman army as auxiliary. Tsiakamas was from a wealthy background and hired as bodyguards the notorious Skoubraious brothers. His life trajectory was shaped by the assassination of his two brothers in 1906 by a Greek named Mitrogiorgos under the orders of the Macedonian Committee, and in 1908 by the Greek chieftain Louka Kokkino. His blood feud did not go unnoticed by Bekir. After 1908 the "Prince of Krania" was integrated into the Ottoman security apparatus and was assigned duties to guide units of the Ottoman gendarmerie that patrolled Vlach settlements. During the Balkan Wars he served with the rank of captain.[57] For this reason Greek sources refer often to *tourkoroumanikes symmories* (turk-romanian bands).[58]

As it seems, the Metropolitan was a very dangerous person and both Bekir and Tsiakamas had many reasons to want him dead. All these events were taking place, the exact same period were Enver Bey convinced the Central Committee of the CUP in Salonika to wage a counter-insurgency war in Libya which lead to the formation of the special organization.[59] One cannot be certain about who gave the final order for the execution. Still it goes without doubt that the assassination further polarized local communities. The constant exchange of accusations and the identification of the perpetrators along ethnic lines created rumours and certain dynamics that shaped the locals' mental framework. For the Greek Christians of Grevena the assassination of their beloved Metropolitan was a plot by the Young Turks, the Greco-Turks (Vallahades), and the Vlachs. This exploding synthesis detonated at the beginning of hostilities and the intensity of violence was greatly determined by these local dynamics.

---

57 Papadimitriou, *Selides Istorias ton Grevenon*, 172, 228, 235, 369.
58 IAYE, 122, 7, apo Monastiri pros Kendriki Ypiresia, 06/10/1911.
59 IAYE, 122, 7, apo Monastiri pros Kendriki Ypiresia, 23/11/1911; IAYE, 122, 7, apo Siatista pros Kendriki Ypiresia, 24/11/1911. Eugene Rogan, *I Ptosi ton Othomanon*, trans. Eleni Asteriou (Athens: Alexandreia, 2015), 15–16.

Bekir's Insurgency

> On my way I was thinking the future of Grevena and we were crying silently with my
> good friend (the kaimakam) for the misery that has fallen to our homeland. I went to
> my village and from there to Kirasti. From there we had more time to gather forces
> to recapture Grevena.[60]

With these words Bekir described his feelings when the news about of the
invasion of the Greek Army arrived. The initial days of hostilities found the
Ottoman commander in Grevena who immediately arrested local notables as
hostages in order to use them as leverage.[61] Bekir was fully aware that he had
been completely cut off from reinforcements and that the defence of Grevena
was not feasible because the city was unfortified. Defending ground in his
village appeared as the only viable alternative. Along his way, he recruited
five hundred Vallahades from Muslim villages[62] and he handed over weapons
to Tsiakama so that to arm his supporters.[63] He additionally took measures in
order to prevent from being deprived from his base of support. Declaration of
martial law and intimidation in case of surrender were amongst the measures
implemented.[64] In his attempt to convey a message that this fight was to the
death he made a move with a high symbolical meaning by not evacuating his
family from Tsourchi. This was one of the most fateful decisions that made the
war even more personal for the Ottoman captain.[65] Bekir's appeal to Ottoman
patriotism was well received by the Vallahades because they followed in great
numbers the Bektashi order, as Albanians did. The multiple faces of Islam
functioned temporarily as glue in some cases during the wars and this certainly
was correlated with the declaration of a *reconquista* by the Balkan states.

In this light we must consider more closely the behaviour of local Muslims
and Vlachs regarding the prospects of resistance. The measures taken by Bekir
instigated certain dynamics that caught civilians in the cross fires. The frame

---

60   Cited in: Vagelis Nikopoulos, *Grevena 1912–1940 Photographika Dokoumenda kai Tekmiria.*
61   Eyal Ginio, "Mobilizing the Ottoman Nation during the Balkan Wars (1912–
     1913): Awakening from the Ottoman Dream", *War in History* 12, no. 2 (2005): 172.
62   GES/DIS, *O Ellinikos Stratos kata tous Valkanikous Polemous*, Vol. I, Appendix (Athens,
     1932), 352.
63   Papadimitriou, *Selides Istorias ton Grevenon*, 369.
64   Georgiou Mylona, *E Drasis ton Andartikon Somaton en Makedonia kata ton Ellinotourkiko
     polemo* (Volos: Thessalia, 1913), 20, 29.
65   Cited in: Vaggelis Nikopoulos, *Grevena. 1912–1940.*

of reference of the local populations had been shaped by collective memories from the endemic violence of the Macedonian proxy war and the Young
Turk era.[66] Every village had different incentives and this depended on prewar
grievances, violent practices inflicted upon neighbours, and personal blood
feuds. While it is true that a lot of Vallahades might have wanted to avoid
fighting, this got really complicated because of the imposed pressures and the
conduct of war. The fight for the kaza of Grevena was mainly conducted by
irregular formations and it was closer to a counter insurgency type of warfare.
The main units that were dispatched from the Greek side were comprised,
among others, by Cretan Macedonian fighters who belonged to the "Scouts",
paramilitary formations that were created on the eve of the Balkan Wars
and operated as auxiliaries to the regular army.[67] Captains such as Georgios
Katechakis and Dikonymos Makris had earned a notorious reputation because
of their struggle against the IMRO and Bulgaria. Ioannis Karavitis one of the
main chieftains in the fight for Grevena writes: "Turkish (Vallahades) villages
are willing to surrender but they want the regular army to do so because they
have misunderstood and are afraid of us. Only a few fanatics are preventing
them."[68]

Although we should take with a grain of salt the captain's presumption
about the numbers of those willing to surrender, it still reflects the situation
in some extend. This reality was acknowledged also by Greek officers who
knew that discipline was something very difficult to attain in irregular units.
Colonel Ippitis who was in charge of an independent mixed detachment that
operated in the area had forced individual captains to swear an oath for disciplinary behaviour.[69] For that reason, Captain Katechakis who enjoyed respect
was appointed as leader of the operations.[70]

Another essential factor that should not be overlooked concerned the
abundance of weapons that existed in the Macedonian hinterland. More

---

66   On the role of collective memory especially the ones that not related to official state
      narratives see: Hanna Kienzler & Sula-Raxhimi, "Collective Memories and Legacies of
      Political Violence in the Balkans." *Nationalities Papers* 47, no. 2 (2019): 173–181.

67   Konstantinos Mazarakis Ainian, *Apo to Makedoniko Agona stous Valkanikous Polemous*
      (Athens: Ethniko Istoriko Mouseio, 2016), 118.

68   Ioannis Karavitis, *O Valkanotourkikos Polemos* (Athens: Petsivas, 2001), 155.

69   Istoriko Archeio Mouseiou Benaki (AMM), Archeio Panagioti Dagkli, Folder 30, Ekthesi
      Pepragmenon ypo anexartitou Miktoy apospasmatos Ant. Pyrovolikoy Antonioy Ippiti
      kata tin ekstrateia 1912–1913, 2.

70   Karavitis, *O Valkanotourkikos Polemos*, 109.

than two decades of revolutionary activity and proxy war had converted the European parts of the Ottoman Empire into a gigantic arsenal.[71] Villages were armed to the teeth,[72] while a lot of villagers possessed weapons for hunting activities that could be used to form militias for self-protection. In this precarious position for the locals was about to be added a vicious circle of violence and retribution signalling the last days of the Ottoman rule in the kaza.

Everybody knew that the crucial battle is about to be given in Bekir's main base of defence, his village Tsourchli. This village was segregated in two districts along religious lines. Its population according to a 1920 census numbered 1,172 people. Christians and Muslims in some occasions were relatives and some theories support that some Albanian speaking families relocated there by Ali Pasha of Tepelenë in the early nineteenth century.[73] Mixed villages of this kind had been the locus of co-existence in the late Ottoman era as well as the first places that this coexistence was disrupted. Tsourchli experienced the rise of inner communal tensions in the years before the war. The murder of the Metropolitan had created frictions. The tense debate after the assassination polarized the community of Tsourchli and cultivated suspiciousness among friends and foes. This situation brings in mind the concept of "antagonistic tolerance" that is used by anthropologists for the Balkan case in order to explain some of the main premises for inner-communal violence. The different ethno religious groups in the late Ottoman era, while they coexisted this did not mean that they embraced each other's values, but rather tolerated them. The most obvious example of this fragile modus vivendi concerned competition for space for religious sites. Once prewar dominance was interrupted, violent outbreaks were anticipated, since the competing groups tried to shift or retain the existing status quo.[74]

The battle for this village witnessed fierce brutality by both sides and the employment of counter insurgency methods. The opening of hostilities began with an act of retribution when Vallahades executed the local Christian priest

---

71 Ramazan Hakki Oztan, "Tools of Revolution: Global Military Surplus, Arms Dealers, and Smugglers in the Late Ottoman Balkans, 1878–1908," *Past & Present*, 237 (November 2017): 167–195.

72 Karavitis, *O Valkanotourkikos Polemos*, 146.

73 Michalis Kalinderis, "Symvoli eis tin Meleti tou Thematos ton Vallaadon", *Etaireia Makedonikon Spoudon*, (1977): 321–354.

74 Robert Hayden, Erdemir, A., Tanyeri-Erdemir, T., Walker, T.D., Rangachari, D., Aguilar-Moreno, M., López-Hurtado, E., and Bakić-Hayden, M., *Antagonistic Tolerance: Competitive Sharing of Religious Sitis and Spaces,* 1st ed. (London: Routledge, 2016), 10–11.

and his sons.[75] The arrival of the first Greek units did not meet with any resistance and this was perceived as a practice of appeasement for the fear of Greek
irregulars.[76] Yet, things escalated when snipers hidden in the Muslim district
started firing at Greek squads. This was a plan of a coordinated attack by
Bekir who intentionally left civilians inside so that to distract his enemies and
to conduct a successful counter attack with troops hidden in nearby hills.[77]
After the initial failure, Greek units arrived with reinforcements and this time
Tsourchli fell. The Cretans surrounded the Muslim district and burnt it to the
ground. In the battle Bekir's brother died and his mother along with other
family members were captured and transferred to Grevena.[78]

An orgy of violence followed in which women and children were indiscriminately killed.[79] This was definitely an act of retribution because of the
involvement of locals. As in the Franco-Prussian War and the German occupation of Belgium in 1914, enemy aliens were considered legitimate targets.[80]
Still, it was more than that. The Austrian consul in Janina specifically underlines in his report the involvement of Bekir in the assassination of Aimilianos
attributing to the annihilation of Tsourchli the notion of what is described by
historian Alan Kramer as "dynamic of destruction".[81] This act was not only
about revenge. It also entailed a symbolical meaning. For Greeks, the village
was the snake's nest and everything that represented had to be vanished.[82]

The same fate awaited other villages involved in the assassination of the
Metropolitan. The operating units that conducted the fight had received specific orders: disarmament of villagers that assisted Bekir or total destruction.[83]
That was typical counter insurgency measures that aimed to deprive the enemy
from manpower. These villagers had already been supplying Bekir and they
were left with no alternative but to fight. The news that had been arriving

---

75   GES/DIS, O Ellinikos Stratos kata tous Valkanikous, 207.

76   AMM, F. 30, p. 8.

77   Georgiou Milona, E Drasis ton Andartikon Somaton (Volos: Thessalia, 1913), 19–21.

78   Nikolaos Davaris, Imerologio Stratiotou Dimitriou Davari (Athens, 2003), 26.

79   Osterreich haus und hof fun stadt archiv (ÖS, HHStA), PA, XII, Konsulate Janina,
     Tellegram aus Hrupista to Janina, November 1912.

80   Mark Stoneman, "The Bavarian Army and French Civilians in the War of 1870–1871: A
     Cultural Interpretation". War in History 8, no. 3 (2001): 273–274.

81   ÖS, HHStA, PA, XII, Konsulate Janina, 23 November 1912, no.91.

82   Alan Kramer, Dynamic of Destruction. Culture and Mass Killing in the First World War
     (Oxford: Oxford University Press, 2007).

83   AMM, F. 30, p. 7; Dimitriou Chatzopoulou, Oi Garivaldinoi sti Machi tou Driskou
     (Athens: Fexis, 1914), 17–18, 20.

daily about relentless massacres, brutalized the belligerents and made the pros-pect of surrender less tempting. But there was another factor that deteriorated the position of the Vallahades. Contemporary Greek sources describe them as fanatics that actively denied their Greek identity by converting to Islam. That was a commonplace perception especially among Cretans whom frame of reference was shaped by the disruption of inner communal relations in the island of Crete among Christian and Muslim -Greek speaking- inhabitants. In their eyes, the ultimate proof of the disloyalty of the Vallahades was that they collaborated with the archenemy of Hellenism, the man who embodied the quintessence of Muslim oppression.[84]

The roots of this rival yet might be deeper reflecting long standing resent-ments. Many Vallahades possessed large estates and were Beys. According to historian Giannis Glavinas the Balkan Wars provided the perfect opportu-nity for the banishment of the existing status quo.[85] This became even worse for Beys that sided with Bekir.[86] The demise of the existing socio economic reality led in many occasions villagers to attack their neighbours by stealing live stocks, confiscating lands or pillaging properties. Recent grievances could be reflected by the intervention of irregulars to prevent reprisals between neighbouring villagers. These practices generated another violent dynamic correlated with the element of reciprocity. One of the multiple facets of vio-lence in wartime is that once it occurs, it has the tendency to incline towards a self-perpetuating action-reaction mechanism.[87]

This chaos disrupted logistical supply.[88] The creation of militias by locals was one of the measures taken to form a new security apparatus.[89] Nevertheless, this was not always feasible with old bandit leaders who plagued the area,

---

84 Stavrou Kelaidi, *I drasi ton Ethelondikon somaton Kriton en Makedonia* (Athens, 1913), 23–24, 102.

85 Giannis Glavinas, *Oi Mousoulmanikoi Plithismoi stin Ellada* (Thessaloniki: Stamoulis, 2013), 302.

86 Mylona, *E Drasis ton Andartikon Somaton*, 75.

87 Isabel Bramsen, I. "How Violence Breeds Violence: Micro-Dynamics and Reciprocity of Violent Interaction in the Arab Uprisings", *International Journal of Conflict and Violence*, 11 (2017): 2.

88 GES/DIS, *O Ellinikos Stratos kata tous Valkanikous Polemous*, 168. When a militia recruits its members from the same constituency as the insurgents, the militia is less likely to target civilians, as doing so would mean attacking their own community: Stanton, J. A. "Regulating Militias: Governments, Militias, and Civilian Targeting in Civil War", *Journal of Conflict Resolution* 59, no. 5 (2015): 899–923.

89 Kelaidi, *I drasi ton Ethelondikon somaton Kriton en Makedonia*, 92.

especially in the kaza where the vast majority of native Macedonian fighters were former brigands.[90] The loyalty of those people was fluid twisting among personal aspirations and irredentist ideals. Some chieftains employed tactics of extortion in order to fund their units.[91] For instance, the two alleged assailants of Aimilianos, Zikos and Ramos during the Wars intensified their murderous activities. Zikos executed 72 Vallahades because they refused to fulfill his economic demands.[92]

Rumours circulated quickly leading Bekir to harden his stance against Christian villages.[93] The decision to leave his family back drove him to orchestrate a campaign to retake Grevena. The imminent news about the attack created chaos in the city and hundreds of inhabitants evacuated to seek shelter to Thessaly, in the Kingdom of Greece.[94] Bekir's actions attracted the attention of the Greek high command becoming public enemy number one. Crown Prince Konstantinos himself offered a 10,000 drachmas bounty for his head.[95] Until the middle of November the situation was almost out of control. Bekir had expanded his operational base in Janina by instigating a terror campaign.[96] According to Greek reports, he collaborated with local Vlachs while, his units had been involved in destruction of churches and massacres of civilians.[97] With his irregulars he recaptured for a short time Grevena and evacuated the city after pillaging, albeit this was not his order but independent actions by Albanians and Vallahades.[98] Only a few Vlachs had remained when it was retaken.[99]

Since the outbreak of hostilities bands of Vlachs collaborated with Bekir and participated in raids against Greek speaking villages initiating a vicious circle of vendettas. Sometimes they united with Vallahades as it was the case of a mixed detachment of 470 men that engaged in skirmishes with a Greek cavalry squad.[100] Greeks bands accordingly targeted from the very beginning

90   Koliopoulos, *Brigands with a Cause*, 225.
91   Papadimitriou, *Selides Istorias ton Grevenon*, 249.
92   Papadimitriou, *O Ethnomartis Mitropolitis Aimilianos*, 172.
93   IAYE, 14, 8, 1913, apo Epitropo Kozanis pros Kendriki Ipiresia, 2/2/1913.
94   Empros: 15/12/1912.
95   Mylona, *I Drasis ton Andartikon Somaton*, 75.
96   Demetrius-John Cassavetti, *Hellas and the Balkan Wars* (London: Fisher, 1914), 147.
97   IAYE, 1913, 14, 8, Kakoseis Bekir Aga.
98   Karavitis, *O Valkanotourkikos Polemos*, 217. Bekir's main purpose was to release his mother from prison.
99   Chatzopoulou, *Oi Garivaldinoi*, 19.
100   Istoriki kai Ethnologiki Etaireia (IEE), Archeio Stefanou Metaxa, Ekthesi Taxiarchias Ippikou, 10/1912.

Vlach populations who begun to flee to the northern parts of the vilayet.[101] In a lot of occasions these attacks had the character of score settling. That was the case of a unit of 150 men from Vlach villages Avdella and Perivoli that tried to burn down the Greek speaking village of Tista (Ziakas) and engaged in a battle with armed villagers. This act was not coincidental. The particular village supported financially chieftains that were the main rivals of the Vlachs in the area.[102] Krania, which was the base of the infamous Tsiakama, was stormed and its population indiscriminately massacred. The raid was conducted among others to track down the teacher. Tsiakamas was eventually murdered outside Grevena after an unsuccessful attempt to surrender.[103]

This seemingly tactical convergence between some Vallahades and Vlachs could shed light to local responses in times of mass violence. United against the common enemy appeared to be the main incentive for this alliance. Recent historical experiences and tensions brought in some occasions Greek speaking Muslims and Vlach Speaking Christians together in the kaza. Bekir tried to capitalize the momentum by employing notions of ottomanism. For both groups the Greek national movement represented a fatal threat. The inclusion into the Hellenic Kingdom meant restrictions in civil liberties particularly for their language and Church. For the Vallahades it would have jeopardized old landowning prerogatives. In a more personal level, some individuals have participated in actions against Greek bands and were targeted beforehand. These motivations which were mixed with fear ended up to the support of Bekir's endeavour.[104]

Apart from common interests, however, there was the appeal of Bekir's persona which presented many elements that scholars ascribe to warlords. These were: military experience, authority to inspire obedience, political ambition, interest in civilian affairs, and a high tolerance for risk.[105] The warlord phenomenon made its presence in a large scale in the Russian civil war (1918–22) when numerous "Whites" opposed the Soviet regime and controlled vast territories imposing their own para-states. It was also a pattern followed in the Asia Minor campaign in 1919–22, when the Greek army faced

---

101 ÖS, HHStA, PA, XII, Konsulate Janina, 23 November 1912, no.91.

102 AMM, F. 30, pp. 14–15.

103 ÖS, HHStA, PA, XII, Turkey, Balkankrieg, 386, Janina 17/11/1912, no.89.

104 See more on: Giannis Gklavinas, "Oi Vallaades tou Voiou Kozanis 1912–1924 mesa apo tis ektheseis toy ypodioikiti tis Eparchias", *Valkanika Symmeikta*, 12–13 (2001–2002): 7–9.

105 Joshua Sanborn, "The Genesis of Russian Warlordism: Violence and Governance during the First World War and the Civil War", *Contemporary European History* 19, no. 3: 198.

enormous challenges especially in its advance deeper into Anatolia, where the ethnological composition favoured the Muslim element and proved to be a hostile ground for the invaders. Certainly the Ottoman captain possessed the above qualities and had the war been prolonged, he might have ended up as a powerful regional actor with his own base of support and his example in that sense paved the way for this phenomenon.

Eventually, after six months of counter insurgency the Ottoman lieutenant evacuated the area. His war was over for now. In May, 1913 he sent two letters to the notables of Grevena expressing his concerns about the mistreatment of Muslims promising revenge. He also denied every accusation about his actions during the Balkan Wars by mentioning that although he did not support publicly the cause of Hellenism, because he is "Turk and son of a Turk", he had always had respect for Greeks. However, the actions of his "new patriots" as he refers to them had been a disgrace allowing the rape of Ottoman women and the purge of loyal Turks. In the end he is closing by sending regards to his fellow Greek and Albanian co-patriots.[106]

Bekir's letters were written with a very emotional tone implying deep sadness and anger. For the Ottoman commander the Greeks were totally disrespectful and constituted the most important factor for the loss of the rule of law and rise of ethnic hatred. Masculinity and honour were concepts underpinning his words and the violation of Muslim women is mentioned twice in the letters. His response was typical of a CUP officer who had devoted his life to the preservation of the Empire. It was also a representative example of perceptions that were fuelled after the end of the Balkan Wars about the betrayal of the non-Muslims and the trauma for the loss of their homelands.[107]

In the summer of 1913 Bekir relocated to Bucharest and tried to recruit bands to conduct a new guerrilla war in Macedonia.[108] Shortly after the termination of the Balkan Wars he was sent to Albania in order to organize a conspiracy that aimed to promote a Muslim Prince for the Albanian throne. This attempt failed and Bekir was imprisoned but eventually Prince William of Wied pardoned him.[109] For his service in the army during the Balkan Wars

106 Istoriko Archeio Makedonias (IAM), Phakelos, 78A, 7/2/1914, pp. 42–43.

107 Erik Jan Zürcher, "Macedonians in Anatolia: The Importance of the Macedonian Roots of the Unionists for their Policies in Anatolia after 1914", *Middle Eastern Studies* 50, no. 6 (2014): 970.

108 IAYE, F. 8, 1913, apo Proxeneio Constantsas pros Ypoyrgeio Exoterikon, No 173, 3/7/1913.

109 Bekir wrote books about his experiences as an officer and his political ideology. Mehmed Tutuncu, "Grebeneli Bekir Fikri Bey Albay Thomson'a Karşi 1914 Avlonya Olayı

he was named as "the hero of Grevena". Ultimately, having crossed Greece, Yemen, Albania, Italy, and Romania he was killed in combat thousands of kilometres away in Erzurum in the depth of the Ottoman Empire during the offensive of Enver Bey in the Caucasus in early 1914.[110]

**

This chapter showed in what way pre-war cleavages and intimacy were significant determinants for the locals to engage in violent acts. In this puzzle key figures such as Bekir played a crucial role to politicize and enhance a strife that had different variations, but already existed. As Benjamin Fortna maintains in his biography about of the Circassian Esref Bey, these kinds of individuals represented the rapid demographic change of the late Ottoman era and the way that personal networks worked for these agents.[111] The life trajectory of Bekir reflects also in the micro level the fluidity of identity formation and the mechanisms of transition from empires to nation states. It is a historical irony, how Bekir, a Greek speaking Turk, and Aimilianos, a Turk speaking Greek greatly affected the events in a small region on the eve of war.

For the historian, on another level, it is quite challenging to discern whether the motivations were political or personal. What can be said with certainty is that this violence had an intimate form. Besides, intimacy had another facet. Christians in many occasions aided Muslims, while Vallahades and Vlachs that opposed Bekir received an exceptional treatment. These individuals managed to survive because of their benevolent behaviour in the previous years.[112] Still, the violence that preceded the wars created a "culture of paramilitarism" that stimulated certain dynamics.[113] The Balkan Wars constituted a catalyst for social transformation and the crystallization of this antagonistic sense was informed by a mixture of personal, political, and socioeconomic factors.

[Grebeneli Bekir Fikri Bey against Colonel Thomson: The Case of Vlorë 1914]". Düşünce ve Tarih 3, no. 31: 40, 42.

110 Elsie Robert, *Historical Dictionary of Albanian History* (London: Tauris, 2012), 179–180.

111 Benjamin Fortna, *The Circassian: A Life of Eşref Bey, Late Ottoman Insurgent and Special Agent* (London: Hurst, 2017).

112 Kelaidi, *I Drasi ton Ethelondikon Somaton Kriton*, 122; Glavinas, *Oi Mousoulmanikoi Plithismoi stin Ellada*, 304.

113 Concept borrowed by Gingeras, *Sorrowful Sorrows*.

· 3 ·

AN UNDECLARED WAR IN THE SIDELINES: THE PARAMILITARIES AND THE LOCALS

A hatred fed with blood is not easy to fade away.[1]

Konstantinos Karavidas, diary, 1912

In Strumica the Bulgarians have been waging a war like the one in 1904, but this time it is even fiercer. It is a matter of time until half of the {Greek} population will immigrate.[2]

Greek Ministry of Foreign Affairs, 1912

The abovementioned quotes describe in an eloquent way the turbulent legacy of the decade that preceded the Balkan Wars. The first one is an abstract coming from the diary of the soldier Konstantinos Karavidas. There, the author recounts his conversation with a local Greek priest in the district of Giannitsa, in nowadays Greek central Macedonia. The clergyman described how local villagers denied their race because of actions of Bulgarian comitadjis during the Macedonian proxy war and how they recovered when Greeks sent units to confront this threat. The second is an official source addressed to the Greek Ministry of Foreign Affairs by the commissioning Governor of Strumica who conveyed an urgent message about an anti-Greek campaign waged by the Bulgarians in the autumn of 1912.

These testimonies are of crucial importance so as to understand the instrumental role of violence in shaping the locals' mental world. The rivalry between Greece and Bulgaria, despite the creation of the military alliance and the temporary halt in hostilities was resilient on the ground level. The

---

1 Gennadios Vivliothiki, Archeio Karavida, Folder 115, 1, pp. 128–130.
2 IAYE, F.6, 8, Pros ton Ypodioikiti Stromnitsas, 1913, p. 8.

dynamics of the Macedonian proxy war were still active and the outbreak of war only intensified them. When this was combined with the Balkan states' appetite for land and neglect to the spirit of the alliance, it led to an undeclared war in the sidelines similar to 1904–8 which culminated a climate of violence and retribution.

In this chapter I analyze this undeclared war through the interaction between the paramilitary groups and the locals and partially revisit the causes of the Second Balkan War. Traditional historiography has engaged with the outbreak of the Inter-allied war mainly through the lenses of high politics, disregarding the agency on the ground level.[3] Only recently some studies opened the discussion underlying socio-cultural factors, yet the role of non-traditional combatants in the context of the Balkan Wars has not been adequately analyzed.[4] The phenomenon of paramilitarism is linked with transformations in warfare as well as with wider state-society relations.[5] Groups such as the IMRO, the Bulgarian comitadjis, and the Greek Scouts operated as auxiliaries to the regular army, and were comprised of men who had confronted each other in the proxy war that was fought over Macedonia in the first decade of the twentieth century. In the autumn of 1912 they met again ostensibly as allies and were tasked with reconnaissance, sabotage operations and to recruit local populations. In these areas, where Greek and Bulgarian troops made contact with each other skirmishes broke out well before the war against the Ottomans ended. Pressures steaming from local agents, serving both national and personal agendas, drove policies that generals and politicians adopted, and generated an explosive climate. The actions of these groups that fought for the causes of Greece and Bulgaria and pursuit individual agendas ultimately deteriorated inter-allied relations leading in a bloody finale in the summer of 1913.

***

Captain Konstantinos Mazarakis Ainian (1869–1949) was forty two years old when he received orders by the Greek high command to create a new corps to assist the regular army in August, 1912. "Captain Akritas", as he was widely known, was an experienced fighter who operated in Ottoman Macedonia

3 Georgi Markov, *Bûlgarskoto Krushenie 1913* (Sofia: Bûlgarska Akademiya na Naukite, 1991).
4 Wolfgang Höpken, "'Modern wars' and 'backward societies': The Balkan Wars in the History of 20th Century European Warfare", in *The Wars of Yesterday*, ed. Boeckh, Rutar.
5 Ugur Ümit Üngör, *Paramilitarism: Mass Violence in the Shadow of the State* (Oxford: Oxford University Press, 2020).

in the area of mountain Vermio near the city of Naoussa, nowadays Greek Macedonia. He belonged to the generation of officers who had been stigmatized by the defeat against the Ottomans in 1897 and was in agony to find an opportunity to prove his worth.[6] Mazarakis seemed the ideal candidate to undertake this task. He was aware of the challenges that guerrilla warfare entailed, particularly the complex relations with the local populations.[7] The new unit which was about to be formed was named "proskopoi", which literally meant boy-Scouts.

One of the basic reasons that led to the creation of the Scouts was that the Greek army lacked substantial cavalry units for reconnaissance operations.[8] Intelligence gathering and preparation of the ground facilitated the advance of the regular army. The most reliable and effective way to achieve that was by reactivating the old networks of the Macedonian proxy war. On the eve of the declaration, old fighters, locals and from mainland Greece were recalled to arms and dispatched to Ottoman Macedonia. However the situation was not the same as in 1904–8. This time they were parts in a struggle for national liberation and they needed no more to operate underground.[9]

One of the things I want to remind is that these individuals had a different frame of reference from ordinary soldiers or civilians. First of all they were familiar with the area. Second, they had recent memories from the Macedonian proxy war. Some of them were involved in vendettas with members of rival organizations, while others had postwar agendas such as taking advantage of their bases of support to become local patrons. As Helen Katsiadakis contends, the Macedonian Struggle was a school for violence. Criminals were mixed with ambitious captains, schoolteachers, and priests leaving a legacy of mistrust and violence among locals.[10] While the regular army "trusted" the Bulgarian army, the Scouts were very reluctant to cooperate because of the Macedonian Struggle.[11] It did not thus constitute a surprise that tensions emerged from the early stages of the war.

6 Idryma Meleton tou Chersonisou tou Aimou, O *Makedonikos Agonas. Apomnimoneumata* (Thessaloniki, 1984), 175–180, 232–234.

7 Spyros Karavas, *Mystika kai Paramithia apo tin Istoria tis Makedonias* (Athens: Vivliorama, 2014), 135–145.

8 Ioannis Mazarakis, *Ta ethelontika somata ton proskopon kata tous Valkanikous Polemous, 1912–1913,* Vol. 2 (Athens: Deltion tis Estorikes kai Ethologikes Etairias, 1989), 183.

9 Dakin, *The Greek Struggle for Mecedonia,* 499–594.

10 Helen Katsiadakis, The Balkan War's Experience: Undestanding the Enemy, in *War in the Balkans,* ed. Pettifer -Buchanan, 230–235.

11 IEE, Archeio Konstantinou Mazaraki Ainian, Polemoi 1912–1913, Proskopoi, p. 13.

Most importantly, the Scouts had a twofold agency: the official and the personal. The official included all the tasks assigned by the Greek High Command. The Scouts were a valuable source of manpower with local knowledge. They were not only aware of how to wage a proxy war but were also knowledgeable on the dynamics of ethnic cleansing especially when dealing with "enemy civilians". This capital was also used for personal gains representing the other side of their agency. All these individuals had been involved in local affairs and awaited, in the summer of 1912, a major geopolitical shift to transpire. The declaration of war by the Balkan alliance brought significant changes in the socio-political landscape offering opportunities. Service to the motherland was a key credential that paved the way for new careers in the state apparatus paying off long lasting services. Being part of the national crusade was a promising apprenticeship, particularly for army officers who pursuit to get rid of the stigma of the 1897 war.[12]

This struggle for power inevitably prompted dynamics of competition between rival factions in Ottoman Macedonia. The bad blood of the previous years was a central factor that generated violent dynamics in the micro level. In an ethnically mixed area where the future was uncertain the local chieftains had serious reasons to act pre-emptively so that to gain the upper hand. Paramilitary bands spearheaded the allies' advance because they were familiar with the local terrain and allegedly with the ethnological composition. Mazarakis was accompanied by a number of prominent chieftains who were praised for their service and had important social clout.[13] Their objective was to capture all the passages from the city of Drama to the Nestos River, east of Salonika, and crush the operating bands of the Bulgarians and the IMRO. Moreover, they were tasked to secure arsenals with war material. Food supplies were about to be provided by the occupied lands.[14] According to official information the scouts were comprised by 77 units of Cretans numbering 3,556 men, nine native units from Epirus of 446 men and nine from Macedonia numbering 211. From other parts of Greece the scouts numbered 1,812 men.[15]

Similarly, Bulgarians reactivated their own comitadji networks. In that case however it was more complicated. The split within the ranks of the IMRO

---

12 IEE, Mazarakis, p. 33.
13 ÖS, HHStA, PA, XII, Turkei, Der Kampfen zwischen Turken und Griechen vom 18–27 October 1912, no 162, p. 3.
14 IEE, Mazarakis, pp. 1–6, 21.
15 Yet, the number of local chieftains that fought in the war in significantly higher and cannot be recorded due to lack of detailed data.GES, *Epitomi Istoria*, 16.

regarding the Young Turk Revolution and the trajectory of the Macedonian question had generated a fratricidal war. A tactical convergence was eventually attained just on the eve of war when the adversaries put aside temporarily their differences. The Bulgarian High Command in the end of September ordered the cells stationed in Bulgaria to start organizing bands.[16] The Central Committee of the IMRO made a public appeal. The most combat experienced and prominent guerrilla leaders who had been fighting since the Ilinden uprising responded positively.[17]

Serbia too mobilized chetnik formations that numbered around 2,000 to 4,000 men. Major Vojin Popovic led the strongest unit which participated in the decisive battle of Kumanono (23–24, October) which opened the way to the Serbian army for the conquest of Macedonia. Other detachments also operated in Kosovo and the Sanjak of Novi Pazar and their main task was quite similar to the scouts and comitadjis. Their composition was consisted of officers and NCOs as well as volunteers and locals.[18]

Way before the advance of the regular armies, armed bands grabbed swiftly pieces of land establishing control ostensibly on the behalf of their country.[19] In these newly formed units, at the beginning, the presence of local volunteers was quite strong. Hristo Silianov an experienced fighter who operated in the Gramos mountain in Pindus recorded how locals from a diverse professional background (students, workers, builders etc.) enlisted by expressing concerns that many of them lacked combat experience. Recklessness and lack of morale represented a constant phenomenon affecting the coherence of these units.[20]

The original tasks of the paramilitaries included actions that aimed to undermine the enemy from within through sabotage operations such as: cutting off lines of communication, blowing up bridges, railway lines, disarmament of garrisons, and providing intelligence. The experience from their underground modus operandi in the late Hamidian era had made them quite effective in subversive activities.[21] Moreover, the paramilitaries were tasked

16 National Library Sofia, Folder 24, ae: 7, 1, 22/9/1912.

17 Cyril Kosev, *100 Godinata ot Podviga na Balgarite v Balkanskata Voyna* (Sofia, 1986), 86–87.

18 Dmitar Tasić, "Repeating Phenomenon: Balkan Wars and Irregulars", in *Les guerres balkaniques (1912–1913): Conflits, enjeux, memories*, ed. Catherine Horel (Bruxelles: Peter Lang, 2014), 29–30.

19 Stiliyan Kovachev, *Zapiski na Generala ot Pehotata* (Sofia, 1992), 166.

20 Hristo Silyanov, *Ot Vitosha do Gramos*, (Sofia Izdanie na Kosturskoto blagotvoritelno bratstvo, 1920), 13.

21 In 1903 two impressive terrorist hits in Salonika were achieved when an anarchist group with links with the IMRO the "gemidzhii" (boatmen) sunk in the harbor the French

to train the locals and encourage them not to flee. This ambiguous practice that aimed to create enclaves of support as leverage in the peace negotiations entailed intimidation, spread of inaccurate information, and assurances for protection.[22]

The first actions of the scouts took place in the Chalkidiki peninsula south of Salonika. Days before the outbreak of war irregular troops landed and started organizing a guerrilla campaign. They gathered material from hidden warehouses from the Macedonian proxy war and recruited locals.[23] At the beginning the whole operation seemed a huge success. Greek and Bulgarian bands had managed successfully to cut off communication and telegraphic lines. The Austrian consul in Salonika reported that the locals were supporting en masse the war endeavour and that Greek bands were moving swiftly in Chalkidiki assisted by inhabitants who look sympathetic.[24] The Austrian diplomat here is touching a thorny issue: the interaction with the locals. The importance of the latter is constantly underlined by Mazarakis because they held the key to success. Food supplies, recruits, and clothing were entirely dependent on their willingness. Their familiarity with the terrain, their networks of volunteers, and their knowledge of local dialects was essential for gathering intelligence and to activate spy networks. In mixed villages in the contact zone between Greece and Bulgaria, in the kaza of Salonika, the dispatch of agents became imperative. Local villagers and units of scouts had the fragile task to penetrate occupied villages deep into the Bulgarian zone and disrupt lines of communication.[25] Intelligence networks in the Pangaion Mountain, which extended the regions of Kavala and Serres, were formed by people familiar

commercial boat "Guadalquivir" and blew up the branch of the Ottoman bank. Two other major attacks took place in 1911 and 1912 in the cities of Shtip and Kochani in the Manastir vilayet respectively which resulted in several casualties: Giannis Megas, *Oi Varkarides tis Thessalonikis. I anarchiki Voulgariki omada kai oi vomvistikes energeies tou 1903* (Athens: Troxalia, 1994); Ryan Gingeras, "The Internal Macedonian Revolutionary Organization: 'Oriental' Terrorism Counterinsurgency, and the End of the Ottoman Empire", in *The Oxford Handbook of the History of Terrorism*, ed. Carola Dietze and Claudia Verhoeven (Febr. 2014), https://doi.org/10.1093/oxfordhb/9780199858569.013.019.

22 Unemployment has already pushed people to immigrate and war exacerbated the situation leading many people to attempt to immigrate to the US but the new political authorities created obstacles. IAYE, 1913, 6, 3 apo Mavroudi pros Ypourgeio Exoterikon, No 41284, 8/2/1913.

23 IEE, Mazarakis, p. 21.

24 ÖS, HHStA, PA, XII, Turkei, am Salonich 19/10/1912, no 157, pp. 1, 3.

25 IEE, Mazarakis, p. 2.

with the weapons and uniforms of Bulgarians destined to operate as double agents.[26] Local Macedonian guerrillas were utilized in addition to safeguard the Greek occupation because of their appeal to native populations.[27] After the surrender of the Ottoman army in Salonika the scouts' responsibilities further expanded by undertaking cleansing operations of bands that were created by former Ottoman-Macedonian soldiers that pillaged the mainland.[28]

Nevertheless, the view of the Austrian diplomat was somehow biased not necessarily reflecting the full picture in the ground level. While it is true that locals participated to some extent, this had variations and depended on multiple factors. In order to fully grasp their incentives we need to adopt a more nuanced approach by taking into consideration two main motivators: the strategies for survival and the struggle for resources. The first phase of war, that lasted until the end of November was a mayhem in which the Ottoman security apparatus collapsed and the Balkan states had not consolidated their rule. Acts of revenge and pillaging was an everyday phenomenon involving numerous actors. Captain Papakostas a veteran of the Macedonian proxy war and native from Old Greece expressed frustration about the challenges he encountered at the beginning of the campaign. His unit was one of the first that arrived in Chalkidiki and the chieftain asked from local notables to provide animals for transportation as well as men for recruits. In his communication with Mazarakis, he expressed disappointment about the reluctance of the locals to volunteer and he ultimately managed to double his strength only by recruiting Christian deserters from the Ottoman army.[29]

Reluctance was also reflected in the testimony of a priest in the town of Ierissos in Chalkidiki who characterized the scouts as bandits and his claims in some occasions were not unfounded. Several Macedonian guerrillas had obtained notorious reputation because of their ambiguous practices, while some of them had become persona non grata in local communities. Such an example was Captain Georgios Giaglis, a native captain from the abovementioned town. The case of Giagli is particularly important because he was one of the chieftains in the very fragile zone in the kaza of Salonika where the

---

26 IEE, Archeio Papavasileiou, Folder 3, No 84699.

27 Notable examples were: Chatzigeorgiou from Gevgeli, Grolio to Visoka, Avramidi from Karatzova and Mita from Soho. IEE. Mazarakis, p. 14.

28 ÖS, HHStA, PA XII, Turkei, Liasse XLV/3, Balkankrieg, 387, Beilage zu Vertaulichem Bericht, No 56, 19/11/1912.

29 IEE, Mazarakis, Ekthesis peri tis katholou draseos sto yp 'eme soma mechri simeron, Vasileios Papakostas, 28/12/1912, pp.1–3.

Greek and Bulgarian presence overlapped. Giaglis operated in the area of Serres during the Macedonian proxy war and he was recalled to Athens in 1906 after a public outcry because of the massacre of 36 Exarchist civilians by his band for reprisals for the assassination of some family members of one of his close associates.[30]

The perception moreover of the priest brings to the surface again one of the initial points of this chapter: the frame of reference and recent traumatic memories. For the local people, the war constituted a turmoil and the situation was way more critical because they were called to take serious decisions in a short period of time. A representative example that shows how violence affected loyalties is the example of the destruction of the village of Kriva near the town of Kukuch (Kilkis), nowadays Greek central Macedonia. This particular village was wiped out and its population brutally massacred in October 1912, while two versions for the events exist. The first one, reproduced by the Greek press supports that it was the Ottoman gendarmerie that bombarded the village as a form of punishment for the reaya betrayal. Indeed, this was a common Ottoman practice in retreat to target civilians as a form of retaliation especially Christian notables.[31] The second version of the Austrian Consular presented a more complicated story. According to this narrative, the massacre of villagers was committed by Bulgarian Christian bands because the inhabitants did not join immediately the war effort.[32] Kriva was an important base and arsenal for comitadji activities in the late Hamidian and Young Turk era. After the outbreak of hostilities a unit of the Ottoman gendarmerie arrived and the locals showed submissive behaviour in order to avoid reprisals. Meanwhile, two Slavic speaking chieftains named Dankov and Gioupchev were heading to the village. Along their way, their band was reinforced by Christian deserters of the Ottoman army and locals peasants leading a unit that numbered 250 men. A siege followed and because the village's houses were built out of stone the comitadjis bombed it with artillery. When the Ottomans retreated the band massacred the remaining population and left the bodies to freeze in open air. This version of the story opens the way for a lot of interpretations and

---

30 For more information see: Vasileios Pappas, O Chalkidiotis Makedonomaxos Kapetan Giaglis. I iroiki Drasi tou Enoplou Somatos toy sti Chalikidiki, Nigrita Serron kai Agio Oros (Ierissos Chalkidikis, 2011).

31 ÖS, HHStA, PA, XII, Turkei, Liasse XLV/3, Balkan Krieg, Baron Braun, Athen, 23/12/1912, No 4885.

32 Christos Indos, Valkanikoi Polemoi, 1912–1913. Ta Gegonota sten Periochi tou Dimou Paionias (Thessaloniki: Kyriakidis, 2012), 44–48.

shows the multiplicity of the motivations. One may assume that the comit-adjis showed what fate awaited people that wanted to remain neutral, and to show who was now in change, and indeed this might be plausible explanation. A couple of weeks before the outbreak of war Greek guerrillas Lazos Dogiamas and Athanasios Betsis from the neighbouring Kastaneri were assassinated by Dankov and Gioupchev. This act had the character of score settling but also belonged to the first phases of the undeclared war when prominent comitad-jis were trying to eliminate potential opponents in an attempt to establish their own feuds.[33] The local villagers who joined probably were driven by some revenge motivations or looting and the deserters most likely wanted to plunder. We cannot be certain about which version of the story is valid. Yet, these violent dynamics forced the locals to reconsider their stance. The power vacuum that was created by the departure of the Ottomans was partially sub-stituted by irregulars. Requisition, food deprivation, and endemic violence led many people to seek refuge and protection by aligning and offering services. The Balkan peasant was amid a painstaking dilemma. Used to appease the Ottoman forces they were now caught in uncertain territory where no one was clearly dominant and danger lurked throughout.[34]

This did not mean however that the agency of natives was confined to a passive role. Formation of militias was the most vivid example of their involvement. Militias in civil wars are generally defined as armed groups that operate alongside regular security forces or work independently of the state to shield the local population from insurgents.[35] Unlike typical irregulars units, which were comprised by a mixture of experienced fighters, natives or recruits from abroad, militias were many times immobile units created for self defence.

In my suggested typology in the context of the Balkan Wars, broadly fall three categories. In the first belonged militias that were created by villages that actively participated in the Macedonian proxy war and coordinated their actions beforehand with the Balkan states, as well as Muslim populations armed by the Ottoman military. Those militias assisted the regular army and comitadjis either as auxiliaries or volunteers. The way to establish linkage between the militias and the irregulars was as follows: when a comitadji unit arrived in a village the heads of the militia welcomed them. In case of attack

---

33   Konstantinos Dogiamas, *Oi Makedonomachoi Adelfoi Dogiama* (Thessaloniki: University Studio Press, 2009), 10–12.

34   ÖS, HHStA, PA, XII, Turkei, am Salonich 19/10/1912, no 157, pp. 1,3.

35   Corinna Jentzsch, "Stathis N Kalyvas, Livia Isabella Schubiger, 'Militias in Civil War'", *Journal of Conflict Resolution* 56, no. 5: 755–769.

the militia was obliged to fight with the irregulars.[36] In the area of Kreshna, today south-western Bulgaria, the outbreak of the war found many local Slavic speaking populations siding with the invading forces. They warm welcomed in several occasions the troops by offering bread and celebrating by ringing the church's bells to praise the liberation.[37] Furthermore, volunteers provided espionage services that aimed to penetrate the Ottomans' intelligence system.[38] These were valuable information about the positions of the enemy and hostile militias hidden in houses.[39] Some villages not only provided information but also participated in armed comitadji activities.[40] Militia and irregular forces in the wider area of Salonika numbered almost 3,000 men and were involved in the burning of at least five Muslim villages leading Muslims to act accordingly.[41] In the Kastoria district local bands and militias contributed to the war effort by capturing 2,300 Ottoman POWs.[42]

The second category entailed ad-hoc militias. In this case the male population of a village was armed in order to protect civilians from raids.[43] The usage of force by locals had a detrimental effect expanding this vicious cycle in some cases. Such an example was the Turkish village of Takova near the city of Drama when a Muslim militia murdered two Bulgarian gendarmes to avenge the pillaging of their village by comitadjis prompting an immediate reaction from Bulgarians who sent a group of volunteers to hunt them down. The fear of reprisals led approximately 200–400 Muslims from nearby villages to take up arms and flee to the mountains to conduct guerrilla warfare.[44]

The third type was the product of the Greek High Command's order n. 513. This was an initiative taken for security reasons. In order to safeguard the newly captured areas and nationalize the locals the male members of each community ought to vow to the Greek flag and form militias. Similar practices were adapted to the Bulgarian and Serbian zones so as to contain somehow

36 Leon Trotski, *Ta Valkania kai oi Valkanikoi Polemoi*, trans. Paraskevas Matalas (Athens: Themelio, 1993), 287.

37 Tsentralen Voenen Arhiv, (TsVA), Fond 64, Op. II, del. 2, Dnevnik 3/7 na Peshotna Brigada, 5/10/1912, p. 6.

38 TSVA, F 64, Op II, d 2, 1/10/1912, p. 3.

39 TSVA, F 64, Op II, d.2, 26/10/1912, p. 7.

40 TsVA, F 64, Op II, d 2, 7/10/1912, p. 8.

41 TsVA, F 64, Op II, d.2, 28/10/1912, p. 9.

42 Georgi Bakalov, Christo Matanov, Plamen Mitev, Ivan Iltsev, and Roumiana Marinova, *Istoria tis Voulgarias*, trans. Georgios Christidis (Thesalloniki: Epikentro, 2015), 308.

43 Spyros Melas, *Oi Polemoi tou 1912–1913* (Athens: Vlassis, 1972), 57.

44 IAYE, 6, apo Serres pros Koromila, 8/2/1913.

the chaos of the first weeks of war and accelerate the assimilation of new territories.[45]

The disarmament of these militias was a tricky business especially when conducted by non-regular units as it was often accompanied by pillaging and retribution. For instance, a turbulent situation took place in the district of Florina. In this area, the Greek 5th division was defeated by a surprising counter attack in the city of Sorovitz (Amyntaio) and local Muslim militias were a key part of this success. A lot of Greeks-Patriarchists retaliated when the army advanced once again and the investigation showed that the vast majority of locals were armed under the guidance of the Patriarchist Metropolitan of Florina with weapons probably confiscated by the retreating Ottomans. On another occasion, on November, 24 in the mixed village of Zelenitch (Sklithron) the followers of the Exarchy and some Greek Patriarchists pillaged the Turkish district leading the military authorities to take measures to protect Muslims.[46] A similar turmoil occurred in the kaza of Kastoria where challenges from the disarming of Muslims occurred. While Muslim villages initially seemed compliant, this changed when news about the arrival of units of the Ottoman army arrived.[47] Probably around 2,000 militia men operated in the district of Kastoria.[48]

These attitudes maybe explained by a series of socio-economic and practical factors. Whole communities were found suddenly armed and having relatively the ability to act freely. As discussed in the previous chapter, war appeared as an opportunity and a lot of prior resentments escalated especially between peasants and landowners.[49] This struggle for survival naturally went hand in hand with another struggle equally important: the one for resources. Control of food supplies is a key priority in warfare. Pre-war logistical systems are quickly dismantled and replaced by the ones who orient everything toward the war effort. However, this transition does not occur immediately and a fragile period of lawlessness provides opportunities. That was by no means an exceptional attitude implying a savage Balkan mentality. Imperial borderlands in East Central Europe witnessed such events. The anarchy created by the invasion of the Russian army in Hapsburg Galicia drove locals to participate

45 IEE, Mazarakis, p. 29.

46 Geniko Epiteleio Stratou/Dieuthinsi Istorias Stratou (GES/DIS), F. 1635/13/6, pp. 1–3.

47 GAK, Archeio Tsondou Varda, Apo Zoto pros Varda, 27/2/1913, No 186.

48 GAK, Archeio Varda, Apo Kolokotroni pros Varda, 25/11/1912, No 165.

49 Tasos Kostopoloulos, *Polemos kai Ethnokatharsi. I Xechasmeni plevra mias Dekaetous Exormisis* (Athens: Vivliorama, 2008), 30–58.

in plundering making no distinctions to ethnicity or religion.[50] Lithuanian peasants along with Cossack troops looted their Jewish neighbours and participated in pogroms in Eastern Europe in 1915.[51] Similarly, villagers in Ottoman Macedonia raided warehouses of local Beys, looted Muslim properties and committed reprisals to avenge the atrocities of the retreating Ottoman army.[52] The following report for the British Consul General in Salonika offers a very vivid picture:

> The passage of the allied troops was immediately followed by a species of Jacquerie. The peasants, whether metajers (remnants of the reaya system) or free villagers throwing themselves ravenously upon the property of the land owners, carrying all off such cattle, grain or other farm produce as the soldiers had not already consumed, the agricultural implements, the furniture and even the windows and planking of their houses cutting down their trees, devastating their gardens and destroying much they could not carry away.[53]

The report continued by stating that this behaviour not only concerned Turkish Beys but also Christian and Jewish landowners and that the peasants were redistributing lands. Attempts to restore order failed and agents sent by the Balkan states were either intimidated or murdered. This form of violence was commonplace in borderland regions when a system collapses and socio-economic grievances pre-exist.[54] Similar incidents were reported in the districts of Drama and Kukuch (Kilkis) in the Bulgarian sector. In Kilkis local militias participated in massacres of Muslims with the approval of Bulgarian officers.[55] In some areas apart from the eradication of the Muslim element, which was almost total, confiscation of lands and redistributing of properties took place.[56] Flora Karavia a painter who followed the expedition of the Greek army offers a very vivid image of the city Florina:

50 Christoph Mick, "Legality, Ethnicity and Violence in Austrian Galicia, 1890–1920", *European Review of History: Revue européenne d'histoire* 26, no. 5 (2019), 767.
51 Balkelis *War, Revolution, and Nation-Making in Lithuania,* 23.
52 Melas, *Oi Polemoi tou 1912–1913,* 43, 109–129.
53 FO 195/2453/3010/1-2, Balkan Situation Political and Military, Consul General in Salonika, 29/4/1913, No 37, pp. 1–2.
54 For a more detailed analysis see: Thomas Kühn, ed. "Borderlands of the Ottoman Empire in the Nineteenth and Early 20th Centuries", *The MIT Electronic Journal of Middle East Studies,* 3 (Spring 2003).
55 ÖS, HHStA, PA, XII, Turkei, Bulgarische Gewaltakten im Distrikte Kukuch (Kilkis, Avret Hissar), No 187, 23/11/1912, pp. 1–3.
56 ÖS, HHStA, PA, XII, Salonich, 13/12/1912, No 187.

Florina is a mosaic of nationalities. Here the Turks are majority, around seven to eight thousand. The many mosques indicate its Muslim character. The Greeks are around 4,000 and the Bulgarians 2,000 {…} Houses investigations are about to take place for the relentless plundering and a commission represented by Greek and Bulgarian priests is going to facilitate the process because the presence of the cross here is much more important than any police provision {…} People are characterized as schismatic or Patriarchic. Many of them are relatives. They all speak the Macedonian idiom which the Bulgarians barely understand and the Greeks not at all {…}[57]

As a matter of fact, offering material incentives proved to be the key to involve more actively the locals and captains such as Vasil Chekalarov was fully aware of that.[58] Born in 1874 in the Slavic speaking village of Smerdesh (Krystalopigi) he enlisted in the ranks of the IMRO becoming a leading member. He participated in the Ilinden uprising and he was one of the main adversaries of the Greeks in the area by setting up a band with his close associate Pando Kliashev.[59] At the beginning of war his unit aided the Greek army. Captain Tsondos Vardas who was an old foe of Chekalarov and the man that replaced Pavlo Mela was coordinating activities of Greek bands in that sector. Vardas was receiving worrying reports from Greek chieftains about the activities of comitadjis that disarmed Muslims and extorted Greek villages by confiscating crops and livestock.[60] Captain Lolos Apostolidis complained to Varda about the activities of Chekalarov who had, according to his testimony, instigated a whole illicit trade network by re-selling confiscated crops and arming with the highest quality of weaponry the followers of the Exarchy.[61] Chekalarov's enterprise is crucial to understand the essence of the double agency mentioned at the beginning of this chapter. The kaza of Kastoria was an ethnically mixed area and especially the mainland was inhabited by a majority of Slavophope populations. The Macedonian proxy war was fiercely waged in the previous years and a lot of blood had been shed. Chekalarov knew that his position, in contrast to chieftains in other sectors,

---

57 Thaleia Flora Karavia, *Endiposeis apo ton Polemo tou 1912–1913* (Athens: Idrima gia ton Koinovouleutismo kai tin Dimokratia, 2012), 43, 74.

58 Uğur Ümit Üngör, "Mass Violence against civilians During the Balkan Wars", in *The Wars before the Great War*, ed. Geppert and Mulligan, 77–84.

59 For more info see: Vasil Chekalarov, *Dnevnik, 1901–1903* (Sofia: Sineva, 2001); Ryan Gingeras, "'Scores Dead in Smerdesh': Communal Violence and International Intrigue in Ottoman Macedonia," *Balkanistika,* 25 (2012): 75–98.

60 GAK, Archeio Varda, apo oplarchigo Konstantino Papastavrou pros kapetan Tsondo, 11/12/1912, 141.

61 GAK, Archeio Varda, apo oplarchigo Lolo Apostolidi pros kapetan Tsondo, Kastoria, 144.

was very vulnerable owing to the fact that he had to confront the Greek army without the assistance of conventional forces. The creation of bases of support thus was imperative in order to prevent a Greek annexation. The only way to attain that was by aligning with the locals. Subsequently, his actions were both political and personal in nature. On the one hand, by controlling resources he made a tempting case to the war ravaged populations to join his ranks providing food and protection. One the other, it was an ideal timing to expand his personal influence becoming a local patron.

Chekalarov's practices were rather the rule than the exception. Offering goods and especially land was a very effective way to shape loyalties and generate new patronage networks. This was a typical divide et impera tactic employed by the Ottomans too in the late Hamidian era particularly in the eastern provinces of the Empire where the land issue lied in the heart of tensions between Kurds and Armenians.[62] In Kilkis Muslims populations from neighbouring villages evacuated to Salonika before the arrival of the Bulgarian army. The ones that failed to depart were killed and their lands redistributed to local Christians. When some of them tried to return in the spring received death threats. For instance, a local notable named Hadji Hussein was informed that his estate had been destroyed by the notorious comitadji Mito from Moravtcha who sent emissaries to warn the former not to even consider getting back. Mito furthermore, confiscated live stocks, and instigated a state of terror.[63]

Another dimension of war as a pillaging enterprise represented the issue of banditry. This social phenomenon was far from over in the Balkans in the early twentieth century. Several criminal elements utilized the war to their advantage. By pretending that they were fulfilling official duties they were confiscating goods and soon became a source of serious concern. The line that distinguished a bandit from a scout was very thin. The locals had their own interests and needs and could not simply comply on demands of people without uniforms. Grievances over the presence of bandits soon rose from locals. Notables throughout Macedonia had been protesting about a state of lawlessness, even until the summer of 1913, by claiming that a lot of irregulars pretend to be scouts so that to pillage and plunder and get away without punishment.[64] The chieftains in response accused the natives as the actual

---

62 See more on Klein, *Margins of Empire*.

63 FO 195/2453/3010/1-2, Enclosure No 4, in Consul General Lamp's dispatch No 44, 14/5/1913, pp. 6–7.

64 IEE, Mazarakis, Ek Genikou Stratigeiou, Serres, 4/7/1913, p. 2.

perpetrators initiating a blame game. That was the case for the community of Vlatchi in Florina whose inhabitants faced charges by a chieftain who claimed that the villagers were prevented by his unit from plundering Turkish houses.[65] The committee of the village responded by denying everything, stressing on how law abiding and helpful had been to the regular forces by providing food and shelter to a whole Greek battalion.[66] This example indicates the agency of the locals who knew how to articulate a proper language to the military authorities pursuing group interests.

Crown Prince Konstantinos was concerned over the actions of militias and the scouts and eventually forbid recruitment unless these units were controlled directly by officers. General Panagiotis Dagklis, the Greek Chief of Staff, in late November issued a decree on the activities of Greek and Bulgarian bands and ordered law enforcement and court-martials. Moreover, he demanded the disarmament of dangerous natives and adviced toleration only to units that officially cooperated with the army.[67] In late 1912, a lot of locals were disbanded and only the most trained were kept in service in order to preserve order in the contested territories, boost the morale of the locals, and counterbalance Bulgarian propaganda, and comitadji activities.[68]

The blame game was quickly transferred to the higher echelons of the Greek and Bulgarian High commands. The Greek side claimed that Bulgarians were playing a double game underreporting the numbers of irregulars or denouncing their actions. In contrast, the Greek scouts, the Greek High Command claimed, was a coordinated body affiliated to the army, whereas the comitadjis were criminals. The Bulgarians claimed similar things about the scouts and showed zero willingness to remove their paramilitaries especially from the contact zones.[69] Not surprisingly, comitadji activities constituted a major source of friction in the kaza of Salonika. In the areas captured by the scouts there was defiance by Bulgarian units who did not recognize the former as regular army.[70] The contact zones of Nigrita and Pangaio had been occupied

65 GAK, Archeio Varda, apo Papastavrou pros Varda, En Darda, 12/12/1912, No 171.

66 GAK, Archeio Varda, Pros ton kyrion Georgion Tsondon Lochago tou Pyrovolikou, En Vlatsi, 24/11/1912, No 162.

67 GAK, Archeio Varda, apo Geniko Stratigeio Stratou Thessalias pros tas Merarchias kai apasas tas Stratiotikas Archas, No 170.

68 IEE, Mazarakis, pp. 23–24.

69 GES/DIS, F. 1635A4, Ellines Proskopoi kai Voulgaroi Komitatzides. Stratiotis Aneu Stolis, No 19, pp. 1–2.

70 IEE, Mazarakis, p. 15.

by the chieftains Giagli and Papakosta.[71] Giaglis sent alarming reports that Bulgarian units were not only unwilling to reimburse for the confiscation of goods but also pillaged villages and coerced locals to join the Exarchy.[72] The band of the native scout Douka one the other hand was accused for a series of abuses while Bulgarians seriously questioned the utility of paramilitaries by mentioning that although they have been helpful at the beginning of the campaign, they turned up into a plague.[73] Within the first two months of 1913 at least twelve incidents occurred (skirmishes, assassinations, arrests, band clashes.) in this undeclared war involving the locals, the scouts, comitadjis and the army.[74]

Things went out of control in February 1913 amid the siege of Edirne when General Mikhail Savov, the Bulgarian Chief of Staff, made an appeal to irregular units to reach the port of Malkara (Tekirdağ) in Eastern Thrace to assist the regular army. The siege had reached a critical point and Bulgarians had concentrated all their efforts to this crucial fortress. A Serbian division was assisting too, however stubborn resistance and malaria had led to a stalemate.[75] The need for reinforcements was imperative. Yet, this order was fiercely rejected by bandit leaders almost in a threatening tone. The refusal to abandon their operational bases was representative of the gravity of local networks. The connection with the local socio-economic environment was essential for paramilitaries. Prominent leaders functioned as shady governors in those areas given the absence of robust state control. They knew that their authority was temporary therefore they had to be constantly present safeguarding prerogatives in order to remain influential brokers. Leaving was equal to suicide since losing leverage and material profits would force them to plunder to live for another day.[76]

Greeks shared similar concerns and suggested a plan for gradual evacuation and replacement with regular units.[77] Prince Nicholas, the military

71 IEE, Mazarakis, p. 22.
72 IEE, Mazarakis, From Oplarchigo Georgio Giagli pros ton Sevaston Archigon Konstantino Mazaraki, En Nigrita, 28/11/1912; Ibid., 29/11/1912.
73 GES/DIS, F. 1635A48-9.
74 IEE, Mazarakis, No 25.
75 For more info see: Syed Tanvir Wasti, The 1912–13 Balkan Wars and the Siege of Edirne, *Middle Eastern Studies* 40, no. 4 (2004), 59–78.
76 Foreign consuls even expressed concerns about the inadequacy of regular troops to control them in case of mutiny. ÖS, HHStA, PA XII, Turkei, Liasse XLV/3, Balkankrieg, 389, Am Salonich, No 30, 5/2/1913.
77 GES/DIS., F. 1635A4 10–14.

governor of Salonika insisted that the contested area must be evacuated by irregulars.[78] Until February, the scouts were officially disbanded and the military authorities implemented a measure to arrest armed individuals without uniforms.[79] That had a significant ramification due to the fact that anyone could be arrested on the grounds of being an irregular.[80] A joined Greco-Bulgarian commission was formed in April 1913 to investigate violations but it reached a deadlock.[81] Interestingly, the legacy of irregulars and this conduct of war had a long lasting effect in the Austro-Serbian front in WWI leading Habsburg military authorities to obsessively invest in dealing with this threat targeting indiscriminately civilians. This practise also continued in the eastern front way after the armistice in the former imperial borderlands in East-Central Europe.[82]

The eruption of the Second Balkan War brought paramilitaries to the surface once again. The war among the allies dropped the façade and opened the Pandora's Box for score settling. In the summer of 1913 the scouts and the comitadjis were about to spearhead the advance of the army and take part in a major ethnic cleansing campaign.

78 TsDA, F. 176, Op. 2, AE: 1212, Ministerstvo na Vŭnshnite Raboti, 11/3/1913, No 163.
79 GES/DIS., F. 1635A4, 16–18.
80 GES/DIS., F. 1635A4, 23.
81 Tsentralen Dŭrzhaven Arhiv (TsDA), F 176, Op. 2, ae 1212, Commission Mixte Greco-Bulgare, 5/4/1913, pp. 266–326.
82 Jonathan E. Gumz. *The Resurrection and Collapse of Empire in Habsburg Serbia, 1914–1918* (Cambridge: Cambridge University Press, 2010).

· 4 ·

AN UNDECLARED WAR IN THE SIDELINES: THE MILITARY OCCUPATION

The Greek propaganda that had roots from the Young Turk era continues its destructive work against us. Soldiers, civilians, educated people, and irregulars are trying to undermine the Bulgarian cause by targeting the language, the churches, and the schools.[1]

General, Hristo Hesaphtsiev

With these words, General Hristo Hesaphtsiev, the commanding officer of the Bulgarian garrison in Salonika, depicts in what he perceives as a war that was waged by the Greeks behind the frontlines. On a daily basis he was receiving reports for the ordeal of the Bulgarian population in the kaza of Salonika that ultimately led him to convey a warning to his superiors about a campaign by Athens to make these lands Hellenic.[2] One cannot deny the validity of this testimony. Indeed with a careful look at the archives the researcher can verify what the Bulgarian General was claiming. Nevertheless, this viewpoint is partial and does not reflect the picture in its totality. The Greeks waged no less a proxy war in the sidelines than the Bulgarians and the Serbians. It was exactly these dynamics that the belligerents induced that resulted to the violent outcome in the summer of 1913.

The Balkan States, as I mentioned in previous chapter, had initiated in the nineteenth century overlapping state building projects. Once the war started their aim was to rapidly establish full control and annex territories. This was about to materialize in a threefold way: politically by establishing administration, economically through taxation, and culturally by targeting

---

1   TsDA F. 176, op 2, ae 1212, No 13, 8/1/1913, p. 50.
2   TsDA, F. 176, Op. 2, ae 1228, 8/1/1913, p. 61.

and wiping out the local elites (teachers, priests, and notables). In this conquest numerous agents were utilized to penetrate the enemy territory and solidify enclaves of support destined to be used when score settling among the allies would ensue. This multifaceted war which included paramilitaries, civilians, agents, and the army is going to be unravelled in this chapter. The main focus of attention will be the dynamics of the military occupation and the different nuances of the concept of collaboration.

My theoretical approach builds on literature that perceives ethnic cleansing as a dynamic process that is related to multiple factors. Space, among others, affects both the production and construction of violence and it is always associated with specific incidents that transpire in a given area.[3] As Umit Ungor argues about the Armenian genocide, the intensity of killings throughout Anatolia varied spatially. These variations depended on the geographic conditions, the conduct of social elites, the inter-communal relations, the proximity to the front, and the settlement patterns.[4] This framework is be really helpful because similar preconditions applied to the Balkans during the wars. For instance, in order to explain the intensity of violence in the vilayet of Salonika one cannot disregard the fact that this was a contested territory with a simultaneous presence of the Greek and Bulgarian army. Moreover, we cannot scrutinize violence in the Western and Eastern parts of Macedonia where Greeks and Bulgarians had a free hand, without taking into account the interactions with the locals and discern the violent dynamics among urban centers and the rural mainland. Hence, this chapter is divided in two parts. The first will provide an analysis of the contested zone of the kaza of Salonika and its surroundings, whereas the second assesses the dynamics of the occupation in places captured by Greeks and Bulgarians independently.

***

The occupation of Salonika was the catalyst that deteriorated Greco-Bulgarian rivalry. This multi-ethnic city that numbered approximately 160,000

---

3 Carter Wood, "Locating Violence: The Spatial Production and Construction of Physical Aggression", in *Assaulting the Past: Violence and Civilization in Historical Context*, ed. Watson, Katherine D. (Newcastle: Cambridge Scholars Publishing, 2007), 28–29.

4 Umit U. Ungor, "Explaining Regional Variations in the Armenian Genocide", in *World War I and the end of the Ottomans. From the Balkan Wars to the Armenian Genocide*, ed. Hans Lukas Kieser-Kerem Oktem, Maurous Reinkowski (London: IB Tauris, 2015), 242–243; See also: Ümit Kurt, "Theatres of Violence on the Ottoman Periphery: Exploring the Local Roots of Genocidal Policies in Antep", *Journal of Genocide Research* 20, no. 3 (2018): 351–371.

inhabitants: 64,000, Jews, 25,000 Muslims, 22,000 Greeks, and 10,000 Slavic speaking became the apple of discord.[5] When Konstantinos Raktivan, the newly appointed Greek Minister of Justice reached the capital of the vilayet to receive his post he had to deal with immense challenges. The presence of the Greek and Bulgarian armies, in combination with a refugee crisis, thousands of prisoners of war, and a multiethnic synthesis signalled an imploding situation.[6] The Bulgarians who had never accepted the Greek occupation entered the city and stationed a division in the Hamidiye district.[7] Quarrels among the allied units occurred everyday while robberies and violent incidents from irregulars that had infiltrated made the Salonikans' life miserable.[8]

Ethnic violence was intense not only against Muslims but against to the Jewish community. Numerous anti-Semitic incidents took place especially in the autumn of 1912. Greek authorities were very suspicious of Jews because they did not join the celebrations and showed preference to the annexation by Bulgaria as the lesser evil.[9] The Jews were in a perilous position. War had interrupted commercial activities and paralyzed local economy. Starving refugees and deserters had forcefully occupied hospitals and synagogues.[10] Raktivan tried to decompress the crisis by evacuating 25,000 Ottoman POWS and forming the Cretan gendarmerie.[11] The gendarmerie ameliorated somehow the situation but did not solve the problem entirely. In many occasions soldiers were escorted by local residents that pursued revenge leading the attacks. The British Consul mentioned that hostility between Greeks and Jews was not a surprise.[12] Unlike other communities throughout Greece, the loyalty of the Sephardic Jews was in doubt because the Salonikan community was reluctant

---

5   Stoyan Nikolov, "Sadbata na Balgarite v Solun predi i po Vreme na Valkanskite Voini (1912–1913)", *Makedonski Pregled*, 2 (2008): 59.

6   Yura Konstantinova, "The Race for Salonica", *Études balkaniques* 49, no. 2 (2013): 44–67.

7   Balgarskata Akademiya na Naukite (NA), Archiv Hristo Hesaphtsiev, Fond 42K, opis 1, a.e. 575.

8   Konstantinos Raktivan, *Egrafa kai Semeioseis Apo ti Doiikisi tis Makedonias* (Thessaloniki, 1951), 19.

9   Gelber, N. M., D. Florentin, Adolf Friedmann, and G. F. Török. "An Attempt to Internationalize Salonika, 1912–1913." *Jewish Social Studies* 17, no. 2 (1955): 105–20.

10 Rena Molho, *Oi Evraioi tis Thessalonikis. Mia idiaiteri koinotita* (Athens: Patakis, 2014), 240–251.

11 Christos Christodoulou, *Oi Treis Tafes toy Chasan Tachsin Pasa* (Thessaloniki: Epikentro, 2012), 228.

12 FO 195/2446, His Britannic Majesty Consulate General Salonika, No 162, 17/11/1912, pp. 520–521.

to shift its allegiance from the Ottomans. The stark contrast in the attitude of the Greek state was reflected by the treatment of the Romaniote Jews of Janina who were Greek speaking and their greekness was not in doubt.[13]

Another source of friction between Greece and Bulgaria constituted matters of religious jurisdiction. There was a struggle for urban space from the very beginning when Greeks and Bulgarians occupied the churches of St. Dimitrios and St. Sofia respectively.[14] The five largest mosques that sheltered Muslim refugees were quickly converted into churches. Debates between the Greek sub-perfect Perikli Argyropoulo and the Bulgarian Metropolitan Evlogio regarding the jurisdiction of the Bulgarians denoted another crisis.[15] The attempt of Bulgarians in early 1913 to hold a religious service almost led to an open clash.[16]

At the same time, IMRO cells were active in Salonika. Jane Sandanski's band entered with the Bulgarian army while on the eve of war the prominent chieftain Todor Alexandrov and future leader of the IMRO- infiltrated in disguise. Alexandrov's intent was to financially aid the endeavours of the organization by intimidating and extorting local Bulgarian merchants.[17] The Greek occupation was something completely unacceptable by the leaders of the IMRO and soon took actions to undermine that. On November, 13 the Central Committee of the organization held a meeting in the city expressing several concerns about the Macedonian question. Particularly, they focused on the hostile treatment of Greeks and Serbs to "Bulgarian-Macedonians" and pressured the Bulgarian Government toward a more decisive intervention by sending a memorandum to Tsar Ferdinand.[18]

Greek authorities were aware and deeply concerned about the presence of IMRO cells. In the middle of November a gigantic blast polluted the air in the barracks in the Karaburun fortress, where the POWs were kept, creating panic in the Jewish and Muslim quarters. The Greek military was led to the

---

13 Evdoxios Doxiadis, *State, Nationalism and the Jewish Communities of Modern Greece* (London Bllomsbury, 2018), 100–101.

14 FO 195/2452, His Britannic Majesty Consulate General Salonika, No 5, 23/1/1913, pp. 2–3.

15 TsVA, Fond 1647, Op. 2, No 179, No 520, 8-13/1/1913, pp. 28–33.

16 ÖS, HHStA, PA, XII, 386, Am Salonich, No 194, 19/11/1912, p. 2.

17 Under the name Zafirov. ÖS, HHStA, PA, XII, 386, Am Salonich 19/10/1912, no 157, p. 5.

18 Dimitar Gotsev, *Ideyata za Avtonomiya Kato Taktika v Programite na Natsionalnoosvoboditelnoto Dvizhenie V Makedoniya i Odrinsko 1893 – 1941*, (Sofia: Izd. BAN, 1983, 1983), 33–36.

district of the Mosque Souk Shou that sheltered three hundred Bosnian refugees. It was firmly believed that this act was machinated by Bulgarian bands that wanted to discredit the new authorities in European public opinion by presenting them as incapable of maintaining the rule of law.[19] The issue of terrorism was employed as an excuse to initiate arrests and classify individuals as "enemy aliens".[20] Teachers especially those that worked at the St. Cyril and Methodius Bulgarian Men's High School as well as merchants, students, and other civilians were targeted.[21] Districts inhabited by Bulgarian speaking were searched for weapons and bombs increasing hostility of the Slavic population.[22] The terrorist threat reached an apogee in March 1913 due to the assassination of the Greek King George I. Regicides were a common phenomenon in Fin de siècle Europe performed by movements with a complex structure operated by national and international cross-border networks. This case however constituted an exception because it took place during wartime and almost paralyzed the city.[23] In the first hours after the event outraged Greek crowds were seeking avenge targeting Muslims and Jews and only when the Greek identity of the assassin (Georgios Schinas) was given to publicity further escalation was averted.[24]

Anyhow, the establishment of state control and the presence of foreign personnel confined to some extend violence in Salonika until the summer of 1913.[25] On the contrary, what was happening in the countryside was an entirely different story. Decision makers in Greece, Bulgaria, and Serbia knew that the Balkan conquest was a scramble for land. The rapid defeat of the Ottoman army accelerated this process rendering the quest even more urgent. Since in the treaty among the allies a clear distribution of lands had not been agreed, it became obvious that this was a rally for the more decisive and the

19 ÖS, HHStA, PA, XII, 386, Am Salonich 15/11/1912, p. 3.
20 For more on this concept see: Annette Becker, "Captive Civilians", in *The Cambridge History of the First World War*, I, ed. Jay Winter, 3 Vol. (Cambridge: Cambridge University Press, 2013).
21 Atanas Karayanev, Poslednite dni na Balgarskata targovska gimnaziya i zatochenie na o. Trikeri.
    Spomenat se sahranyava v TSarkovno-istoricheskiya arhiven institut s inv. № 10847.
22 ÖS, HHStA, P.A, XII Turkei, 438, 3148, 20/06/1913.
23 Vivien Bouhey, "*Anarchist Terrorism in Fin-de-Siècle France and its Borderlands*," Oxford Handbooks Online (February 2014), accesed October 2020.
24 IAYE, 1912,2,4, apo Thessaloniki pros Ypourgeio Exoterikon, No 3080, 2/6/1913.
25 Mark Mazower, *Salonica, City of Ghosts: Christians, Muslims and Jews 1430–1950* (London: Harper Perennial, 2004), 335.

more effective. Political and military leaders in Sofia, Athens, and Belgrade were well aware of the importance for the peace negotiations to have solid claims based on ethnological grounds. The only viable solution thus was to generate de facto situations by instigating social engineering campaigns. The Balkan League mobilized all human and material resources in a daily battle for expansion that engaged the locals to a point of no return. This multifaceted war reflected the reactivation of the mechanisms of the Macedonian proxy war. Persecutions of suspicious elements, provocation of the opponent, dispatch of agents, and establishing of control wherever possible, constituted the means in this battle over the space and its people. The military authorities employed old techniques in order to compel the locals to take sides. Inevitably people that collaborated were considered as enemies generating a new security threat. After a point, so as to legitimize persecutions the Balkan states classified whole communities as harmful for national interests. Eventually, this vicious cycle planted the seeds for score settling in the Second Balkan war.

The concept of "hostile" civilians was not something new. Its origins could be traced back in the Thirty Years War.[26] The term civilian has been used in different concepts. Typically it implies a distinction between members of the military and the civil sphere. In the concept of a total war this distinction becomes more blurry due to the mobilization for the war effort. The Balkan Wars in that sense may be characterized partially as total in the zones of occupation because the allied states involved intentionally local inhabitants. For this case, particularly helpful is the concept developed by historian Jay Winter who uses the term "civilianization" of war. Civilianization is a phenomenon that describes the changing nature of warfare after 1918 and how civilians became primary targets by military command centers. The Balkan war in the sidelines was a war against civilians and its decentralized character that necessitated requisition of supplies resembled the Eastern front in many ways.[27]

One of the by-products of the civilianization was a new nuance about the forms of collaboration. This particularly concerned Slavic speaking populations. For Bulgarians, the Slavic speaking followers of the Patriarchate were

---

26 Erica Charters, Eve Rosenhaft, and Hannah Smith, eds., *Civilians and War in Europe 1618–1815* (Liverpool University Press, 2012), 10–11. See also: Philip G. Dwyer, "'It Still Makes Me Shudder': Memories of Massacres and Atrocities during the Revolutionary and Napoleonic Wars", *War in History* 16, no. 4 (2009): 381–405; Mark Hewitson, "Princes' Wars, Wars of the People, or Total War? Mass Armies and the Question of a Military Revolution in Germany, 1792–1815", *War in History* 20, no. 4 (2013): 452–490.

27 Winter, *The Day the Great War Ended*, 4–5.

not simply considered enemy civilians but as Bulgarians who actively denied their race and sided with the enemy. The "Graecomans" represented the most dangerous category and serious corrective measures needed to be taken in order to put these people "back on track". Similarly, people that were loyal to the Exarchy represented for Greeks and Serbians the fifth column that operated from within.

Rumeli was an imperial borderland and in many ways the dynamics of the occupation were quite similar to the Eastern front during World War I. As in parts of Eastern Europe, the plans of the belligerent states collided with certain realities on the ground. That was a typical challenge in borderland territories that changed hands. Difficulties were encountered by Austrians and Russians in Galicia and Ukraine that witnessed turmoil over the course of 1918 making the implementation of any occupation regime impossible.[28] As Joshua Sanborn shows in his study about the Tsarist Empire, the Russian military replaced civilian authorities by trying to implement total control, creating new security zones, regulating economic life and suppressing civic activities. Yet, in spite of the original intentions of the war planners these actions, instead of forming a new administrative order they generated anarchy.[29] That was even more intense in the area under study because in the kaza of Salonika, the simultaneous presence of the armies of Greece and Bulgaria and the absence of a demarcation line converted it to the most fragile contact-zone.

In order to depict accurately this complex reality useful is to discuss the reports communicated by local officials and officers of the army. These documents while impartial and biased many times, they still reflect the knowledge production that shaped the mental world of decision makers. Direct manifestations that defied the allied presence such as capturing and policing villages and violating the zones of control were part and parcel of this story. General Theodorov the commander of the 7th Rila Division had been receiving worrying news since the autumn of 1912. The Greek army in the villages around the Langhada valley around Salonika had removed Bulgarian administration and sent agitators who propagated against Bulgaria.[30] In the same area grievances had been expressed about the taxation of villages, while Followers of

---

28 Mark von Hagen, *War in a European Borderland: Occupations and Occupation Plans in Galicia and Ukraine, 1914–1918* (University of Washington Press, 2007).

29 Joshua Sanborn, *Imperial Apocalypse. The Great War and the Destruction of the Russian Empire* (Oxford: Oxford University Press, 2014), 40.

30 TsDA, Fond 176, op. 2, No 2199, pp. 159–160.

the Patriarchate in the mixed Muslim-Christian village of Goliam Bechik (Megali Volvi) threatened their co-villagers to pay taxes to the Greek army.[31] All these actions, the reports concluded, reflected a carefully orchestrated plan by Athens that intended to occupy these lands.[32]

Bulgarian General Valkov, the Governor General in Macedonia, in his first proclamation commanded the immediate disband of irregulars.[33] He ordered moreover a tighter police control against Muslims and Greeks who did not cooperate in the Bulgarian zone which resulted to a selective violence campaign based on lists of potential enemy civilians.[34] That was followed by Greece and Serbia in their zones generating a new dynamic of violence. Although targeting of certain individuals constituted a common practice in the previous decade, this was about to be systematized in a state level. Individuals that participated in the Macedonian proxy war were high on these lists which did only concern armed bands but also numerous agents or simply people who were perceived as such. This opened the Pandora's Box. Teachers, priests, notables, civil servants, and locals who had collaborated in the past or even expressed dissatisfaction for the regime change were labelled and became targets.[35]

Such an example was the village of Cyxo, 55km from Salonika (Sochos) where a detachment of Greek soldiers showed hostility to Bulgarian civil and military authorities and instead of helping in the disarmament of the population, they distributed arms to Greek and Turkish inhabitants.[36] The attitude toward this village was not coincidental. Sochos was the base of the Dumbalakovs' a prominent IMRO family. One of their members, Dimitar along with the Bulgarian officer Petar Durvingov organized the Macedonian-Adrianople volunteer corps.[37] Greek garrisons additionally were stationed in suspicious villages such as Zarova (Nikopoli) in the Langhada valley to supervise activities. Zarova offered volunteers to the IMRO and had a militia under the leadership of Mikhail Dumbalakov from Sochos.[38] Conquered villages by

31 TsVA, F 1647, op 2, d. 25, No 106, 2/4/1913, p. 106.
32 TsDA, Fond 176, op. 2, 22/11/1912, No 1170.
33 NA, Fond 42K, opis 1, a.e. 590.
34 TsVA, F 1647, op 2, d. 16, No 329, 19/1/1913, p. 54.
35 Kalyvas, The Logic of Violence in Civil War, 173–209.
36 NA, Archiv na Christo Heschaptsiev, Fond 42K, opis 1, ae 694, 22/2/1913, pp. 1–3.
37 For more see: Mikhail Atanasov Dumbalakov, Prez plamŭtsitie na zhivota i revoliutsiiata (Sofia: Xydoznik, 1937).
38 IAYE, F. 1913, 8, 4, Voulgariki Parousia sti Makedonia, Octovrios 1912, pp. 1–3.

the Bulgarian army were retaken by Greek soldiers who ostensibly wanted to track down armed bands but in essence they were recruiting militia men.[39] Metropolitan Evlogios kept a detailed list of wealthy Bulgarian villages that had been occupied by Greeks and Serbs adding that the allied authorities silently endorsed plundering, arrests, and forceful replacement of teachers and priests. For instance, in the village of Sveti Ilija (Profitis Elias) the Exarchate priest was given ultimatum to change affiliation to the Patriarchate,[40] while in the kaza of Salonika shutting down of Bulgarian schools was reported.[41]

The Bulgarian Metropolitan refers to a very important threat and probably the most direct form of continuation of the Macedonian proxy war: targeting of priests and teachers. In the disputed zone of the kaza of Salonika the presence of the clergy and educators was a great asset to keep the locals committed to the national cause. This reflected also a crucial dimension of the mentality of the communities in Rumeli. Local elites were the only intermediary that they could rely on. Decades of irregular activities and weak state presence had constituted them as the only brokers with the outside world that protected them and communicated their needs. The psychological shock of their loss made people more prone to manipulation. Persecution of teachers and priests showed how the recent historical background shaped the trajectories of violence. The difference this time was the direct involvement of the official state machinery which utilized forced assimilation methods within the zones of occupation. That was also a pattern followed in East Central Europe in WWI. Targeting the leadership and intervening in the educational system was also a phenomenon that made its presence in Poland, where German authorities started a program of cultural propaganda though the expansion of a patronized educational network which aimed to classify "inferior" ethnic-groups under a German framework.[42]

The situation by Greek sources was no differently depicted. In Meleniko (Melnik), a village in South Western Bulgaria inhabited by a majority of Greek Patriarchists the treatment of civilians by the Bulgarian army was like enemy aliens followed by forced recruitment of youngsters.[43] Abuses in case of refusal to comply were commonplace. A priest and three individuals from the village

39 TsDa, F 176, op. 2, ae 1212, No 3030, 21/2/1913, p. 80.

40 TsDA, Fond 176, op. 2, ae 1228, No 1531, 25/12/1912, pp. 35–71.

41 TsVA, F 1647, op 2, d. 34, No 33, 13/1/1913.

42 Vejas Liulevicius, *War Land on the Eastern Front: Culture, National Identity, and German Occupation in World War I* (Cambridge: Cambridge University Press, 2000), 122–127.

43 IAYE F 1912, 2,1, apo Meleniko pros Raktivan, 13/11/1912.

of Goumenissa near Kilkis were imprisoned with the accusation that they sold livestock to the Greek army.[44] In Chorovista (Agios Chiristophoros), a Greek Patriarchate village involved in the Macedonian proxy war, was appointed a Bulgarian secretary who forced the inhabitants to pay him a monthly salary of five liras.[45] In the mixed village of Savgiako (Vamvakophito) near Serres locals were appointed as gendarmes and asked their co-villagers to join the Exarchy. The refusal of the latter to comply led to the merciless beating of some of them until the rest eventually denounced the Patriarchate. The case of Savgiako is an indicative example of recent inner-communal tensions that escalated in the war. This village was contested by Patriarchists who had managed to restrain the influence of the Exarchate followers.[46] On another case, a report signed by the notables of a Greek Orthodox community blamed the local secretary, a former comitadji named captain Koevski, for a reign of terror by imprisoning, torturing, and starving the locals because they were followers of the Patriarchate corrupted by Greek money.[47]

Those dynamics distinguish in way the Balkan case from other borderland territories of the First World War. Joined occupation of a certain territory paves the way for competition and in that sense what happened in the Greek-Bulgarian case was not exceptional. Another Balkan country, Romania during WWI had certain parts administered directly by Germany and Austria leading the Central Powers to an open antagonism.[48] However, there was as essential difference with the kaza of Salonika: the legacy of the Macedonian proxy war and the intentions of the allies to annex directly this area which did not exist in the Romanian case. As Koevski's example indicates, this bandit leader who had been involved in the bloody local affairs was very irascible to Slavic speaking people that, in his eyes, betrayed their country for bribes. For Bulgarians, the Followers of the Patriarchate who cooperated with the Greek army were not simply dangerous civilians but rather traitors: co-nationals who decided to side with the enemy and backstab their fatherland.

Nevertheless, while these reports represented in some extend the reality, at the same time they can be misleading as the classification in many ways

---

44   GES/DIS F 1635B4, No 19, pp. 9, 21.
45   GES/DIS F 1635B5, No 19, 8/1/1913, p. 44.
46   GES/DIS F 1635B5, No 19, 20/12/1912, p. 27.
47   GES/DIS F 1635G1 apo Socho pros Thesalloniki, No 58, 26/1/1913, pp. 8–10.
48   Lisa Mayerhofer, "Making Friends and Foes: Occupiers and Occupied, in First World War Romania, 1916–1918", in New Perspectives in First World War Studies. Series, ed. Heather Jones, Jennifer O'Brien, Christoph Schmidt-Supprian (Leiden: Brill, 2008), 139.

was a top town process. Sometimes the officials communicating this information had preconceived ideas about the ethnological reality. This knowledge was based on intelligence gathered from the period of Macedonian proxy war and the Young Turk era that categorized villages in lists of loyalty. In order to understand these notions it is useful to take a look at Mazaraki's list about the ethnographic composition in East-Central Macedonia:

> Between Axios and Gallikos: almost all villages are suspect and linked with Kilkis, a stronghold of *Bulgarianism*. In some villages we have some trustworthy Greeks. Right of the Axios River: Petrovo, Mpozets, and Giouvesna some enclaves of support exist as well as some friendly Turkish villages. Gallikos and Amaxitis road: villages Greek speaking and Greek loyal. Macedonian speaking are not reliable. Serres and Chalkidiki: Sochos, Berovo, Chorouda, and Visoka loyal especially the two ones that were Greek speaking. Zarovon, fanatical pro Bulgarian. Nigrita and the surrounding Greek villages are fanatical Greeks. Also, Turkish villages sympathetic {to our cause}. Pangaion Mountain: either Greek speaking or loyal and the Turkish are friendly. Axios River and Doirani Lake: divided among Greeks and Bulgarians. Mountain Belles: actively pro Greek Turkish villages because of forced Christianization. Kilkis: fanatical Bulgarian 8,000 inhabitants. Strymonas valley and Serres: in Macedonian villages there is sympathy to the Greek cause. Drama: Greeks and Macedonians.[49]

Not taking sides or trying to keep distances was perceived as an act of weakness or even betrayal. For this reason, in the vocabulary of these reports specific words were used. As "low" or "broken" morale were classified villages who eventually complied with the enemy becoming deviators. Particularly, villages with low moral were considered the ones that were more susceptible to "break" implying probably places that changed affiliation due to terror. Words such as "chauvinist" or "fanatic", one the other hand referred to villages that were operational bases of irregular units and had sealed their fate to a point of no return. Framing a village either as low morale or fanatic gave legitimization for counter measures. That was the case when some villages from the Kastoria district wanted to sign a petition advocating the Bulgarian cause prompting the Greek consul Nikolao Mavroudi to admit that: "If we do not use extreme terrorist measures it would not be easy to prevent the signing of the report."[50]

---

49 IEE, Mazarakis, Genikes Plirofories peri tou ethnikou fronimatos ton en ti zoni ton epichiriseon katoikon, pp. 26–28.
50 IAYE F 1913,9,1 apo Mavroudi pros Geniki Dieuthinsi Politikon Ypotheseon, No 2755, 26/1/1913.

While it is true that the villagers many times selected sides, this did not necessarily mean that their motivations were always clear. That was commonplace phenomenon in ethnically mixed areas in the First World War. In Galicia Poles, Ukrainians, and Ruthenians switched several times from being victims to perpetrators of violence participating in looting accompanying the army, while Austrians and Russians relied on them for information employing local tensions. This practise deteriorated relations between ethnic-groups in a whole new level from the pre-war era.[51] The policy of reinforcing ethnic markers enhanced suspiciousness between neighbours as it was the case of Catholic peasants in Lithuania who were considered more trustworthy than Germans and Poles by Russian authorities.[52] Likewise, the Russo-Ottoman engagement in the Caucasus was particularly strong due to a long history of imperial involvement in a borderland territory.[53]

In Ottoman Macedonia surely some communities or individuals intentionally took part and identified themselves along certain ethnic lines. Yet, strategies of survival combined with promises for a better future and protection were also part of the game. For example, not providing supplies was perceived as an act of betrayal while it can be a plausible scenario that the peasants wanted to use the crops to their own use. The war occurred right after the harvest period and many warehouses were stuffed with agricultural products. Participating in plundering raids could have been motivated by ethnic violence but credible also is the scenario of economic incentives and fear in a period of lawlessness and state collapse. This action-reaction process had been feeding daily the rivalry creating deadly dynamics. All these factors brings in mind what American political scientist James C. Scott called as "every day forms of resistance" and "the weapons of the weak" as he refers to any action (food dragging, false compliance, sabotage etc.) that opposed the extraction of labor and recourses from the peasantry.[54]

The dangerous game to create local enclaves of support determined behaviours and generated ground for retribution. Most importantly, these

---

51 Elisabeth Haid, "Galicia: A Bulwark Against Russia? Propaganda and Violence in a Border Region during the First World War", *European Review of History: Revue européenne d'histoire* 24, no. 2 (2017), 208.

52 Balkelis War, *Revolution, and Nation-Making in Lithuania*, 20.

53 Peter Holquist, Forms of Violence during the Russian Occupation of Ottoman Teritory in Northern Persia, in Bartov-Weitz, *Shaterzones of Empires*, 339.

54 James C. Scott, *Weapons of the Weak: Everyday Forms of Peasant Resistance* (New Haven: Yale University Press, 1985), 29.

reports affected decision making from the bottom up. The worrying situation and the prospect of not emancipating the "enslaved brothers" or even worse abandoning them to a new oppressor informed views from the lower to the highest levels of policy decision.

This did not mean, however, that actual agents were not operating on the ground. The presence of agent provocateurs constituted one of the most detrimental effects of the policy of the Balkan states and a significant dimension of the undeclared war. Their activities, which primarily entailed political agitation, not only generated a sense of insecurity but also provided opportunities for the apparatuses of the Balkan states to proceed to wide scale persecutions. Such as an example was the leader of the Bulgarian Catholics, Bishop Epifan Sanov whose actions were praised by Sofia. Sanov for the Bulgarian high command was the man who battled Greek propaganda in the Young Turk era and made the peasantry to embrace their language and feel proud that they are Bulgarians.[55] During the war Sanov donated 8,500 leva for the erection of a new church in the village of Roshlovo (Gerakario) in the Kilkis district, to attach Bulgarian Catholics to their motherland.[56] Bringing closer populations that belonged to the Uniate Church was a political manoeuvre that showed how Bulgaria was willing to accommodate different doctrines in order to satisfy the major Catholic powers' that were involved into Balkan affairs, namely Austria and Italy. For that reason, local bishoprics were perceived in many occasions by Balkan military administrations as factors that undermined stability either by acting as self-proclaimed representatives of locals or as national agents.[57] Bulgarian authorities also utilized agents when they became alarmed because of peasants abandoning the Exarchy by sending agents to the Greek zone in early 1913. Greeks tracked down a Bulgarian priest from Chroupista (Argos Orestiko) in the kaza of Kastoria and a man named Kyriazi who were spreading rumours about the arrival of the Bulgarian army trying to agitate the locals.[58] Also reports mentioned that Bulgarian MPs toured inside the Greek zone so that to instigate a revolt to the loyal populations of the Exarchy.[59]

Raktivan from his base in Salonika gave an order to "special employees" to assist the inhabitants of Kavala, Serres, and Drama against Bulgarian

55 TsDA F 176, op 2, No 218, 19/2/1913, p. 241.

56 TsVA, F 1647, op 2, d. 34, No 6533, 6/4/1913, p. 136.

57 Polina Chokova, "The Activities of Nevrokop Bishopric in the Period of the Wars 1912–1919", *Istoritseski Pregled* (In Bulgarian), 1–2, 85–88.

58 GAK, Archeio Varda, Kastoria pros Varda, No 176, 18/2/1913.

59 IAYE F 1913,9,1 apo pr. Nikolao pros Geniki Dieuthinsi Politikon Ypotheseon, No 2152, 20/1/1913.

pressures. The Greek Minister refers as special employees to people that were actually agents tasked to provide support to the locals who had been morally "compromised" and started to comply with Bulgarian authorities.[60] Individuals such as Philippos Kontogouris, an experienced agent of the Macedonian proxy war and former vice consul at the consulates of Manastir and Salonika, were about to coordinate a network of agents but most importantly to convince local Patriarchists not to evacuate the area in order deter the weakening of the Greek presence in the Bulgarian zone.[61]

***

This tendency was reflecting dynamics of the occupation. The ongoing undeclared war was cultivating daily a toxic climate. In the urban centers occupied entirely by Greece and Bulgaria the situation was yet even worse. Key cities in the Eastern, Central and Western parts of Macedonia had their commercial and daily activities disrupted and its population experienced a harsh occupation.

Kavala was one of the first cities that surrendered and was handed over to irregulars who committed violations. These initially were against Muslims in the form of selective violence. In particular, few days after the surrender a group of Muslims were led with their hands tied to the outskirts of the city. The official explanation was that they were prisoners of war to be sent to Salonika. But the testimony of an American employee in a US tobacco company suggests otherwise. According to this version, at least 150 men were executed on the spot and as it seems this was not an indiscriminate act of violence but a carefully selected move. The assailants had prepared beforehand a list of prominent local Muslims.[62] The man in charge was Hristo Tchernopeyeff a leading member of the IMRO and the head of the branch of Strumica. Under his orders the Ottoman civil servants were incarnated.[63] With these two actions the Muslim leadership was decapitated and shortly afterwards problems with the Greek populations rose.

Kavala was a prosperous port city and a major tobacco producer. In the late nineteenth century tobacco production was a main source of revenue for the Bulgarian economy making the annexation of utmost

---

60   IAYE, apo Raktivan, Thessaloniki, 22/10/1912, No 36654.
61   IAYE F 1913,9,2, apo Raktivan pros Geniki Dieuthinsi Politikon Ypotheseon, No 23924, 22/1/1913.
62   ÖS, HHStA, PA, XII, 386, Turkei, pp. 598–599.
63   FO 195/2446/3010/1-2, British Consulate Kavala, 16/12/1912, No 315.

importance.[64] Still there was an impediment. Bulgarians were underrepresented into the city which was mainly inhabited by Greeks, Jews, and Muslims.[65] Thus something needed to be done in order to alter the population synthesis. Elimination of the "alien middle class" was a subsequent practice. The Balkan states were fully aware that a basic premise to achieve control in urban centers was by containing the activities of wealthy city dwellers. These strata of people were considered as a Trojan horse and were targeted in a systematic way. That was for a variety reasons. They were in control of trade and possessed important resources. They were mainly literate, well connected with foreign embassies, and had voice in the public sphere through their newspapers. Many of them have been involved in the Macedonian proxy war. Economic means like heavy taxation of merchants and boycotting of commercial activities were the first to be implemented. Economic warfare was not a novel weapon in Ottoman Macedonia. It had been utilized during the period of the Macedonian proxy war and gave to economic affairs a nationalizing character. Most importantly it has been employed by the Young Turks especially against Greeks after 1909.[66] At the same time intensifications of pressures of local Greeks continued. People who actively participated in the Macedonian proxy war were targeted. Some were compelled to change names and stop using the Greek language in public.[67] Moreover the Austrian and French post offices were suspended in an attempt to impose censorship and Bulgarian laws and taxation were applied.[68]

In the city of Serres a major crisis of a difference nature erupted due to a forced recruitment campaign for the creation a local militia. This logic of the Bulgarian military in that case followed a certain pattern also applied in a way by the German Military administration in the Ober Ost, where Field Marshalls Hindenburg and Ludendorff tried to subjugate all sectors of the economy and society into the war effort. While it is true that in the German

64 Mary Neuburger, *Balkan Smoke: Tobacco and the Making of Modern Bulgaria* (Ithaca; London: Cornell University Press, 2013), 46.

65 Eyal Ginio, "Enduring the Shift from an Empire to Nation-State: The Case of the Jewish Community of Kavala during the First Balkan War", in *Jewish Communities between East and West*, ed. Anna Machera and Leda Papastefanaki (Ioannina: Isnafi, 2016), 175–179.

66 Doğan Çetinkaya, *The Young Turks and the Boycott Movement: Nationalism, Protist and the Working Classes in the Formation of Modern Turkey* (London and New York: I.B. Tauris, 2014).

67 IAYE, En Limeni Panagias Thassou Vasileios Skourletis pros Archigo tis Moiras tou Aigaiou, 6/12/1912, No 169.

68 FO 195/2451, Vice Consulate Kavala, No 2/8, 20/1/1913.

case there was a rather different background and Bulgarians did not want to convert the wider area into a colony as Germans aimed, the issue of forced recruitment presented some similarities that need to be taken seriously into consideration about the totalizing logic of war.[69] The forming of a local militia would enmesh people deeply and track down enemy aliens accelerating the assimilation process. This divide and conquer tactic ultimately compelled the inhabitants to take sides.

This decision was taken due to a series of events in the military front. Rumours circulated in the autumn of 1912 had it that Greek agents had penetrated deep into the Bulgarian zone.[70] The Greek Metropolis of Serres was accused for using excuses as pretext to send Patriarchate priests for propaganda purposes. This climate led the tightening of the security regime against potential agitators.[71] The fall of Janina alarmed Sofia. In February 1913, a dense concentration of army units and irregulars numbering approximately 3,000 men was noticed in the wider area. This was perceived as a hostile act since the Greeks having conquered Epirus they had free hand to dispatch all of their forces to Macedonia.[72] Given that the bulk of the regular army was in Eastern Thrace the need for the creation of a local force to safeguard the area was imperative. Eventually at the beginning of April the Serres Brigade was formed. It was comprised by two regiments numbering in total 4,000 men with local roots and 32 officers of the Bulgarian army.[73]

Many Patriarchate followers in the kaza of Serres saw that as an unacceptable practice leading tensions to new levels. The first coordinated actions took place in early 1913 when some mixed villages from the district sent a petition to the Greek Prime Minister. The authors, after praising their loyalty and contribution against Bulgarian bands during the Young Turk era they warned about the attempts of forced Bulgarization. According to the villagers, because all the measures to make the locals subjugate had failed, Bulgarians resorted to violent methods urging for help to the King and the Prime Minister.[74] The associations and guilds of the city followed thereafter by

---

69   Christian Westerhoff, "'A kind of Siberia': German labour and occupation policies in Poland and Lithuania during the First World War", *First World War Studies* 4, no. 1 (2013): 55.

70   TsDA, Fond 176, op. 2, ae 1228, No 1531, 25/12/1912, pp. 35–71.

71   TsVA, F 1647, op 2, d. 16, No 320, 19/2/1913, p. 53.

72   TsDA F 176, op 2, ae 1212, No 2248, 25/2/1913, p. 106.

73   OHHSTA, PA XIII, Turkey, XLV/3, Evidenzbureau, No 1200, 10/4/1913.

74   IAYE, 1913, 9,5, apo Serres pros Venizelo, 2/1913.

signing a petition in favour of Greece and founding a committee to assist the Greek effort. These petitions had eventually a detrimental effect for the locals as they were used as proofs of betrayal. Although the ultimate purpose of the locals was to avoid being conscripted, their actions had serious repercussions creating dynamics for retribution in the Second Balkan War being classified as potential agitators.[75]

The crisis from the formation of the brigade led many Patriarchists "voluntarily" to change affiliation. Sixty five people from the village of Egri Dere (Ardino) signed a letter that recognized the Exarch as their religious leader. The interesting part is that in one of the reports a Bulgarian officer makes a significant revelation. In order to prove the spontaneity of their act he underlines that those people took this decision without any kind of pressure.[76] The officer unintentionally admits that pressure was an actual mean utilized to shape loyalties. In other occasions, local Christians signed forms declaring support to the Exarchy in the format of the following document:

> The inhabitants of the village of Boumplikioe (Drama district) Bulgarians by birth, who until now recognized the authority of a foreign Greek Patriarchate, hereby declare loyalty to our national church, the Exarchy. We would kindly ask you to be pleased and welcome us in the sacred Bulgarian church.[77]

This source is a very important historical testimony to grasp perceptions regarding the issue of conversion. The local villagers, having acknowledged their ethnicity and mistake they ask for a second chance promising loyalty to the motherland. Deviation was a thin red line. Once crossed, it automatically rendered individuals or whole communities as traitors. Another example was a petition by 40 people stating that in the Drama district Greek agitators were asking pressures to recognize the Patriarchate and tried to impose the Greek language while they responded by founding their own Exarchate church, expelling Greek teachers. This petition represented a sign of obedience of the local villagers who in order to be considered as reliable they needed to present tangible proofs. Stating loyalty to the Exarchy was a tactic to keep at good odds with the administration and apparently the best way to do that was by showing active participation in the undeclared war.[78]

75 IAYE, 1913, 9,5 apo Serres pros Ypourgeio Exoterikon, No 6020, 13/2/1913.
76 TsVA, F 1647, op 2, d. 34, 24/5/1913, p. 108.
77 IAYE, F 1913,9,5, apo Dimarcho Boumplikioe pros ton Archimandriti Cyril Dioikiti Eparchias Dramas, 25/1/1913.
78 TsVA, F 1647, op 2, d. 34, No 30/11/1912, p. 106.

Tensions took place in the city of Drama too. Patriarchate urban dwellers had been complaining about restrictions in commerce and requisitions without compensation while the Bulgarian sub prefect of Drama conducted an investigation on occasions of murder and pillaging by irregulars.[79] Greek inhabitants were afraid of reprisals by Bulgarians regulars and irregulars and tensions with incoming refugees. Mass exodus from the countryside caused an imminent humanitarian emergency. The new authorities needed to shelter and feed thousands of refugees as well as the army. Muslims from surrounding areas arrived to the city being nervous owing to the fact that some of them had been involved in violent acts. Negotiations started between notables and foreign consuls to deter violent outbreaks while the latter tried to persuade the incomers to return to their homes but the suggestion was rejected.[80]

The occupation in the Greek sector followed similar patterns. As in Eastern Macedonia, pressures and economic incentives drove people to join the Patriarchate and abandon the Exarchy while different techniques were employed. In the mixed village of Zelovo (Andartikon) in the kaza of Florina which was populated by Patriarchist and Exarchist families, the Greek authorities made lists about religious affiliations and through intimidation and coercion tried to convert local Exarchists.[81] As historian Emily Greble points out, practices of citizenship in periods of transition were quite ambiguous and groups that wanted to keep their language or religion were perceived as backward and ultimately undesirable.[82] That was the case in the village of Laghen (Triantafyllia) where a gendarme declared to the villagers that they should identify as Greeks shall they wanted to stay otherwise they must leave the country.[83] Many arrests of Bulgarian elements also transpired in the area of Vodena (Edessa), Veroia, and Pella in the central part of today's Greek Macedonia.

79 FO 195/2451, Vice Consulate Kavala, No 1/7, 11/1/1913.

80 ÖS, HHStA, PA XII, Turkei, Liasse XLV/3, Balkankrieg, 386, Am Kavala, No 343, 8/11/1912. Consuls since the early nineteenth century functioned as crucial intermediaries in the Balkans by trying to protect civilians and capitalize their political leverage as representatives of the Great powers. In general on this issue see: Holly Case, "The Quiet Revolution: Consuls and the International System in the Nineteenth Century", in *The Balkans as Europe*, ed. Timothy Snyder, K. Younger, 110–139.

81 TsVA, F 1647, op 2, d. 25, No 877, pp. 188–193.

82 Emily Greble, *Muslims and the Making of Modern Europe* (Oxford University Press, 2021), 90.

83 TsVA, F 1647, op 2, d. 25, No 177, 23/1/1913, pp. 169–171.

Another phenomenon that made its presence in the interlude between the wars was denunciation. Denunciation was common place in multi ethnic empires in WWI. In Austria- Hungary the army received information for internal enemies by neighbours or people that were in close proximity to the front or occupation zones and received rewards.[84] Likewise, militias by Patriarchists obtained executive powers and patrolled.[85] Officers and gendarmes forced local priests to swear oaths to Greece and conducted house inquiries to track down Exarchists.[86] In Jenidže Vardar (Giannitsa) followers of the Patriarchate with the encouragement of Greek troops tried to occupy Bulgarian schools and churches, while in Edessa the entrance of Greeks troops was accompanied by a series of robberies against Exarchists in which Patriarchists seem to have participated.[87]

In the spring of 1913 the fear of subversive activities led to the tightening of security measures in the Greek zone. The outcome was the controversial decree number 7674 issued by a local official named Ratzelos. This decree gave extended power to authorities for conducting arrests of nationally dangerous elements. The justification behind this decision was that in Veroia, Edessa, and Florina the presence of Bulgarian bands that were operating since the Macedonian proxy war, had committed numerous crimes and propagated the arrival of the Bulgarian army. The massive arrests that took place consequently alienated the locals and[88] overcrowded prison networks.[89]

In the Serbian zone the dynamics of violence had similar roots. The only difference was the actors at play. The vilayet of Kosovo was inhabited by concrete Muslim Albanian enclaves and Slavic speaking populations that fell under the jurisdiction of the Exarchy. The Serbian army encountered a hostile environment along the way in Macedonia and Northern Albania facing problems akin to Greeks and Bulgarians. The locals many times were not willing to contribute to the war effort providing food supplies. Disarmament

---

84 Tamara Scheer, "Denunciation and the Decline of the Habsburg Home Front during the First World War", *European Review of History: Revue européenne d'histoire*, 24 (2017): 214–228.

85 TsVA, F 1647, op 2, d. 25, p. 181.

86 TsDA, Fond 172, op. 2

87 TsDA, Fond 176, op. 2, 29/11/1912, pp. 1–6.

88 IAYE, F 1913,5,5 apo Mavroudi pros Ypourgeio Exoterikon, No 17079, 5/6/1913.

89 As a solution it was adopted the deportation of these people with probably destinations Egypt and Crete with the charge that they are enemies of the nation: IAYE F 1913,5,5 En Thesalloniki to Tmima Stratias pros Ypourgeio Exoterikon, No 10432, 8/5/1913.

and requisitions did not work effectively and the regular army was involved in reprisals.[90]

The Ottomans had equipped local Muslim Albanians of Kosovo which were reluctant to hand over weapons to Serbians. On the October 27, 1912 the commander of the Third Serbian Army issued a surrender order with the threat of death penalty. This partially born fruits leading to the seizing of 5,000 weapons in Pristina but it did not prevent all violent incidents especially in central Kosovo where public executions were performed to irregulars.[91] The appeal of Serbian authorities to Albanian chieftains to surrender weapons led many of them to seek shelter in the mountains. One the contrary, the entrance of the Serbian Army in Prizren and Pristina was met with a sense of relief by local Serbian Christians who greeted them with joy.[92] This did not come as a surprise. The natives that tended to embrace the war effort wanted to safeguard an exceptional treatment and in some occasions employ the new authorities to settle old accounts. However, not only practical reasons constituted the driving force behind these attitudes. Some people in fact shared national enthusiasm especially those who were repressed by the Ottomans and assisted the national causes of the Balkan states. The same happened with the Greeks in Salonika and Kastoria or the Bulgarians in cities in Eastern Macedonia.

The Serbians implemented administrative functions in December 1912 when King Peter I promulgated the "Decree on the Organization of the Liberated Areas". This legal document composed by four chapters, provisioned municipal and judicial duties. The fourth chapter was the most controversial as it proclaimed Orthodox Christianity as state religion and reintroduced the "Law of arrest and persecution of Outlaws of 1895". This law, which was not in effect since 1905, provided a legal base to hunt down people that were considered enemies of the state paving the way for wide scale persecutions.[93] According to some scholars, Kosovo preserved even after the wars frontier characteristics (contested region) leading Belgrade to govern

90 Danilo Šarenac, "The Forgotten Losses. Serbian casualties from the Balkan Wars 1913–1913", *Analele Universității Ovidius din Constanța-Seria Istorie*, 10–11 (2013): 91–92.

91 Mile Bjelajac, The Austro-Hungarian Creation of a "humanitarian" Pretext, 144–145.

92 Dušan T. Bataković, "Serbia, the Serbo-Albanian Conflict and the First Balkan War", *Balkanica* 45 (2014): 342–343.

93 Miroslav Svirčević, "The New Territories of Serbia after the *Balkan Wars* of 1912–1913. The Establishment of the First Local Authorities", *Balcanica*, 44 (2013): 291–293.

the area essentially as a colony considering cultural and political hegemony against Albanians as a legitimate right.[94]

This situation additionally embittered relations with Bulgaria and the IMRO. The Central Committee of the IMRO and the Metropolitan of Skopje Neofyt signed a protest in December 1912 condemning Serbian occupation. In particular, they outline how the populations in Skopje were Bulgarians due the *Berat* given by the Sublime Porte to the Exarchic Metropolitan in 1870 and how they had been fighting Serbian propaganda ever since. To support this claim they provide a table of statistics and underlined the attacks by Serbian and Albanian irregulars. They also accused the new authorities that they banned Bulgarian language describing the administration as "the second period of slavery".[95] Interestingly this report touched upon a very thorny issue about the existence of a distinct Macedonian identity. By presenting the populations of the sanjak of Skopje strictly as Bulgarians it opposed directly with what many revolutionaries of the IMRO had fought for. Yet, this can be partially explained by the tactical allegiance between the organization and Bulgaria. This allegiance reached a peak in the Serbian controlled zone in the end of 1913 when two full scale IMRO uprisings against Serbian rule ensued in the areas of Tikves and Ohrid-Debar, nowadays North Macedonia.

As thing were gradually moving on to the summer of 1913 the hostility between the allies was deepening. The locals having been caught up in the middle were forced to participate in the undeclared war. The moment the proxy war became official, deadly dynamics were unleashed signalling an orgy of violence.

Decent into Chaos: The Second Balkan War in Macedonia

They are arkoudiareoi (bear like). They are not capable but waging war and they are more bloodthirsty than then Turks. If a new war breaks out we are not going to leave anything in Bulgaria.[96]

Archive, Paraskeva Family,, letter, 15/6/1913

94 Ger Duijzings, *Religion and the Politics of Identity in Kosovo* (New York: Columbia University Press, 2001), 8.

95 They use the word *robstvo* which refers to the Ottoman era. TsDA, Fond 176, op. 2, ae 1228, No 1531, 25/12/1912, pp. 35–71.

96 ELIA, Archeio Oikogeneias Paraskeva, 15/6/1913.

The war against the Bulgarians is not the same as the Turks. The hatred among the two races has exploded and created strife.[97]

Archive, Chrysanthakopoulou, letter, 15/5/1913

The abstracts from these letters come from private collections and are both dated a short time before the eruption of the Second Balkan War. One cannot but notice the utilization of stereotypes regarding the perceptions of the authors about Greece's most dangerous opponents. A whole generation in Greek and Bulgarian schools grew up with stories from the medieval era which described the monstrosities committed by the Byzantine Emperors and the Bulgarian Tsars.[98] The educational system in late nineteenth century Greece employed ethnic hatred in order to render Macedonia as a symbol of national magnitude. In that sense, violence obtained a cathartic meaning aimed to balance the fierce anti-Hellenism of Bulgarians.[99] This factor combined with the shared lived experience in Ottoman Macedonia and the dynamics of the military occupation culminated a deadly mixture. Years of rivalry between two states that had mobilized a significant proportion of their societies in this ongoing undeclared war had generated dynamics of destruction.

The decent into a finale of mass violence in the summer of 1913 was thus hardly a surprise. Despite the fact that the allies had reached a compromise in London (5/1913), the situation on the ground was reflecting a different reality. Numerous reports from the occupied lands had been informing policies of decision makers from the bottom up. Taxation, restriction of personal liberties, and targeting of the elites in the zones reached a peak in the spring of 1913 inflaming public opinion.[100] In Bulgaria the General Staff was asking immense pressures to Prime Minister Stoyan Danev while Macedonian Groups even threatened the political leadership with execution. After the signing of the peace treaty, the troops of the Balkan armies not only did not demobilize but were reinforced.[101]

---

97 ELIA, Archeio Chrysanthakopoulou, 15/5/1913.

98 Spyridon Sphetas, *Ellino-Voulgarikes Anataraxeis 1881–1908. Anamesa ste Ritoriki tis Dimerous Sunergasias kai tin Praktiki ton Ethnikon Antagonismon* (Thessaloniki: Epikentro, 2008), 128.

99 Basil Gounaris, *Ta Valkania ton Elllinon. Apo to Diaphotismo eos ton A' Pagkosmio Polemo* (Thessalloniki: Epikentro, 2007), 211.

100 FO 195/2453, Consulate General Salonika, No 69, 17/7/1913, pp. 27–28.

101 Lefteris Stavrianos, *Balkan Federation. A History of the Movement toward Balkan Unity in Modern Times* (Northampton: Smith College, 1944), 118, 170.

In the sidelines the rivals were preparing by gathering information and tightening security measures. Influx of weapons and ammunitions to populations that were considered reliable had begun months ago.[102] In the Vardar zone in an area that covered 50 kms between Karasouli (Polykastro) and Giouvesna (Assyros) Greeks detained Bulgarian civilians, especially civil servants working on railway lines. House inquiries were conducted to track down bands and arsenals.[103] Few days before the outbreak of war a new order was released to find capable people so that to encourage the locals in Gevgeli, Serres, Drama, and Kavala and prepare them for a more active engagement.[104] In June, new militias were formed to assist the army.[105] General Manousogiannakis suggested also the reinstitution of the scouts.[106] Their re-branched name was "Sacred Company" a reference to the 1821 Revolt in the Danubian principalities.[107]

In Serres, in the Bulgarian sector soldiers arrested a Greek chieftain and his men and instigated massive arrests in order to tear apart Greek cells.[108] In Kavala suppression of the Greek population intensified. Censorship on the press was absolute and house arrests increased day by day.[109] In May an exodus of Greeks from the Bulgarian zone of occurred.[110] In other occasions, Greeks tried to respond by organizing militias for self-protection.[111] In the vilayet of Manastir Bulgarian and IMRO bands crossed the Vardar River and begun infiltrating the Greek sector.[112]

The surprising attack to Greek and Serbian garrisons in late June 1913 signalled the beginning of hostilities. The contact zone east of the kaza of Salonika was about to face a severe ethnic cleansing campaign. King Constantine gave specific orders to eradicate all "alien elements" in the areas between the Struma and Axios rivers. Vardas was one of the men dispatched

---

102 TsVA, F 1647, op. 2, d. 3, No 144, 28/1/1913, p. 36.
103 ÖS, HHStA, PA XII, Turkei, Liasse XLV/15, Balkankrieg, 438, Am Salonich, No 110, 26/6/1913.
104 IAYE F 1913, 9,1, apo pr. Nikolao pros Ypourgeio Exoterikon, No 2151, 20/6/1913.
105 ÖS, HHStA, PA XII, Turkei, Liasse XLV/15, Balkankrieg, 438, Telegramme des Militarattache in Athen, No 2717, 6/6/1913.
106 GES/DIS, F 1635A4, p. 34.
107 IEE, Mazarakis, p. 29.
108 TsVA, F 1647, op. 2, d. 16, 15/6/1913, p. 129.
109 IAYE F 1913, 9,5 apo Lekka pros Ypourgeio Exoterikon, No 144, 28/4/1913.
110 ÖS, HHStA, PA XII, Turkei, Liasse XLV/15, Balkankrieg, 438, Am Salonich, No 25, 31/5/1913.
111 FO 195/2453, Consulate General Salonika, No 68, 15/7/1913, pp. 2–3.
112 FO 195/2453, Vice Consulate Manastir, No 43, 7/7/1913, p. 2.

to undertake the operation in which the army spearheaded and assisted by paramilitaries and local militias. The experiences of the captain after so many years of irregular warfare would eventually pay off. The war was reaching its final and most deadly phase. The advancing armies of Serbia and Greece infuriated by the scale of massacres of the retreating Bulgarian army and irregulars and being brutalized by the ordeal of combat retaliated in kind. Although the Second Balkan War lasted roughly a month it was way more savage both regarding the conduct and the casualties.[113]

All forms of violence made their appearance, spanning from ethnic to personal and psychological to political.[114] In the mountainous area around Serres burnt villages and destroyed properties could be found everywhere. In the village of Kubalise in the Drama district which had a church under the jurisdiction of the Exarchy, Greek soldiers raped all female population. In other villages people were burnt inside their houses.[115] Leonidas Paraskevopoulos, the commander of the 10th infantry division was communicating letters to his wife about burnt Bulgarian villages all over Gevgelija.[116] The city of Kilkis was destroyed with artillery shelling in order to prevent irregular units from coming back.[117] Its destruction also entailed a message with a high symbolical meaning. This city which was referred to as "the comitadji nest" was the birthplace of Bulgarian Prime Minister Stoyan Danev and the founding member of the IMRO, Gotse Delchev.[118] In the village of Ploska villagers took a comitadji from the hands of the Greek army and executed him accusing him for the assassination of seven notables.[119] A Bulgarian garrison bombarded the town of Doxato and massacred its inhabitants. Women were violated and notables were arrested and kept hostages.[120] Captain Mazarakis headed a unit that went to Serres in which the retreating Bulgarian army had started to

113 GAK, Archeio Varda, apo Archigo Stratou Katochis, Konstantino pros Varda, No 262, 27/6/1913.
114 Dieuthinsi Istorias Stratou, *Ekato Chronia apo toys Valkanikous* (Athens: GES/DIS, 2014).
115 TsDa, F 176, op. 2, No 4695, 7/8/1913, p. 211.
116 Leonidas Paraskeyopoulos, *Valkanikoi Polemoi, 1912–1912. Epistoles pros ti Sizigo tou Koula* (Athens: Kastaniotis, 1998), 373–374.
117 IEE, Mazarakis, p. 32.
118 Manolis Sofoulis, *Imerologio apo tous Valkanikous Polemous* (Athens: Grigoris, 2007), 74–75. See also: Léonidas Embiricos, « Kilkis 1913 : territoire, population et violence en Macédoine », *European Journal of Turkish Studies* [Online], 12 (2011), Online since 21 May 2012.
119 ELIA, Archeio Metaxa, p. 12.
120 FO 195/2453, Consulate General Salonika, No 74, 28/7/1913, pp. 209–210.

destroy and he tried to organize committees to prevent locals from plundering.[121] After his departure the Local Archbishop organized a militia which engaged in combat with the retreating Bulgarian army who burnt down the Greek district and assassinated many civilians inside their houses.[122] In the northern villages from the city local Exarchists joined the abuses.[123] Mass massacres of civilians and burning down of houses took place in Drama and Demi Chisar (Sidirokastro) by the Bulgarian army and comitadjis who executed on the spot 140 notables.[124]

The narration of atrocious acts can continue but the aim of this chapter was to illuminate the dynamics that resulted to this orgy of violence. The undeclared war between the allies was building deep animosity. The bad blood in the lower level and the mutually exclusive irredentist projects on the top were two different channels that detonated this powder keg. Once the façade of the alliance fell off, nothing was able to reverse it. Yet, as Jochen Böhler contends about the Eastern Front in WWI, instead of seeing the tremendous levels of violence in East Central Europe as a seminal catastrophe we should try to understand them as a period of transition between the nineteenth and the twentieth century. The war was a catalyst that allowed state practices that existed before 1914 to be officially applied into a massive scale.[125] Imperial borderlands such as Macedonia changed hands and involved the locals resulting to violent outbreaks. As the next chapter on Pomak Christianization and the war in Thrace presents, these territories become spaces for ethnic cleansing altering permanently the ethno-religous map of the Balkans.

---

121 IEE, Mazarakis, p. 32.

122 FO 195/2453, Consulate General Salonika, No 73, 25/7/1913, pp. 186–187.

123 IEE, Mazarakis, Ekthesis tou ypo tou Tagmararchi Pyrovolikou Mazarakin Ainian Konstantinon Somatos Proskopon kata tous Ellino-Tourkikon kai Ellino-Boulgarikon polemous, p. 5.

124 ÖS, HHStA, Generalkonsulat, Saloniki, 459, Aus Serres do Wien/Athen, Juli 1913; For a detailed list on atrocities by all belligerents see: ÖS, HHStA, PA XII, Turkei, Liasse XLV/15, Balkankrieg, 438.

125 Jochen Böhler, "Generals and Warlords, Revolutionaries and Nation-State Builders", in *Legacies of Violence: Eastern Europe's First World War*, ed. Jochen Böhler, Wlodzimierz Borodziej and Joachim von Puttkamer (Oldenburg: Degruyter, 2014), 53.

· 5 ·

NOTIONS OF VIOLENCE AND ETHNIC CLEANSING IN THRACE AND THE POMAK CHRISTIANIZATION

The Turks could not believe how things have changed. Now they need to bring light for the cigarette of the former obedient reaya. This until recently was the opposite.[1]

Priest, Ivan Dochev, Memoirs

This abstract comes from the diary of the Exarchist priest Ivan Dochev who was in the city of Edirne when it was captured by the Bulgarian army. These kinds of sources are representative of people that operated as agents of the Balkan states and brought specific perceptions about the roots of ethnic violence. Yet, while the priest's opinion reflects somehow the enmity that had been cultivated among Christians and Muslims in the Second Constitutional period, the story of Thrace is rather more complicated.

In this chapter, I tackle with notions of violence and ethnic cleansing in Thrace in tandem with Pomak Christianization. The reasons that led to this structure is that, first, Pomak communities existed both in Macedonia and Thrace. Second, and this especially concerns Western Thrace, the presence of the Bulgarian military and the dynamics of the occupation brought together more closely Muslims and Greeks producing a short term tactical convergence. The campaign to convert Slavic speaking Muslims to Christianity not only undermined the Bulgarian war effort and alienated the locals but also added another layer to the rivalry against Greece. The "production" of newly Christianized followers of the Exarchy perceived by Athens as a hostile act

---

1 Ivan Dochev, *Saga za Balkanskata voina. Dnevnik na sveshtenik*, ed. Lizbet Lyubenova (Sofia: Iztok-Zapad, 2012), 182.

because those communities fell automatically under the jurisdiction of the Bulgarian church.

This chapter is going to be divided in three parts. In the first, I examine notions of ethnic cleansing in Eastern Thrace with a particular focus on the Greek-Orthodox communities. The second traces a process in Western Thrace where a tactical convergence in the summer of 1913 led to the establishment of an independent political entity: the Republic of Giumiurdzhina (Komotini). In the third, I discuss the position of Pomaks during the occupation and the dynamics of forced conversion.

***

The historical trajectory of the vilayet of Edirne was in many ways defined by its geostrategic location. Thrace served as a bridge between Europe and Asia Minor while according to some historians it was a buffer-zone among the various cultural entities of Anatolia, the Aegean, the Balkans, and the Pontic regions.[2] In late nineteenth century the projects of the Balkan states encompassed Thrace. Yet, for a number of reasons the position of the vilayet of Edirne did not allow the clear articulation of the irredentist goals for Greece and Bulgaria, as in Macedonia. First, it was the geography itself. While in the western part of Thrace the mountainous rage of the Rhodoppes is dominant, in the eastern around Edirne the landscape is characterized mostly by plains. These kinds of territories were not ideal for the development of irregular activities. Bandit units during the winter months were vulnerable and needed shelter. Isolated villages in Macedonia and Epirus offered coverage but in Eastern Thrace that was way more difficult to attain. Another reason was the close proximity to the imperial center due to the existence of a developed transportation network composed by 1,300 kilometers of railway that connected Istanbul to Edirne.[3] Most importantly however it was the ethnological composition itself. According to moderate estimations, during the Balkan wars in the vilayet resided 1,185,189 people in total. Among them were: 648,624

---

2   Mehmet Özdoğan, "Eastern Thrace: the Contact Zone Between Anatolia and the Balkans", in *The Oxford Handbook of Ancient Anatolia*, ed. Gregory McMahon-Sharon Steadman, Online Publication Date: Nov. 2012.

3   Philip Ernest Schoenberg, "The Evolution of Transport in Turkey (Eastern Thrace and Asia Minor) under Ottoman Rule, 1856–1918", *Middle Eastern Studies* 13, no. 3 (1977): 365.

Muslims, 357,102 Greeks, 127,459 Bulgarians, 21,683 Armenians, 25,149 Jews and around 5,000 people from other ethnic groups.[4]

Despite that, Greece and Bulgaria attempted to increase their influence in the region. The creation of the Exarchy in 1870 had already generated a multifaced rivalry. One of them was urban antagonism. In the city of Komotini in Western Thrace for example the apple of discord became property and land purchases. Throughout the 1870s and the 1880s, Patriarchist followers created obstacles to Exarchists, while the latter eventually managed to acquire lands and founded the suburb of Kavakli. The acquisition of land offered the privilege to the buyer to automatically register as legal resident.[5] The annexation of Eastern Rumelia by Bulgaria in 1885 was a turning point that activated more direct involvement leading Athens and Sofia to establish irredentist networks using as blueprint the Macedonian proxy war. Officers operated in disguise while Sofia encouraged the creation of commercial agencies that functioned under the auspices of consulates. In the late 1890s the first Bulgarian agencies in the cities of Dedeagats (Alexandroupoli) and Edirne were established.[6]

In 1905 the experienced diplomat and protagonist of the Macedonian proxy war Ion Dragoumis received commission to go to the port city of Alexandroupoli having been assigned a very significant task. That was to persuade local villagers to buy land in response of the Bulgarian policy of settling farmers in the border zones.[7] Dragoumis was a man well aware of the ethnographic dynamics. His aim was to encourage people to emigrate to Macedonia and Thrace and to promote the establishment of an Agricultural Bank. The main concept behind his line of thought was that the nation was composed by two elements: the land and the people inhabiting the land.[8] Dragoumis was assisted in his endeavours by Athanasio Soulioti Nikolaidi another experienced agent of the Macedonian proxy war. Nikolaidis, as I

---

4 FO, 195/2453, Population in Thrace, statistics, British Embassy Constantinople, 29/7/1913, 165. Also we have sub-divisions such as the Roma and the Gagauzes who were Turkish speaking Orthodox Christians.

5 Vasilis Koutsoukos, *Apo tin Autokratoria sto Ethnos Kratos. Opseis tis chorikis Ensomatosis tis Thrakis* (University of Crete, Unpublished PhD Thesis, 2012), 110–111.

6 Aleka Strezova, "Bulgarian Commercial Agencies or Consulates in the Ottoman Empire Foundation, Development, Influence and Personnel (1896–1912)", *Historical Review*, 3: 81–82.

7 Lena Divani, *I Edafiki Oloklirosi tis Elladas* (Athens: Livanis, 2000), 373–374.

8 Michalis Kaliakatsos, "Ion Dragoumis and 'Machiavelli': Armed Struggle, Propaganda, and Hellenization in Macedonia and Thrace, (1903–1908)", *Journal of Modern Greek Studies* 31, no. 1 (May 2013): 66.

mentioned in previous chapter, had gained specific expertise in boycotting and waging economic warfare against the followers of the Exarchy. The leader of the "Thessaloniki Organization" (1906) was transferred on the eve of the Young Turk revolt to the imperial capital and created along with Dragoumi the "Constantinople Organization". The internal structure of the organization was similar to the Salonikan but the task of the Istanbul shell was even more crucial as it was responsible for equipping the Greek populations in the vilayet of Edirne and economically boycotting the Bulgarian element.[9] Meanwhile, the irredentist organization in Athens named "Panellinia Organosis" (PO) was founded. The PO's objective was the coordination of irregular activities in Rumeli. In the branch that concerned Thrace native notables and teachers from the cities of Lüleburgaz, Ortaköy, Babaeski, Vizii, and Uzunköprü were recruited. While irregular activities in Thracian soil were not as intense as in Macedonia they still existed. In the vilayet of Edirne the two significant centers that supported the Bulgarian cause were located around the cities of Bunarhisar and Lüleburgaz.[10]

Given this composition, it comes with no surprise that cooperation of locals was not something assured. While certain boundaries between communities for prevention of tensions existed, transgressions of those boundaries were not uncommon. Friendships among neighbours, attendance to festivities, and religious syncretism blurred the lines creating impediments to the agents of the national causes.[11] As Paraskevas Konortas asserts in his study on the kaza of Giumiurdzhina, regardless of the attempts of Athens and Sofia, many villagers still considered themselves as members that belonged to a religious community instead of a national.[12]

Regarding some economic aspects, Thrace was a major tobacco producer. The city of Isketche (Xanthi) alone produced in the late Hamidian era 1,945,735 tons out of a total that numbered almost six million, while tobacco

9 Ioannis Zelepos, "Redefining the 'Great Idea': The Impact of the Macedonian Proxy War of 1904–1908 on the Formation of Athanasios Souliotis-Nikolaides 'Oriental Ideal'", *Neograeca Bohemica*, 15 (2015): 17–18.

10 Vakalopoulos, *Istoria tis Meizonos Thrakis*, 261–269.

11 Nickolas Doumanis, "Peasants into Nationals: Violence, War, and the Making of Turks and Greeks, 1912–1922", in *Totalitarian Dictatorship: New Histories*, ed. Baltieri D, Edele M, Finaldi G (London: Routledge 2014), 176–177.

12 Paraskevas Konortas, "Nationalist Infiltrations in Ottoman Thrace, ca.1870–1912: The Case of the Kaza of Giumiurdzhina ", in *State-Nationalisms in the Ottoman Empire, Greece and Turkey: Orthodox and Muslims*, ed. Benjamin C. Fortna, Stefanos Katsikas, Dimitris Kamouzis, Paraskevas Konortas (London: Routledge, 2012), 96–97.

cultivation steadily rose until the Balkan Wars. Politically, Edirne was the central urban center that concentrated military and administrative functions. Alexandroupoli became an important transit point after the expansion of the port and the creation of a railway line.[13]

The eruption of the Balkan wars spawned an ethnographic earthquake of tremendous magnitude. Probably, the vilayet of Edirne was affected the most by the wars.[14] In order to analyze in detail the dynamics of violence I need to point out firstly some significant differences between the Thracian and the other war theatres. As Eyal Ginio argues, eastern Thrace was transformed into a "zone of ethnic cleansing" where targeting of civilians and violent deportations became the norm.[15] In the eastern part of Thrace the ongoing siege of Edirne caused major disturbances on the countryside and after a short Bulgarian interlude the area changed hands. The Bulgarian military Governor General Vladimir Vazov was in the city of Lozengrad and from day number one faced a series of impediments. Technically the responsibilities of the Lozengrad (Kırklareli) Governorship were administrative, political, and financial. Still, the most imperative was to gather supplies from the countryside and reallocate them to the army. The second military Governorship in Western Thrace was established in the city of Dimoteka (Didimoteicho) and General Mikhail Savov was the man in charge. From the beginning problems existed due to appointments of district officials who were outsiders from Bulgaria and did not have familiarity with the local population.[16] Perhaps this was one of the greatest challenges that the Bulgarians had to deal with. Although in parts of Macedonia they could rely on the assistance of Slavic speaking populations that was not the case in Thrace. The experienced

---

13 Koutsoukos, *Apo tin Autokratoria sto Ethnos Kratos*, 60, 72.

14 Justin MacCarthy, *Death and Exile: The Ethnic Cleansing of Ottoman Muslims 1821–1922* (Pennington, New Jersey.: Darwin Press, 1995), 155; Antonis Klapsis, Violent Uprooting and Forced Migration: A Demographic Analysis of the Greek Populations of Asia Minor, Pontus and Eastern Thrace, *Middle Eastern Studies* 50, no. 4 (2014): 627; Penka Peykovska, War and Migration in Bulgaria from 1912 to 1926: The Refugee Inflows in the Light of Census Data, *Bulgarian Historical Review*, 1–2 (2017): 229–230; Elisabeth Kontogiorgi, "Forced Migration, Repatriation, Exodus. The Case of Ganos-Chora and Myriophyto-Peristasis, Orthodox Communities in Eastern Thrace", *Balkan Studies*, 35/1 (1994): 15–45.

15 Ginio, *The Ottoman Culture of Defeat*, 70; Ginio, "*Paving the Way for Ethnic Cleansing*: Eastern Thrace through the Balkan Wars (1912–1913) and Their Aftermath," in *Shatterzone of Empires*, ed. Bartov and Weitz, 283–297.

16 Staiko Trifonov, *Trakiiā: administrativna uredba, politicheski i stopanski zhivot, 1912–1915* (Trakiiskia Fondatsia Kapitan Petko Voivoda, 1992), 21–22.

Bulgarian diplomat, Atanas Shopov outlined this problem in his correspondence with the Bulgarian Government by asserting that the vilayet of Edirne was inhabited by many "foreign" elements that rendered the task of keeping these lands really burdensome. On the contrary, in Macedonia, compact Bulgarians populations had fallen under Greek and Serbian rule undermining the national cause.[17] Indeed, one of the factors that determined the levels of violence was that the populations that favoured Bulgarian occupation was perceived by other ethnic groups, especially by Muslims and Greeks, as a fifth column that collaborated with the enemy. This point leads to the last factor that distinct this area from other war theatres. Eastern Thrace was the only territory that was retaken by the Ottomans and became a laboratory of ethnic expulsion. Western Thrace followed a different path resorting to a multi-confessional political experiment.

Thrace at the beginning of war was plagued by plundering raids from irregular troops, army deserters, and thousands of impoverished refugees. Muslims evacuated swiftly to the port of Alexandroupoli in the west, and to the port of Malgara (Malkara) in the east taking food and supplies.[18] Slavic speaking populations around Edirne panicked when they realized that the armies of the Balkan states did not only include Bulgarians but also Serbian cavalry units making the nourishment of troops and the interaction with the locals a source of serious concern.[19] In city of Raidesto (Tekirdağ) in Eastern Thrace there was concentration of a large number of Muslim refugees when it was captured by the Bulgarian military.[20] Many villages had been evacuated while Ottoman army deserters and irregulars were wandering around creating disturbances.[21] In the neighbouring kaza of Airobol Muslim bands murdered many Christians.[22] A Turkish squad accompanied by Muslim irregulars plundered Exarchate villages around Lüleburgaz. The irregulars had become a menace and the Bulgarian army needed to dispatch units to engage in combat to contain them. These skirmishes escalated tensions and intensified violence with collateral losses in human lives and properties. The bands had been utilizing hit and run practices inflicting casualties to the army. Their effect was significant in psychological terms indicating the immense challenge of the

17   NA, Fond, 41k, Op. 1, ae 159, 25/12/1912, pp. 1–2.

18   TsVa, F. 48, op. 5, d 7–8, No 445, 7/10/1912, 34.

19   TsVa, F. 48, op. 5, d 7–8, No 624, 8/10/1912, 40.

20   TsVa, F. 48, op. 5, d 7–8, No 125, 25/10/1912, 116.

21   TsVa, F. 48, op. 5, d 7–8, No 107, 21/10/1912, 101.

22   TsVa, F. 48, op. 5, d 7–8 No 114, 22/10/1912, 104.

pacification of the area given the lack of regular units.[23] One of the measures implemented was to send volunteers led by army officers in counter insurgency operations. These militias included sometimes locals but according to estimations almost 90% of the volunteers that operated in Thrace came from Macedonia.[24] Permission was also given to burn down villages which were used as bases for irregulars.[25]

In February, 1913 new units were formed under the leadership of the former IMRO operative, Alexander Protogerov and were assigned to coordinate the logistical supply of the army to the port of Malkara by gathering material from shops in city centers. These units were staffed by officers and old comitadjis alike.[26] Protogerov was one of the leaders of the Macedonian Adrianople Volunteers (MAV) which was a legion comprised predominantly by Macedonian refugees that resided in Bulgaria and was formed on the eve of the First Balkan War. The MAV in essence was a semi attached unit to the Bulgarian army, totalled 18,870 men, and operated in the Rhodope Mountains.[27]

The occupation of Thracian territories at first was well received by Christians when the spirit of the alliance was still alive. A soldier of Greek origins of the Bulgarian army who crossed the areas of Ortaköy (Ivaylovgrad), Luleburgas, and Tekirdağ recorded wholehearted support by Patriarchate populations.[28] To that, it had definitely contributed a series of massacres and punitive measures by the Ottoman military. The kaza of Malkara was raided by Ottoman deserters resulting to the destruction of at least three villages. Thracian Christian villages in general were targeted for reprisals leading local populations to welcome the Bulgarian army with a sense of relief.[29] In Didimoteicho and Tekirdağ people manifested their support by hanging Bulgarian flags, handing over weapons, and joining militias.[30] Greek

23 TsVa, F. 48, op. 5, d 7–8, No 106, 22/10/1912, 101–105, 112.
24 Anthony Giza, *Balkanskite Darzbavi i Makedonskiya Vapros* (Sofia: Macedonian Scientific Institute, 2001), 70.
25 TsVa, F. 48, op. 5, d 8, No 619, 23/10/1912, 81.
26 TsVa, F. 422, op. 2, d 2, pp. 15–17.
27 Tetsuya Sahara, "The Military Origins of the Tiskilat Mahsusa", 494–495. See more on: Dûrvingov, Petûr, *Istoriia na Makedono-Odrinskoto opûlchenie, Tom Pûrvi: Zhivotûti deistviiata na opûlchenieto v voinata s Turtsiia* (Sofia: Dûrzhavna Pechatnitsa, 1919).
28 IAYE, 1913, 4,3, Antigrafo Imerologiou Omogenous ek Fillipoupolis Ypiretountos ton Voulgariko Strato.
29 IAYE, 1913, 6,8, Apo Episkopo Raidestou Irakleio pros Ypourgeio Exoterikon, 7/11/1912.
30 Dodov, *Dnevnik*, p. 33.

representatives from the districts of Malkara, Tekirdağ, Kesani (Keşan) and Charioupoli (Hayrabolu) sent in December 1912 an urgent appeal to the Governments of the Balkan alliance not to allow the inclusion of eastern Thrace to the Ottoman Empire owing to horrendous treatment of Christian civilians.[31]

These dynamics of violence as in Macedonia involved eventually the locals in a more active way. The Ottomans' punitive behaviour in combination with a state of lawlessness cultivated a ground for retribution. Christians vented their wrath to Muslim villages and in some occasions the evacuation was followed by pillaging with the participation of natives.[32] In the area around the city of Tekirdağ the local priest Grigorios describes the situation in November 1912 as follows:

> I am in the extremely sad position to report that here we have an internal strife. Christians and Muslims are killing each other. Every day Turkish villages are being destroyed by irregulars (Bulgarians and Greeks) and Christian villages by Turks. I am afraid that this is a part of a satanic plan which wants to devastate out homeland.[33]

The chaos also benefited incoming irregulars from Macedonia who raided parts of Thrace.[34] The Muslim inhabitants of Alexandroupoli were terrified because they created a state of terror and massacred at least three hundred civilians in late 1912.[35] That was a typical category of marauders that operated during the Balkan wars taking advantage of the opportunity by pillaging places that they were unknown avoiding identification.

However, the implementation of measures by Bulgarian authorities gradually alienated the Greco-phone and Patriarchist element. The Bulgarian military conducted house inquiries to confiscate goods that came from looting

---

31 IAYE, 1913, 6,8,, Apo Episkopo Raidestou Irakleio pros Ypourgeio Exoterikon, 6/12/1912.

32 Gencho Stainov, *Pisma ot Odrin, 1912–1913. Pisma i snimki ot Balkanskata i Mezhdusayuznicheskata voini, nyakoi ot koito nepublikuvani dosega*, ed. Radina Nancheva (Sofia: Izd. atelie Ab, 2009), 31.

33 IAYE, F, 6, 8, 11/12.

34 In particular, a chieftain named Chakov managed to recruit 130 men in Serres and 80 of them were Greeks members of the band of a certain captain Antoni. Eventually six hundred men were gathered all volunteers from Serres, Nevrokopi and Kavala under the leadership of Tchernopeevf, Tchardakovf, Tchakovf and Taska. IAYE, 1913,8,4, From Consulate Kavala to Ministry of Foreign Affairs, No 76, 28/1/1913.

35 Anastasios Dimitrakopoulos, *O A Valkanikos Polemos Mesa apo ta Archeia tis Istorikis Ypiresias tou Gallikou Nautikou* (Peiraias: Nautiko Mouseio Ellados, 1996), 103,110.

generating tensions.[36] The Greek Vice consul of Lüleburgaz instructed the clergy not to hand over schools to Bulgarian teachers.[37] According to the previous soldier of Greek origins, livestock and provisions were ripped off by locals who reported that the Greek population was caught in a precarious position deprived from their properties.[38] Meanwhile, Greek consular authorities were sending worrying signals for an attempt of Sofia to alter the ethnological composition by relocating Bulgarian peasants to abandoned Ottoman chiftliks and imposing the Bulgarian language.[39] The last practise alarmed Athens. Since the early phases of the existence of the Bulgarian Principality, policies over land control had been used as a vehicle to de-Ottomanize and assure dominance of the Bulgarian state.[40]

Similar problems existed around the city of Edirne where the majority of Muslim villages had been destroyed.[41] A series of murders committed by Bulgarian troops and irregulars against the Patriarchist population led some local committees to appeal to the Great powers.[42] Inside the city the bombardment and long duration of the siege polluted the air while food ratios had been decreased to half undermining the legitimacy of the civilian administration.[43] A delegation of the Red Cross that visited Edirne recorded several damages from arsons and plundering.[44] The Austrian consul was worried sharing concerns with Bulgarian officers about inadequate policing of the newly conquered city.[45]

While these reports should be treated with cautiousness as they expressed official Greek and Austrian views regarding the occupation, they might still be helpful to facilitate the discussion in regard to another dimension of the concept of enemy civilian. War mobilization represents a period of increased

36 IAYE, 1912, 83,8, Ypoproxenio Saranta Eklession pros Ypourgeio Exoterikon, No 446, 30/11/1912.
37 IAYE, 1913,8,4, Ypoproxenio Saranta Eklission pros Ypourgeio Exoterikon, No 13403, 24/4/1913.
38 IAYE, 1913, 4,3, Epistoli Omogenous pou Polemise me to Voulgariko Strato, 10/2/1913.
39 IAYE, 1913, 4,3 Proxeneio Philippoulopeos pros Ypourgeio Exoterikon, No 76, 11/2/1913.
40 Krzysztof Popek, "De-Ottomanisation of Land. Muslim Migrations and Ownership in the Bulgarian Countryside after 1878", Zeszyty Naukowe Towarzystwa Doktorantów UJ Nauki Społeczne, NR 24 (1/2019):85–110
41 FO, 195/2453, From Embassy Therapia to Foreign Office, No 31 25/7/1913, 62–63.
42 ÖS, HHStA, PA, XII, 438, Am Jenikoj, 40, 31/7/1913.
43 ÖS, HHStA, PA, XII, 391, Am Adrianopel, 3/2/1913, 336–344.
44 ÖS, HHStA, PA, XII, 385, Am Adrianopel, No 43, 14/8/1913.
45 ÖS, HHStA, PA, XII, 391, Am Adrianopel, No 201, 9/4/1913.

security measures. In Tsarist Russia in the years 1914–7, nearly 600,000 civilians were affected by these policies which categorized ethnic-groups as friends or foes resulting to mass migrations, ethnic cleansing, and expropriation of land. Historian Eric Lohr who wrote extensively on that issue argued that the driving force behind the persecution of alien nationals was grounded on the perception that enemy civilians have by definition tied their fate to a foreign country.[46]

This point can be further expanded by seeing how this top down process mirrored from the bottom up and informed the minds of the repressed too. A suitable example to grasp this dynamic comes from a report of the Greek Metropolitan of Xanthi. The Metropolitan after acknowledging abuses under the Bulgarian rule he devoted space to address the issue of the Christianization of Pomaks. According to the Greek clergyman, the Christianization was a centrally coordinated plan of the Bulgarian military in compliance with local Exarchists.[47] The focus of the Greek clergyman on to the Muslims' hardships were not driven simply by pure empathy but also reflected a crystallization of a tactical convergence against the common enemy. As we saw in the chapter on Bekir, cooperation between groups that did not share the same religious affiliation was not unusual. People were witnessing that the occupation authorities benefited some ethnic-groups at the expense of others. Once the Bulgarian army left, immediately the "privileged" were converted into new targets. This was even more evident in February 1913 when the first military setback of the Bulgarian army signalled different dynamics between the Western and Eastern parts of Thrace. The retreat of Bulgarians led to a first wave of reprisals against Christian villages by the Ottomans causing a new exodus.[48]

The eruption of the Second Balkan War only deteriorated the situation. Consular authorities blamed the Ottomans that they unleashed numerous criminal elements of Kurd and Arab (meaning broadly non-Turkish speaking Muslims) origin and war wretched refugees to do the dirty job.[49] For instance, when the Ottoman army arrived in Tekirdağ it was accompanied by a number of irregulars, mainly Arabs who attacked villages and in coordination with the

---

46 Eric Lohr, *Nationalizing the Russian Empire: The Campaign against Enemy Aliens during World War I* (Cambridge MA: Harvard University Press, 2003).

47 IAYE, 1913, 9, 5, Ekthesis Mitropoliti Xanthis Anthimou pros Ypourgeio Exoterikon, 7/1/1913.

48 IAYE, 1912, 6,8, apo Ypoproxenio Saranta Eklission pros Ypourgeio Exoterikon, No 65, 1/3/1913.

49 IAYE, 1913,2,4, apo Konstantinopoli pros Ypourgeio Exoterikon, No 892, 27/7/1913.

army massacred civilians especially Armenians.[50] Another worrying report from the Greek consulate in Istanbul mentioned pillages, murders, and rapes by the Ottoman army and paramilitaries as part of an organized plan that pursued to alter of the ethno-religious map by relocating Muslim refugees and expelling Christians.[51] The Greek Patriarch communicated a report listing atrocities around the area of Malkara against Greek populations by describing the perpetrators as "hordes of savages".[52]

The Armenian Patriarch also intervened after massacres against Armenians in the same city by expressing fears of a repetition of the 1909 Adana events.[53] The targeting of Armenians reflected the deadly dynamics that were unleashed from war and the bellicose climate that had been incubated the previous decades. The reference of the Patriarch to the Adana massacres was not coincidental. The Armenian question became one of the most important thorns in the late Hamidian era that stigmatized Armenians since the bloody events of 1895[54] and the Adana massacres (1909). To this it had definitely contributed the fact that many Armenians participated as volunteers in Thrace particularly in the MAV enhancing this vicious circle.[55]

The embassies of the Great powers in Eastern Thrace communicated similar stories describing a state of lawlessness and impunity. Soldiers and irregulars pillaged, and plundered indistinctively some times in the presence of officers. Particularly intense violence was inflicted upon women who suffered the most horrifying abuses.[56] Official Ottoman authorities refuted any kind of responsibility claiming that these were actions committed by criminal elements uncontrolled by the army and the police. Surprisingly, this view was shared by some Greeks officials. A certain Greek priest named Polykarpos claimed that the Ottoman authorities were unable to reinstate the rule of law

50 FO, 195/2453, Vice Consul d' Italie to Foreign Office, 21/7/1913, 72.

51 IAYE, 1913,2,4, apo Konstantinopoli pros Ypourgeio Exoterikon, No 821, 12/7/1913.

52 FO, 195/2453, resume of the report of the Greek patriarch, 80–81.

53 FO, 195/2453, From Armenian Patriarch to Foreign Office, 8/7/1913, 47–49.

54 Boris Adjemian et Mikaël Nichanian, « Rethinking the "Hamidian massacres": The Issue of the Precedent», *Études arméniennes contemporaines*, 10(2018): 19–29; Edip Golbasi, "The 1895–1896 Armenian Massacres in the Ottoman Eastern Provinces: A Prelude to Extermination or a Revolutionary Provocation?" *Papers of the Strassler Center for Holocaust and Genocide Studies* 25 (2015).

55 In 1909 the Young Turk leadership labeled Armenian populations as collaborators of the counter revolutionaries. Tetsuya Sahara, "Paramilitaries in the Balkan Wars: The Case of Macedonian Adrianople Volunteers", in *War and Nationalism*, ed. Yavuz, Blumi, 399–420.

56 FO, 195/2453, From Vice Consul Raidesto to Foreign Office, 25/7/1913, 138–140.

due to lack of men.[57] A similar Greek diplomatic report from Peran attributed responsibility to irregulars, while for the refuges it was mentioned that they were seeking resources to avoid perishing.[58] Eventually a committee by the Metropolitans of Maroneia and Bursa visited interior Minister Talaat Pasha and the latter after acknowledging that some violations might have occurred, he guaranteed immediate measures to be taken.[59]

Admittedly, relations between irregulars and state authorities were ambivalent at the very least. Control of these units was a thorny issue and their presence generated detrimental effects. Nevertheless, as the Balkan states, the Ottoman Empire has had a long standing tradition in employing paramilitaries in order to deny responsibility and keep its hand clean.[60] Recent studies have shown that some massacres in Eastern Thrace were not simply tolerated by the Porte but orchestrated. That was the abovementioned case of Malkara and Tekirdağ where the Ottomans landed paramilitaries and soldiers who started deliberately violent attacks.[61] This policy continued in the Turkish republic during the early Kemalist period especially in Kurdish provinces where bands were played against each other in a game of divide and rule.[62]

On the contrary, the role played by refugees who were employed by the Balkan states is even more challenging to analyze. Refugee accommodation became one of the central problems in East-Central Europe during WWI. Millions of people crossed back and forth imperial frontiers played in the veins of political agendas.[63] Recently ravaged individuals who lost relatives, friends, and properties were used in recapturing operations to assist the army and reclaim the land. Eastern Thrace was probably the most vivid example of the implementation of this policy. One of the factors that encouraged participation of civilians in violent acts was the protection by the regular army and the civilian administration. As we came across from other examples in the

---

57 IAYE, 1913,2,4, apo Polykarpo pros Nomarchi Adrianoupoleos, 7/1913.

58 IAYE, 1913,2,4, apo Peran pros Ypourgeio Exoterikon, No 20870, 17/7/1913.

59 IAYE, 1913,2,4, apo Konstantinopoli pros Ypourgeio Exoterikon, No 803, 7/7/1913.

60 The crisis of the Eastern Question in 1877 and the usage of bashi-bazouks for the Bulgarian massacres had created a historical precedent. Heraclides, Dialla, *Humanitarian Intervention in the Long Nineteenth Century*, 150–51.

61 Darko Majstorovic, "The 1913 Ottoman Military Campaign in Eastern Thrace: A Prelude to Genocide?", *Journal of Genocide Research* 21, no. 1 (2018): 4.

62 Ugur Ümit Üngör, *The Making of Modern Turkey: Nation and State in Eastern Anatolia, 1913–50*, (Oxford: Oxford University Press, 2011).

63 Peter Gatrell, Liubov Zhvanko, eds., *Europe on the move: Refugees in the Era of the Great War* (Manchester: Manchester University Press, 2017).

Balkan Wars, the capturing of territories that favoured friendly ethnic-groups had a dual purpose. On the one hand, it engaged non-traditional combatants in ethnographic engineering campaigns. On the other, it created a hostile environment deterring the repatriation of unwanted neighbours. Many Muslims from the Balkans resettled in Asia Minor after 1913 and had very tenuous relations with Greek Christians that cultivated a climate that ended up to a mass pogrom in the summer of 1914.[64] In the heart of the problem lied the agrarian question which was rooted in the first Muslim migrations from the Tsarist Empire in the 1870s. This struggle for resources that was combined with institutional weakness of the Ottoman state increased pressures on peasants. Naturally, the eruption of war and the ethnographic shift impacted locals and newcomers alike. When the struggle for survival and the struggle for resources were combined, it forced peasants to fight with their own hands in order to secure a property and survive the day after tomorrow.[65]

The Short Term Republic

While the situation was calamitous in Eastern Thrace in Western different evolutions were taking place. The short lived political experiment of the "Republic of Giumiurdzhina" signalled the distinct paths that Thrace followed. While it is true that in Eastern Thrace ethnic cleansing operations occurred and many local Muslims participated in reprisals, the main perpetrators in the Second Balkan War were mainly outsiders encouraged by the official Ottoman state. In Western Thrace where the same policy was not implemented the locals responded differently. In an area that was allocated to Bulgaria at the Bucharest treaty a large local coalition comprised by Muslims, Greeks, Jews, and Armenians attempted to form and independent political entity. The Republic of Giumiurdzhina or "Islamic Republic of Western Thrace" was a short term political experiment that lasted roughly three months (August-October, 1913) and encompassed the cities of Komotini, Xanthi, Alexandroupoli, Koşukavak (Krumovgrad), Kardžali and Mestanli (Momchilgrad).

64 Ther, *The Dark Side of Nation State*, 61–62.
65 Antonio Ferrara, Niccolò Pianciola, "The Dark Side of Connectedness: Forced Migrations and Mass Violence between the Late Tsarist and Ottoman Empires (1853–1920)", *Historical Research* 92, no. 257 (August 2019), 616.

The background behind this evolvement was intertwined with the undeclared war in Macedonia. Throughout the spring of 1913 Athens and Sofia tried to explore potential opportunities for new alliances. Angelos Forestis who represented General Dousmani, the head of the Greek Chief of Staff, visited the highly ranked officers Esat Pasha (the Commander of the Janina Garrison) and Vehib Pasha who were captives in Athens during the First Balkan War to explore the possibilities of cooperation between the Greek and the Ottoman army due to rising tensions with Bulgaria. The plan included the reorganization of an Ottoman Army Corps composed by POWs destined to assist the Greek army in the area east of the Strumica valley. Prime Minister Venizelos himself paid a visit to the Pashas, and Vehib obtained permission to go to Istanbul to discuss this issue with his superiors. The proposal reached a deadlock because, albeit the Ottomans agreed, they asked additionally the islands of Chios and Mitilini.[66]

The Bulgarian side was trying to establish connections with Muslim Albanians who deeply resented Greek and Serbian administration. Jane Sandanski's mission to meet with Albanian leaders was part of this process.[67] This produced results in late June and September 1913 when two full scale uprisings took place in Tikves and Ohrid-Debar, nowadays North Macedonia, where IMRO and Albanian units collaborated.[68]

Greek diplomatic agencies advocated a coordinated effort in Western Thrace against Bulgarian presence by advising closer cooperation between local Metropolitans and Turkish officials.[69] It was also suggested the usage the Greek Patriarch to advocate the idea of an independent movement in Western Thrace.[70] At the same time, Athens had started utilizing influential local Muslim notables as it was the case of three hodjas from Serres who made an appeal for the incorporation of the city to the Greek kingdom.[71] In the summer of 1913, in Eastern Macedonia, local Greek officials requested permission for the formation of Muslim militias in order to confront raids from Bulgarian bands.[72]

---

66 Melas, *The Balkan Wars*, 422–424.
67 See more on: Gabor Demeter, The behavior of Bulgaria towards Albania in 1912–1913, proceeding, 26–27, November, 2012, Tirana (100 years of Albanian Independence).
68 Georgi Georgiev, "Backround and Planning of Bulgarian Albanian Uprising of 1913", in *100 Years from the Ohrid Debar Uprising* (Sofia: 2014), 41–47. (in Bulgarian).
69 IAYE, 1913,2,4, No 18554, 21/6/1913.
70 IAYE, 1913,2,4, apo Kostantsa pros Ypourgeio Exoterikon, No 18554, 21/4/1913.
71 IAYE, 1913, 8,4, apo Raktivan pros Ypourgeio Exoterikon, No 8202, 18/3/1913.
72 Gennadios, Archeio Karavida, F. 113, apo Zoto pros Ypourgeio Exoterikon, No 37–38.

This policy gradually allowed a tactical convergence amongst Christians, Muslims and Jews in Western Thrace. There was already turmoil in Komotini due to rumours that Bulgarians were arming local populations in case of a local revolt.[73] A mixed delegation comprised by eleven notables, expressed complains against the Bulgarian occupation and their objection for the city to be annexed announcing the creation of a provisional government in late August.[74] The first step after the proclamation was to pledge for support to the Ottoman Empire and Greece.[75]

Apart from the Bulgarian element this new political entity enjoyed inner confessional support having representatives from the Greek, the Jewish, and the Armenian communities.[76] Bulgarians were not included because Exarchist populations were targeted as collaborators and many villages were destroyed by locals and incoming irregulars.[77] Ottoman troops attacked Bulgarian villages in the districts around Didimoticho and Greeks villagers seemed to have actively participated.[78] The important Bulgarian textile guild (abadji) in Komotini was effectively destroyed and their properties looted.[79] Refugees that arrived in the city of Charmanli, in southern Bulgaria, recounted atrocities committed by Muslims and Greeks, a couple weeks before the proclamation of the Provisional Government.[80] Yet, one cannot speak with certainty about the overall tendencies of the Slavic speaking populations and it would not have been a surprise if some Exarchists switched to the Patriarchate in order to avoid being expatriated and targeted.

According to information from the Greek Ministry of Foreign Affairs, the Islamic Republic of Western Thrace was populated by 550,000 people: 350,000 Turks 185,000 Greeks and the rest Armenians, Jews and Slavic speaking.[81] Locals willingly staffed the new administrative structures and militias giving

73 IAYE, 1913,2,4, apo Kountourioti pros Ypourgeio Exoterikon, 28/7/1913.

74 ÖS, HHStA, PA, XII, 448, Am Adrianopel, No 60, 9/9/1913.

75 IAYE, 1913,2,4, apo Raktivan pros Ypourgeio Exoterikon, No 27233, 18/9/1913.

76 Vemund Aarbake, and Koutsoukos, Niatchos, "The Independent Republic of Gioumoultzina", 223–227.

77 *Turkish atrocities committed against Thracian Bulgarians*, From a poll conducted by Professor Dr Lyubomir Miletic on the ruins of the Thracian Bulgarians in 1913 (Sofia: Sofia Press, 1987), 37–46.

78 ÖS, HHStA, PA, XII, 448, Am Jamboli, No 62B, 10/9/1913.

79 Staiko Trifonov, *Trakiiā,* 240.

80 ÖS, HHStA, PA, XII, 438, Beilage zu Bericht Sofia, No 47A, 14/8/1913.

81 IAYE, 1913, 2,4, apo Epitropi Aneksartiti Politeia tis Thrakis pros Stefano Dragoumi, No 1109, 18/9/1913.

momentum to the whole endeavour. The composition of the provisional government is a strong indicator about the spatial variations of violence between Western and Eastern Thrace. While in the eastern part, state sponsored ethnic cleansing operations alienated Christians and Muslims, in the west where the Ottomans did not have a free hand the locals responded differently.[82]

The official representation of the Porte in the provisional government was through the close associate of Enver, Suleyman Askeri bey. Askeri was an army officer and member of the CUP with many years of valuable experience in clandestine warfare in Libya.[83] His appearance in Thrace was connected with a decision taken in the aftermath of the January 1913 coup when the doctors Mehmed Nazim and Bahaeddin Shakir started merging several paramilitary forces that formed the nucleus of the Special Organization.[84] As Ryan Gingeras underlines, the rapid collapse of the Ottomans in the Macedonian front reshaped relations with allied paramilitaries. Enver Pasha as the new Minister of war appointed Suleiman Askeri and the Circassian Eşref Sencer Kuşçubaşı to organize a subversive organization that aimed to wage a guerrilla war against the Bulgarian military. In this endeavour prominent paramilitaries participated who forged alliances with local notables for the creation of the Islamic Republic of Western Thrace.[85]

Talaat pasha although initially shared sympathies for the cause of the Provisional Government he soon expressed his inability to assist creating frictions with Askeri. In early October the latter sent a letter to the Interior Minister expressing his determination to fight for the independence of the republic warning that any kind of settlement with Sofia would be considered as an act of betrayal. Talaat one the other hand was asking pressures for immediate ceasefire. A committee sent by Istanbul to implement the treaty was rejected and the revolutionaries gathered 150,000 liras to create a telegraphic agency to communicate foreign ministries and newspapers in Western Europe. A national-guard (militia) was also formed which numbered 40,000 men and

---

82   Tetsuya Sahara, "The Military Origins of the Teşkilat-ı Mahsusa. The IMRO and the Special Forces on the Eve of WWI", in *War and Collapse. World War I and the Ottoman State*, ed. Yavuz, M. Hakan and Ahmad, Feroz (Salt Lake City 2016: The University of Utah Press), 497.

83   Vemund Aarbake, "The Report of Petâr Chaulev to Prime Minister Vasil Radoslavov about the Situation in Western Thrace in February 1914", *Balkan Studies*, 49 (2014): 52.

84   Ungor, "Paramilitary violence in the collapsing Ottoman Empire", 168.

85   Gingeras, *Sorrowful Sorrows*, 58.

was comprised by officers of the army and soldiers that served in local areas Greeks, Muslims, and Jews alike.[86]

Yet, the Republic was not destined to last for long. The Greek state followed Istanbul's policy in order to avoid implications in the peace treaties declaring readiness to withdraw forces from the port of Alexandroupoli.[87] This move sealed the fate of the Republic. Without adequate backing from Greece and the Ottoman Empire and lack of international recognition this political experiment stood helpless. Eventually Western Thrace became a part of Bulgaria until the defeat of the country in WWI when the Treaty of Neuilly (1919) handed over this area to Greece.

The Provisional Government of Western Thrace serves as a tangible example to scrutinize the spatial variations of ethnic cleansing as a combination of the local historical background and the dynamics of the battlefield. Areas that experience periods of transition in wartime are fertile grounds for the development of autonomous movements. These were typically multi ethnic/religious borderland territories in which state control was fragile. The inner confessional alliance of locals against Bulgaria and their willingness to defy Athens and Istanbul shows the importance of the natives' agency who responded in a way that did not necessarily fit into national paradigms. The people that comprised this endeavour wanted to avoid annexation by Bulgaria preferring to create a political entity that incorporated Muslims, Greeks, Jews, and Armenians and not to resort in the same levels of violence as in other places. The Provisional Government of Western Thrace was also a response that aimed to protect the current socio-economic structures by the implications of nation state integration. Perhaps, the 1913 experience built the foundation for a different mode of Muslim-Christian coexistence in Western Thrace which despite certain flaws, hitherto exists.

The Pomak Christianization

Amidst the undeclared war between the allies a forced conversion campaign was underway. Conversion is without a doubt a contested topic in Balkan history. Debates about the degree of the Ottomans' religious tolerance have been at the center of attention. Religion was considered by regional historiographies

---

86 IAYE, 1913, 2,4, apo Konstantinopoli pros Ypourgeio Exoterikon, No 1201, 2/10/1913.
87 IAYE, 1913, 2,4, apo Ypourgeio Exoterikon pros oles tis Presveies stis Megales Dynameis, 18/9/1913.

as the matrix of a distinct identity which was transformed into ethnic in the age of nationalism. As Selim Deringil argues in his work on apostasy in the late Ottoman Empire, the linkage among the religious and national identity was so blurred that any case of conversion implied loss of identity and subsequently denationalization and while Muslim communities embraced converts and facilitated their inclusion (often through marriage) the Ottoman state was more reluctant to accept them.[88]

There are many theories about the origins of the Pomaks. What is certain is that this group could not be easily classified along traditional ethnic lines. As Mary Neuburger puts it, "No Balkan community is more contested, more wrapped in multiple intertwining twisted webs as the Slavic speaking Muslims or Pomaks of the southern Balkan range".[89] Even the term itself is utilized almost exclusively by non-Pomaks and implies a state in between that lacks a crystallized national affiliation.[90] Pomaks mainly resided in Western Thrace, nowadays part of Greece and Bulgaria around the mountainous area of Rhodope. In the late Ottoman era a number was also located in Ottoman Macedonia in the areas of Radoviste, Kilkis, and Petrich. The meaning of the word Pomak literally means "helper". According to a widely accepted interpretation, the origins of this term can be traced back in the period of the first Ottoman invasions of the Balkans when Pomaks provided guidance to the army.[91] In Bulgarian sources they are referred to as "Bulgaro-Mohammedans".

Their vernacular dialect is close to Bulgarian while Pomak communities preserved many Christian traditions. Yet, religion and particularly Sunni Islam constituted the main pillar of their identity. Contemporary anthropological researches have shown the resilience of the religious identity of the Pomaks. Despite their attachment to Islam they do not necessarily identity as Turks by emphasizing the importance of belonging to the umma, the collective

---

88 Selim Deringil, *Conversion and Apostasy in the Late Ottoman Empire* (Cambridge: Cambridge University Press, 2012), 4.

89 Mary Neuburger, "Pomak Borderlands: Muslims on the Edge of Nations", *Nationalities Papers*, 28, no. 1 (2000), 181; For more general information on the issue of conversion in a Bulgarian context see: Maria Todorova, "Conversions to Islam as a Trope in Bulgarian Historiography, Fiction and Film", in *Balkan Identities: Nation and Memory*, ed. M. Todorova (New York: New York University Press, 2004), 129–157.

90 Neuburger, *Pomak Borderlands*, 182.

91 Ömer Turan, "Pomaks, Their Past and Present", *Journal of Muslim Minority Affairs* 19, no. 1 (1999): 70.

community of Islam.[92] Recent studies pertain that the Pomak identity was the construction of a long term process that entailed performance, political struggle, and negotiation.[93]

Bulgarian historians one the other hand argue that the Pomaks were early Islamized Bulgarians, while Turkish historians pertain that they are step tribes related to the Abbasids dynasty. Greek theories categorize them as descendants of ancient Thracian tribes who converted to Islam.[94]

The crisis of the Eastern Question and the war against Tsarist Russia had a pivotal effect to their historical trajectory. Some Ottoman officials considered in the 1870s the usage of Pomaks as potential spies since they were linguistically and culturally accustomed with Bulgarian traditions.[95] Pomaks were involved in reprisals against Slavic speaking populations after the 1876. In early 1878, the prospect of integration of their territories to San Stefano Bulgaria prompted them to organize a revolutionary movement. In total, twenty one villages unified and created a short lived "Pomak Republic" that lasted until the annexation of Eastern Rumelia by Bulgaria in 1885.[96] Their stance during the period of the "Bulgarian rebirth" created bad blood and enmity that played an important role in the Balkan Wars.

In the turn of the century Pomak communities were still based on household economy being both productive and consumptive units. Mandatory inclusion into new national borders, the absence of an educated elite, and socioeconomic isolation led to religious conservatism.[97] Interfaith marriages with Christians were not common, whereas endogamous commitments within the confines of the community constituted the main pattern. Women in most occasions were excluded from inheritance and received no dowry.[98] Their

---

92 Magdalen Lubanska, *Muslims and Christians in the Bulgarian Rhodopes. Studies on Religious (Anti) Syncretism* (Berlin, Boston: De Gruyter, 2015), 17–18.

93 Ali Eminov, "Social Construction of Identities: Pomaks in Bulgaria", *Journal on Ethnopolitics and Minority Issues* 6, no. 2 (2007).

94 Manolis Varvounis, "Historical and Ethnological Influences on the Traditional Civilization of Pomaks of the Greek Thrace", *Balcanica*, 34 (2003): 269.

95 Milena B. Methodieva, *Between Empire and Nation. Muslim Reform in the Balkans* (California: Stanfrod University Press, 2020), 59.

96 Konstantinos Vakalopoulos, *Istoria tis Meizonis Thrakis. Apo ton Othomanokratia mechri tis Meres mas* (Athena: Stamoulis, 2004), 162–163.

97 Krzysztof Popek, "A Body Without a Head". The Elite of the Muslim Minority in the Bulgarian Lands at the Turn of the 20th Century", *Balcanica Posnaniensia. Acta et studia* (Poznań), t. 25 (2018): 137.

98 Ulf Brunnbauer, Families and Mountains in the Balkans, *The History of the Family* 7, no. 3: 333, 337, 341.

economic activities mainly included forestry, small scale animal breeding, and subsistence agriculture. Communication with other communities was scarce due to geographic isolation.[99] According to data, in 1912 the Pomak population numbered 129,042 in the province of Thrace and 56,456 in the province of Macedonia.[100]

The eruption of the Balkan conflict opened a new chapter for the precarious position of this ethno-religious group. The forced assimilation campaign was firstly based on ethnographic dynamics because without the inclusion of Pomaks it would have been unfeasible for Bulgaria to ground solid ethnological claims in Thrace. Yet, the *pokrŭstvane*, the Christianization process by the Bulgarian military and civil authorities not only paved the way for inner communal violent dynamics, but also forged new cross-confessional alliances among the locals. The decision of Sofia to launch a religious crusade changed the rules of the game. Not only Greek but also Austrian and British archival sources confirm that this campaign generated a dual dynamic. On a state level, Athens utilized the opportunity to side with Muslims condemning forced Christianization. On the lower level, Muslims appealed to Greek authorities for protection and occasionally collaborated with Greeks in Thrace in paramilitary activities. In this campaign, after a point, it became impossible to discern the motivations of the perpetrators that committed atrocities under the guise of a new crusade.[101]

Already, since the autumn of 1912 and the initial invasion of Macedonia and Thrace an intense wave of violence against Muslims had been initiated.[102] In many occasions the assailants waited for the departure of regular units to act without constraints. This happened in Strumica when the bands of a certain Chadji Manoff and Djakov pillaged and murdered Muslims after the evacuation of regular Bulgarian and Serbian detachments.[103] In the village of Mouzeni near the city of Sarisaban (Chrysoupoli) in Kavala apart from

99   Kevin Featherstone, Dimitris Papadimitriou, Argyris Mamarelis, and Georgios Niarchos, eds., *The Last Ottomans: The Muslim Minority of Greece, 1940–1949* (London: Palgrave Macmillan, 2011), 21.

100   Myuhtar-May, *Identity, Nationalism*, 52.

101   Vemund Aarbake, "Vasileios Koutsoukos, Georgios Niarchos, The Independent Republic of Gioumoultzina (1913). A New Test for the Young Turk Policy Makers", in *Balkan Nationalism and The Ottoman Empire*, Vol., 3, ed. Dimitris Stamatopoulos (Istanbul: ISIS Press, 2015), 217.

102   ÖS, HHStA, PA, XII, 385, Am Salonik, No 315, 26/11/1912.

103   ÖS, HHStA, PA, XII, 385, Am Salonik, No 203, 9/12/1912.

some Beys who were allegedly killed by locals, all other victims were brutally executed by outsiders, comitadjis with the usage of axes, clubs, and knifes.[104]

Physical eradication was just one of the hardships endured by Muslims. Economic exploitation was another and, as we saw in the Greco-Bulgarian case it was a standard practice to transfer the war burden to the locals' shoulders. Many bands exploited the opportunity to grab properties with the pretext that Muslims were not compliant while local Exarchists quite often played an active role.[105] On October, 28 Michail Dumbalakov accompanied by 150 armed Exarchate villagers disarmed Muslims, established Bulgarian authorities, confiscated crops, and imposed heavy taxation.[106] In Sidirokastro Muslims had all their possessions distributed to Bulgarian villagers and band-members.[107]

Aside from these reports, however, irregulars appeared to be actively engaged in the Christianization campaign which was based on General Savof's order dated in November, 1912. Until the end of the war it is estimated that around 200,000 Pomaks changed religious affiliation.[108] The typical process was as follows. Armed men surrounded villages and an Exarchate priest was delivering a speech. Then, people were baptized with Holly water and sometimes were forced to consume pork. The following abstract is indicative:

> On the afternoon of Sunday, April 13, 4 Bulgarian priests and some 50 armed men arrived at Eski Kavala and collecting the mukhtar and chief men drove them at the bayonet's point into a house when they were called upon to give the names of all the inhabitants of the village, which consists of 150 families all of them were Pomaks. The drawing up of the list occupied some five or six hours. On the morrow the Bulgarians draw all the inhabitants of the village into the mosque at the point of the bayonet. The mosque had by this time been converted into a church. Most of the interior ornaments had been torn down and the minaret destroyed. The inhabitants were thereupon forcibly baptized with full ceremony. Kalpaks with crosses sewn on them were then distributed to each man and head coverings to the women, while each person received a small cross and a paper bearing a number and a Christian name and some pious pictures.[109]

104 IAYE, 1913,8,4, apo proxeneio Kavalas pros Ypoyrgeio Exoterikon, No 92, 4/2/1913.

105 FO 195/2452, Petition of the people of Drenova in the kaza of Nevrokop, 21/12/1913, 63.

106 GES/DIS, F 1635Γ1, apo Socho pros Stratiotikes Arches Nigritas-Pangaiou, 20/3/1913, pp. 18–23.

107 ÖS, HHStA, PA, XII, 385, Am Salonik, No 205, 9/12/1912.

108 Turan, Pomaks, p. 76.

109 FO, 195/2452, From Vice Consulate Kavala to Ambassador Constantinople, No 15/25, 17/4/1913.

An inherent part of this process with high symbolical meaning was the replacement of the fez with the Bulgarian hat. The fez itself was an emblem of hybridity and its ban was crucial for Christianization.[110] Dressing code in remote communities represented cultural norms. Ethnicity and ornament were intrinsically connected because clothing was mostly produced by the communities themselves. Acceptance or rejection of a uniform denoted the willingness of locals to integrate to the national body. Those that rejected to do so were considered suspicious.[111]

Incoming irregulars from Macedonia spearheaded the campaign. The Holy Synod of the Bulgarian Church sent two missions in Thrace and Macedonia to facilitate the process. Those missions were accompanied by bands allegedly for protection. Nevertheless, security services provided by old bandit leaders to the clergy were simply a pretext to cover up the coercive methods at use. Almost always the Christianization was taking place under the watchful eye of irregulars. Tane Nikolov was a representative example of a comitadji involved in the Christianization campaign. Nikolov was a person not unknown in the area. During the Ilinden uprising he participated with his unit in Thrace and afterwards relocated to Macedonia where he forged connections with prominent IMRO leaders. After the outbreak of war he received orders to provide security to the Holy Synod's envoys. With the approval of the chief of staff he partook in activities around the area of Komotini with great zeal and he was accused for a series of crimes.[112] Other bands in Xanthi effectively converted around 1,800 people after resorting to violence, threats, and intimidations.[113] Representatives from 14 areas in the districts of Osmaniye, Djoumaja, and Petrich sent a report regarding Bulgarian atrocities asking from the Greek Government protection. Among others, they mentioned that they compelled them to sign documents showing that the conversion was voluntary.[114]

Pomaks, in principle, were willing to abide to Bulgarian rule but not to change their religion as shown in a protest signed by three delegations from the areas of Tets, and Nevrokopi stating that: "Under no circumstances should we be unfaithful to our ancestral faith and that at the present time we would

---

110 Mary Neuburger, *The Orient Within* (Ithaka and London: Cornell University Press, 2004), 92–93.

111 Ksenija Kolerovic, *The Vlachs and the Serbian Primary School (1878–1914): An Example of Serbian Nation-building* (Unpublished PhD Thesis: University of Manchester, 2015), 155.

112 Myuhtar-May, *Identity, Nationalism*, 91.

113 FO 195/2452, Consulate Salonika to Foreign Office, No 13, 16/2/1913, 56.

114 IAYE, 1913, 4,3 apo Thessaloniki pros Ypourgeio Exoterikon, No 611, 28/2/1913.

defend our religious freedom."[115] In other petitions Pomak communities after acknowledging their kinship ties with Bulgarians they declared readiness to do whatever it takes to comply with the new authorities given that they strived to maintain their traditions and faith.[116] Eventually, in many occasions intimidation, lack of protection, and circulation of horror stories compelled Pomak villages to succumb.[117]

British diplomatic documents arrived at the conclusion that this was part of a coordinated plan from the Bulgarian state. Throughout the spring of 1913 massacres and violation of Muslims in the kazas of Nevrokopi and Rupkus continued. 50 out of 90 Muslim villages in Nevrokopi forcefully converted.[118] Bulgarian inhabitants and local officials were compelling Pomaks while complaints were expressed by a Muslim delegation for acts of forced Christianization by Bulgarian teachers in Pechtsevo and Pancharevo.[119] In the village of Pletena (South-western Bulgaria) Christian villagers instigated a looting campaign against their co villagers and tried to forcibly convert them.[120] The British Consul in Salonika warned that while the Bulgarians would attribute responsibility solely to irregulars,they should not be believed since he witnessed open encouragement of these practices by the military authorities.[121]

Yet, there was another dimension of this campaign that needs further attention related to gendered violence. Rape was a weapon deliberately used during the wars. As Irvin Cemil Schik supports, the usage of this form of violence entailed a symbolical sense of appropriation of territory where the male population is incapable of defending their females generating a masculinity crisis.[122] Gender directed violence was a standard mean in ethnic cleansing. The 1990s war in Bosnia is the most notorious example. Scholars that addressed this issue outline three crucial consequences of this type of attack

---

115 ÖS, HHStA, PA, XII, 392, Beilage zum Bericht, Am Salonik, No 85, 15/5/1913.
116 FO 195/2452, Consulate Salonika to Foreign Office, No 10, 7/2/1913, 49.
117 ÖS, HHStA, PA, XII, 385, Am Salonik, No 212, 27/12/1912.
118 ÖS, HHStA, PA, XII, 391, Beilage zum Bericht, Am Salonik, No 67, 8/4/1913.
119 ÖS, HHStA, PA, XII, 391, From Salonik to Berchtold, No 69, 17/4/1913.
120 FO 195/2452, Position of the people of Pletena to the vice Consul in Kavala, 18/1/1913, 62.
121 FO 195/2452, Consulate Salonika to Foreign Office, No 10, 7/2/1913, 49.
122 Irvin Cemil Schick, "Christian Maidens, Turkish Ravishers: The Sexualization of National Conflict in the Late Ottoman Period", *Women in the Ottoman Balkans: Gender, Culture and History*, ed. Amila Buturovic, Irvin Cemil Schick (London; New York: I.B. Tauris, 2007), 274–304.

to civilians: demoralization of the opponent, an intention to break up the society's structure, and infliction of trauma to the opposite site.[123]

Male survival becomes an existential issue for civilian communities in wartime and the Balkan Wars constituted no exception. Bandits took advantage of the situation and forcibly married widows or wives that their husbands had gone missing.[124] Forced marriages constituted an effective way to convert women owing to the fact that Islam does not allow marriage of Muslim women and Christian men without apostasy. Additionally it represented a channel for enrichment. As I mentioned earlier, Pomak women did not possess dowry hence by getting married, their husbands' automatically obtained their properties. Tolerance to these practises by the authorities served a dual purpose. On the one hand, it altered inner communal structures favouring the expansion of the Bulgarian state. On the other, it offered material incentives and a facade of legitimization to people that committed murderous acts. Another form of women's' abuse represented kidnapping. This constituted a direct way to pressure the afflicted families and comply sooner rather than later.[125]

In order to have a more competent picture however we need to point out some interesting remarks from the Bulgarian perspective about the dynamics of conversion. The official position of the Bulgarian state was represented in the writings of Athanas Shopov. Shopov stresses out the poverty of those communities by underlining a specific aspect. While Pomaks were Muslims, their cultural references were much closer to Bulgarians due the closeness of their dialect to Bulgarian as well as the fact that despite Islamization they preserved a lot of Christian traditions. Cultural affinity and dissatisfaction to the Ottomans were the main pillars to be utilized to facilitate the assimilation process. Shopov moreover advised to align with important local notables because the Exarchy alone did not have the capacity to undertake this task.[126]

In addition, many factors interplayed and sometimes conversion was not the outcome of force but the product of strategies of survival and recent dynamics from the battlefield. Voluntary conversion was not unknown in the Ottoman Empire. The most representative example constituted the Armenian

123 Cheryl Bernard, "*Rape as Terror: The Case of Bosnia*", *Terrorism* and *Political Violence* 6, no. 1 (1994): 35–37.

124 FO 195/2452, Consulate Salonika to Foreign Office, No 2, 5/2/1913.

125 Zeki Cevik, "The Policies that Bulgarian Government Implemented on the Turkish Population during the Balkan Wars", in *Recent Advances in Social Sciences*, ed. Recep Efe, Irina Koleva, and Münir Öztürk (Cambridge: Cambridge Scholar Publishing, 2019), 39.

126 NA, Fond 41k, Op. 1, ae. 156, 21/12/1912, pp. 1–2.

genocide when women got married and orphans were assigned to Muslim families to avoid extermination.[127] In Western Thrace, some Bulgarian accounts claim that conversion was voluntary and in response to punitive behaviours from retreating Ottoman officers.[128] In other occasions, conversion was a reaction to previous oppressive situations as it was the case of a certain Ali Efendi who exploited local Pomak villagers.[129] Money was utilized also as an incentive to abandon Islam and particularly specially allocated funds.[130] This issue during the war acquired publicity and harmed the image of Sofia in Western press. Orders were given to district officials to pay attention not to spread rumours about the opening of Exarchist schools in territories with newly Christianized Pomaks.[131]

Nevertheless, this is not to say that these kinds of testimonies significantly change the main characteristics of the conversion which was primarily involuntary and coercive. This policy eventually proved to be a double-edged sword. While technically it succeeded in substantially enlarging the Bulgarian population, this was only temporary. Pomak communities not only insisted in preserving their ancestral religion but also this policy brought closer Greeks and Muslims in Western Thrace. The Pomaks were about to be a thorny issue during the interwar years once again, but his time they would be divided along new demarcation lines.

127 Lerna Ekmekcioglu, "A Climate for Abduction, a Climate for Redemption: The Politics of Inclusion during and after the Armenian Genocide". *Comparative Studies in Society and History* 55, no. 3 (2013): 522–553.

128 Stoyan Stoyanoff, "Balgaromohamedanski Vapros po Vreme na Balkanskata Voina", in *80 Godini ot Valkansikte Voini* (Sofia: Izdatelstvo na Ministrarstvon na Otbranata, 1995), 142–143.

129 Velichko Georgiev and Staiko Trifonov, eds. *Pokrûstvaneto na bûlgarite mohamedani, 1912–1913: Dokumenti* (Sofia: Academichno Izdatelstvo "MarinDrinov", 1995), 121.

130 FO, 195/2452, From Vice Consulate Kavala to Foreign Office, No 13/23, 15/4/1913, 75.

131 TsVA, F. 1647, op. 2, del. 34, No 159, 30/4/1913, 43.

· 6 ·

THE EPIRUS FRONT: A CASE OF COUNTERINSURGENCY AND THE ALBANIAN FACTOR

In December, 1911 an assassination that took place in the Janina vilayet prompted an investigation by the prosecutor's office in Athens. The victim was a member of a notorious band named the "Fearless" (Atromitoi) which extorted villages for protection purposes. In the belongings of the victim some documents related to the structure of the organization were found as well as a letter written by a Greek officer who requested to border guards to allow passage to its members. Their insignia was a cap and a cross.[1]

Banditry was certainly not a novel problem in that area. Epirus was an imperial borderland contested by Greece, Albania, the Dual Monarchy, and Italy. The main factor that differentiated somehow this vilayet in terms of ethnic antagonism was that the Albanian state was created in the Treaty of London in May 1913, hence there was not an articulated state policy serving Albanian interests. Italy and Austria on the contrary avoided open exposure by intervening by way of using soft power meaning alternative channels such as education, diplomatic, and economic.[2] This part of the Balkans has hardly

---

1   IAYE, 1912.98.8, apo proxeneio Ioaninnon pros Ypourgeio Exoterikon, No 1876, 27/12/1911.

2   Alex Tipei, *Influence, Development, Civilization: French Soft Power in Early Nineteenth-Century Eastern Europe and the World* (working title) manuscript based on doctoral

attracted any interest hitherto in historical inquiries. Yet, it still deserves attention. More than other war theaters the conduct of war in that region, apart from the siege of the capital, mainly involved irregular units; therefore, the role of this chapter is to open the discussion by trying to shed some new light and offer a fresh perspective regarding the quality of violence, the Albanian ethno genesis, and the origins of the Northern Epirus/Southern Albania Question.

***

In order to be acquainted with the history of Epirus it is necessary to have an eagle's eye view at the human geography the period that preceded the war. The Janina vilayet was founded by an administrative reform in 1864 and covered almost 17,200 km spanning across the four Sanjaks of Berat, Gjirokaster, Janina, and Preveza. In population terms, Orthodox Christians outnumbered Muslims in a percentage of 55% to 45%. Christians were classified to three major ethno-national groups depending on their vernacular: Greek, Albanian, and Vlach. The Albanian speaking populations were subdivided among the Tosks of the South, the Liaps who resided in the western part of Epirus, and the Chams of Chameria who were Sunni Muslims and Orthodox Christians. Around 2,502 Jews and 3,200 Greek speaking Muslims lived in Janina (tourkogianniotes). The cities of Janina, Vlorë, and Berat were the main administrative centers. As Nathalie Clayer notes, in contrast to other territories inhabited by Albanians in which powerful beys and Pashas dominated, in Epirus the Tanzimat reforms succeeded to install a system of effective taxation, functioning courts, and military conscription. This in turn, gradually, undermined powerful local patrons.[3] The agrarian question, as in other parts of Ottoman Rumeli, was intense. The vast majority of arable lands in Preveza, Phillipiada, and Paramithia belonged to Muslim landowners with strong links to the Ottoman state while Christians (Greek and Albanian speaking) formed the bulk of the cultivators.[4] Heavy taxation to the latter had created a sense of solidarity against Muslim landowners.[5]

---

dissertation: "For Your Civilization and Ours: Greece, Romania, and the Making of French Universalism" (Indiana University, Bloomington, 2016).

3 Clayer, *Oi Aparches tou Alvanikou Ethnikismou*, 104–112.
4 Spyros Ploumidis, "Nuances of Irredentism: The Epirote Society of Athens (1906–1912)". *The Historical Review/La Revue Historique* 8 (2012): 151–159.
5 Divani, *I Edafiki Oloklirosi*, 426, 433, 445.

The vast majority of Epirus Muslims were Albanian speaking and followed the Bektashi order with the exception of Chams.[6] The Chams were a distinct group and their identity was fiercely contested by Greek and Albanian circles. Some Greek intellectuals developed theories in the late nineteenth century that claimed that these people were Islamized locals rather than migrant Turks- using as argument the kinship and family ties between Christians and Muslims in Chameria.[7] Chams indeed were an ethno-cultural group comprised by Orthodox Christians and Sunni Muslims. They resided in the wider area of the northern part of the city of Preveza, today Greek Epirus. According to historian Lampros Baltsiotis, in late nineteenth century the Albanian movement had not gained significant momentum among local Muslims of Chameria aside some certain members of the elite who had joined Albanian Clubs (Bashkimi).[8]

From the Greek perspective, the geographical confines of Epirus were as follows. The first part was the "liberated one" which included the areas of Tzoumerka and Arta and was granted to Greece after the crisis of the Eastern Question in 1875–8. The second part the "non-liberated" entailed the six sanjaks of: Preveza, Resadije (Igoumenitsa), Janina, Gjirokaster, Vlorë, and Berat. It also included the sanjak of Korçë which was part of Ottoman Macedonia. Ecclesiastically the area was divided in Bishoprics each with its own Metropolitan. Overlapping national agendas was not an exception in the vilayet of Janina as the new born Albanian national movement developed its own claims. Particularly the santzaks of Vlorë, Gjirokaster, and Korçë encompassed the so called "Northern part of Epirus" which was the bone of contention between the two countries for decades after the war.[9]

The evolutions in early twentieth century and the systematization of the proxy war did not leave unaffected the neighboring vilayet of Janina. As in Macedonia, in 1906 a secret organization was formed in Athens named the "Epirote Society". Its founding members, officers Spyros Spyromilios and Panagiotis Dagklis belonged to the gendarmerie and the army respectively, and both had roots from Epirus. The branch that operated in Janina shared similar responsibilities to the Macedonian Committee in Manastir. Members were expected to recruit people, gather intelligence, and prepare the ground

---

6 Glavinas, *Mousoulmanikoi Plithysmoi stin Ellada*, 28–31.
7 Divani, *Ellada kai Meionotites*, 218–220.
8 Lambros Baltsiotis, « The Muslim Chams of Northwestern Greece », *European Journal of Turkish Studies* [Online], 12 (2011), 2–3.
9 IAYE, 1912, 123, 1, Epiros geographika oria kai ethnographia, Chapter 4.

for subversive activities. The society additionally pursued to cede control of schools and appointment of teachers to the Greek consulate which provided diplomatic cover. Cooperation of the Orthodox Church was imperative and the Metropolitan of Janina, Gervasios became a central figure.[10] Many Greek Epirotes spanning from different strata of the local society partook in activities that aided the endeavors of the organization. Although in name the agenda was oriented to the external dimensions of Greek nationalism, it used propaganda to induce armed struggle. That was the message conveyed by Michael Lando a reservist officer and leader of the directorate's organization in Janina. However, cooperation of locals was not untroubled because there was an inherent difference in the notions of irredentism between the agents of the society and the "communalism" of native notables. While for the former the motherland of every Greek was solely the Greek state, for the latter it was rather more relative. Elites in urban centers in the vilayet perceived their community as homeland. Members of the Epirote society from old Greece called that localism (topikismos) entailing a pejorative connotation generating tensions within the ranks of the movement.[11]

In tandem with Greek irredentism, its Albanian antithesis had begun taking form. The rise of nationalism arrived relatively late for the Albanian case probably in the 1850s. It was in this period that a vibrant class of merchants from Elbasan, Vlorë, and Berat with links in Italy inaugurated a process of spiritual "rebirth". At the core of this rejuvenation was the linguistic issue because a written form of Albanian language did not exist. The 1875–8 crisis of the Eastern Question gave prominence to the Albanian question through the formation of the Prizren League, the first body destined to articulate demands for the creation of a separate state.[12]

Nevertheless, Albanianism was neither a monolith ideology nor something fabricated by émigré circles in Europe. As every other Balkan national movement, similarly the Albanian was a project under a constant process of negotiation depending on pragmatic needs. By and large, those promoting Albanianism tried to coexist and accommodate notions of Ottomanism while men such as Ismail Kemal, one of its disputable leaders, functioned in a complex set of social roles and contradictory expectations.[13]

---

10   Vasileios Anastasopoulos, *Bizani, 1912–1913* (Athens: Gnomon, 2012).
11   Ploumidis, Nuances of Irredentism, 170.
12   Divani, *I Edafiki Oloklirosi*, 433.
13   Blumi, *Reinstating the Ottomans*, 74, 168.

A thorny issue for Albanian activists was the ambivalent interconnection with the Macedonian question. Contested territories were inhabited by Slav and Albanian speaking populations particularly in the Kosovo vilayet.[14] A huge wave of Albanians who fought for the Ottomans in 1875–7 fled from the sanjak of Nis. Until the eruption of the Balkan wars the revolts of Albanians barely enjoyed sympathy by Slavs generating resentment in a regional level. Serbia's intention of neutralizing the Albanians was controversial. Actions based on the Macedonian model were not feasible in Kosovo. Albanians were armed, consisted the majority, were predominantly Muslims, spoke a different language, and there was no rival organization like the IMRO. The Austrian Annexation of 1908 triggered a series of events and pushed Serbia's government to focus elsewhere, but not only towards Kosovo but also to the Sanjak of Novi Pazar and Macedonia, territories better known as old and south Serbia.[15]

The centralization attempts of Abdul Hamid II and concurrently the Young Turks deteriorated the turmoil in Albanian lands.[16] Perhaps the most challenging events occured in 1911 when in the Gegalik North and the Toskalik South the intense activities of revolutionary bands created unrest leading to the "Gerche Memorandum" which proclaimed the autonomy of Albanian regions functioning as glue between the north and the south.[17]

Yet, in the Janina vilayet the development of Albanianism was distinct in some ways. A peculiarity that altered the historical trajectory of Epirus was the non-straightforward relation of Greek and Albanian nationalism. The connection of Greeks and Albanians was deeply rooted. Albanian speaking Orthodox Christians (Arvanites) became the steam engine of the Greek war of independence and comprised an important number of the overall population of the Hellenic Kingdom. On another level, influential notables such as the Frashëri brothers, key figures and founding members of the Prizren league,

---

14 Fabio Bego, "Beyond the Albanian–Slav Divide: Political Cooperation and National Identities in the Balkans at the Turn of the Twentieth Century", *East European Politics and Societies* 34, no. 1 (2020): 25–47.

15 On the eve of the Balkan Wars the head of Serbian army intelligence, Colonel Apis secretly travelled to Kosovo and met with the experienced Albanian chieftain Isa Boletini in an attempt to persuade Kosovar Albanians to join forces. Bolletini refused the offer saying that despite previous rebellions against the Young Turk regime Albanians will rally as irregulars and defend the Empire. Životić, A.Ž. "Apis na Kosovu 1912. godine". *Vojno-istorijski glasnik*, br, 1–2 (2005): 44–57.

16 Bataković, "Serbia, the Serbo-Albanian Conflict and the First Balkan War", 321, 334–336.

17 George Walter Gawrych, *The Crescent and the Eagle: Ottoman Rule, Islam and the Albanians, 1874–1913* (London: IB Tauris, 2006), 188–189.

were born and educated in an environment heavily influenced by Greek culture. Their notions of Albanianism had a vivid imprint from Hellenism not existent in Northern Albania.[18] For Athens, it was crucial to side with Albanian speaking populations especially to Orthodox Christians so that to contain the expansion of Albanianism. Religious affiliation was utilized as common denominator to attribute ethnic identity and Albanian Christian Orthodox speakers became the most contested group by both sides.[19]

Proxy war, as in Macedonia, became a key method to forge local allegiances. Groups such as the Fearless become dominant in the area employing many times as pretext the cause of the Epirote society compelling locals to join their ranks.[20] The Fearless were simply one of the many groups that operated in the border zone between the Ottoman Empire and the Kingdom of Greece. Geostrategy and the landscape made Epirus the ideal ground for the development of banditry. The Ionian coast and particularly the island of Lefkada was base for numerous groups that raided the vilayet.[21] The attempt to integrate these units to the national causes of the Balkan states was a standard practice but in many ways backfired. These units while they were a valuable source of manpower with experience in the local terrain they could not be easily tamed. In 1909, a major dispute broke out between Metropolitan Gervaseio and the Consul General, Angelo Foresti over that issue. The clergyman made an urgent appeal to Foresti to take immediate measures to contain the activities of bands associated with the Epirote Society. Gervaseios heavily accused these units as criminal groups who alienated locals. Although Forestis acknowledged the existence of the problem he followed a dilatory tactic which enraged the cleric. The position of the Greek consul was really delicate. While, on the one hand it was an unpleasant situation to have to confront his most important religious ally, one the other, he could not blame openly local bands, the only available force at his disposal.[22]

---

18 Clayer, Oi Aparches toy Alvanikou Ethnikismou, 253.

19 Gawrych, The Crescent and the Eagle, 182.

20 IAYE, 1912.98. 8, apo proxeneio Ioaninnon pros Ypourgeio Exoterikon, No 14210, 5/6/1911.

21 Nikolaos Anastasopoulos, I Listia sto Elliniko Kratos. Mesa 19ou aiona—Arches 20ou (Athens: Estia, 2018), 113–114.

22 Athanasios Tsekouras, Apo tou 98ou Ypsomatos. Anamniseis enos Epirotou Agonistou (Athens: Vivliothiki Epirotikes Etaireias, 1979), 142–144. The concern of the Metropolitan would never stop even until the declaration of war reflecting this rivalry among the Church and the Greek state. A couple of days before the war Gervaseios communicated a worrying message about the appearance of a number of criminal elements.

Consequently, the locals were caught amid competing state projects. The hit and run practices of armed groups challenged the already fragile control of the countryside and blurred the picture among political agitators, common criminals, and bystanders. Albanian and Greek "activists" adopted a punitive behaviour to suspicious attitudes considering any declaration of loyalty to official authorities as an act of treason. That was ambiguous however because attribution of the traitor label was many times a vessel to settle personal scores or to masquerade illicit acts as national partisanship. That became apparent in the wars when many units had disciplinary issues. One of the key chieftains associated with the Epirote Society was Ioannis Potetsis, alias captain Voreas. Potetsi's reputation skyrocketed when he wiped out the infamous gang of Skoumbraioi that had been involved in the assassination of the Metropolitan of Grevena, Aimilianos. Captain Voreas never gave up his old activities and continued terrorizing.[23] Ultimately, the exposure of locals in this endemically violent climate had consequences. This, "culture of banditry" as I may call it by paraphrasing Ryan Gingera's concept of the "culture of paramilitarism", which was cultivated in Ottoman Epirus familiarized the peasants with violent practices. Thus, it was not a surprise that during the war locals joined the army in pillaging blurring the unclear boundaries between combatants and civilians. This reference point, I suggest, could be utilized more broadly in order to historicize the determinants for violence in the countryside, particularly in mountainous regions where state control was looser.

Yet, banditry represented just one of the many illegal activities developed in the region. Another form concerned arms smuggling. Arms proliferation had become a very profitable business involving many actors. Albanian notables gained an extra income by this enterprise while Balkan revolutionary networks augmented demand.[24] Epirus was the locus of a business that spanned across the shores of the Adriatic and involved trans-regional networks over the Ionian Sea. The port of Trieste constituted a key transit point.

The stance of the clergyman here is quite interesting since he advised his flock to assist the Ottoman Government and not participate in disturbances by isolating those bands. Probably the reference of Gervaseios had to do with agents provocateur dispatched in the area to instigate a guerilla war mixed with local bandits. ÖS, HHStA, PA, XII, Konsulate Janina 11, aus Vlorë zu Außenministerium, No 38, 9/10/1912.

23   IAYE, 1912.98.8, apo astynomiko epitropo Artas pros astynomiko tmima Pramadas, No 32, 6/6/1911.

24   Selim Hilmi Ozkan, "Arms Smuggling across Ottoman Borders in the Second Half of the Nineteenth Century", *Journal of Balkan and Near Eastern Studies* 18, no. 3 (2016): 297–312.

The transportation was conducted by boatmen who smuggled armaments into the capital via the Janina Lake. Afterwards the weapons were hidden in multiple spots and distributed. The operations were taking place under the cover of darkness and local villagers assisted and paid in kind. Within three to four years, according to the member of the Epirote Society Athanasios Tsekouras, approximately thirty boxes were sneaked into the vilayet.[25] The intensity of this illicit trade reached a peak on the eve of war. The Perfect of Corfu was reporting on a daily basis arms smuggling to Epirus while the police was unable to act.[26] Days before the official declaration of the Balkan Wars Austrian steamships begun transporting boxes with ammunition destined for Albanian revolutionaries.[27]

The Austrians were part of that business following their policy of supporting factions of the Albanian National Movement in order to prevent the overexpansion of Serbia and Greece and safeguard a foothold in the Balkans.[28] The background of this involvement is traced at the beginning of the twentieth century when Austrian Foreign Minister Count Alois von Aerenthal reoriented the Mediterranean policy of the Dual Monarchy. One of the central factors behind Austria's policy was to re-establish stable relations with Russia by accommodating the Tsar's interested in the Balkan Peninsula. In 1907 he promoted economic penetration through the creation of a railway line that connected the sanjak of Novi Pazar with Salonika.[29] Aerenthal took even more energetic actions after the Young Turks' Revolution by suggesting to the Council of Foreign Ministers the annexation of Bosnia-Herzegovina.[30] At the same time, he initiated a dialogue with St. Petersburg. Conversations between the ministers of the two countries had already started a month ago when Aerenthal's Russian counterpart Alexander Izvolski sent him a memorandum outlining the basic principles of his Balkan policy. The main idea was that the Danubian Monarchy could annex Bosnia and as compensation Vienna

25 Tsekouras, *Apo tou 98ou Ypsomatos*, 130–131.

26 IAYE, 1912,45,6, apo Nomarchi Kerkyras pros Ypourgeio Exoterikon, No 26405, 29/8/1912.

27 IAYE, 1912,45,6, apo Nomarchi Kerkyras pros Ypourgeio Exoterikon, No 7825, 15/9/1912.

28 Gynter Bischof, ed., *Austrian Foreign Policy in Historical Context* (UK: Transaction, 2006), 85.

29 Robert Kann, *A History of the Habsburg Monarchy* (California: University of California Press, 1980), 412.

30 It was controlled economically and militarily by the Monarchy since 1878 but was still Ottoman territory.

would provide support to St. Petersburg on the issue of the Dardanelles.[31] This reconciliation did not borne fruit because of Bosnia's surprising annexation which caused serious repercussions.[32] The most important was the creation of the notorious organization "Narodna Obrana", a Serbian irredentist network ardently anti-Austrian which recruited and trained volunteers for military confrontation.[33] After that point the policy of the Dual Monarchy turned steadily against the Balkan Alliance leading to direct intervention in the Balkan crisis of 1912–3.

Italy was the other major player in the Mediterranean arena. Italian interference emerged in the Congress of Berlin when Rome opposed Greek territorial demands in Epirus. The Italians, in geostrategic terms, were investing in the old route of the Via Egnatia which connected the Roman Empire with the Balkan provinces. A more direct involvement was attempted by the activation of commercial networks and schools spreading the Italian language to Albanians after the 1880s. In the wake of the new century this attempt intensified with the establishment of banks branches and prominent companies such as the chemical corporation, Leopoldo Parodi-Delfino.[34] Eventually, in 1912, Rome had managed to control around 25%-30% of commodities' trade in Scutari and Southern Albania. The overall plan of the Italian penetration in Albania was to convert the Gate of Otranto into an Italian Gibraltar. This vision however overlapped not only with Austria-Hungary but also with

---

31 Henry Steed, *The Habsburg Monarchy* (London: Constable, 1914), 244–45.

32 Roy Bridge, *From Sadowa to Sarajevo. The Foreign Policy of Austia-Hungary* (London: Routledge, 1972), 323.

33 Lefter S Stavrianos, *The Balkans 1815–1914* (US: Berkshire Studies in European History, 1963), 119. The "apple of discord" for Austria-Hungary during the First Balkan war was Scutari that was besieged by the Montenegrin army. The overall ambition was to convert this city, which had an important proportion of Catholics, into the Monarchy's port in Southeastern Europe. However, King Nikolas of Montenegro wanted to incorporate it into his domain and thereafter a major crisis erupted. When Eshad Pasa, the commander of the Ottoman garrison, surrendered the Montenegrins entered the city in April 1913. The response from Vienna was immediate. On the 3rd of May General Potiorek, the commander of Bosnia-Herzegovina, made some maneuvers to his troops and he ordered them to be combat ready. A joined naval blockade from the Great Powers led King Nikolas to withdraw his men from the city which was given to the newly established state of Albania: Misha Glenny, "The *Balkans*, 1804–2012: Nationalism, War and the Great Powers" (London: Penguin, 2001), 242–243.

34 Ioannis S. Papafloratos, "The Italian Policy in Epirus (1861–1918)", *Balkan Studies*, 50 (2015): 160–162.

Serbia and Greece who had claims in the North and the South of Albanian inhabited lands.[35]

As the clouds of war were gathering, the situation in the Epirote countryside was deteriorating. Activities of Albanian activists against the new agenda of the CUP created tensions and implicated relations with Balkan Christians. The climate in the vilayet of Manastir was very bitter particularly among Albanians, Serbs, and Montenegrins. The CUP was following an ambiguous policy trying to bribe Albanian Beys and arm Muslim villages in the border with Montenegro.[36] The Greek Patriarchate advised the Metropolitans of Janina and Manastir, in case of an Albanian insurrection, to abstain from revolutionary actions. Same policy was followed by Athens that wanted to tame the Albanian movement by employing support to the Porte.[37] In this climate, the outbreak of war came as a catalyst. The demise of the Ottoman security apparatus and the military campaign would afflict deeply the communal framework of Epirus.

Irregular War in Epirus

There are three categories of soldiers: the regular army, the euzones and the andartes. The last two are more familiar to the romeiko type of war.[38]

Crown Prince, Konstantinos

In this way the Greek Crown Prince describes the different set of combatants that fought in the Epirote Theater. Probably the most interesting part in this statement is that he mentions a particular genre of warfare the so called *romeiko*. Konstantinos here refers (Romios) to a term that originated from the Rum millet and was used to designate the Christian Orthodox flock in the Ottoman Empire. The euzones one the other hand were a specially trained squad for Alpine war, while the term andartes encompassed all other types of

---

35 Vladislav Sotirović, *Serbia, Montenegro and the Albanian Question, 1878–1912*: A Greater Albania Between Balkan Nationalism & European Imperialism (Saarbrucken: Lambert Academic Publishing, 2015), 48–52.

36 IAYE, 1912,104, 7, apo proxeneio Skopia pros Ypourgeio Exoterikon, No 327, 15/8/1912.

37 IAYE, 1912,107, 2, apo proxeneio Konstantinopoleos pros Ypourgeio Exoterikon, No 2095, 7/7/1912.

38 Gennadios, Archeio Karavida, F. 115, 12/11/1912.

irregular units. The euzones and andartes were way more close to the tradition of warfare that emerged in the Ottoman Empire since the era of the legendary klephts (bandits). The mountainous terrain of mainland Greece served as sanctuary for banditry and the development of guerilla activities. This manpower was of crucial importance for the national campaign.

The declaration of war by the Balkan League signaled general mobilization for regular and irregular forces throughout Epirus. The importance of Macedonia and the rally to Salonika rendered this front as secondary priority.[39] Therefore, the need to fill a lacuna in manpower became imperative and the only viable alternative was the usage of locals and volunteers. The Greek Consul in Janina asked for reinforcement of Greek bands in Epirus and requested from officers with local roots to be in charge.[40] From the beginning of war logistical centers were created to effectively coordinate volunteers. Agents operating in urban centers assisted the formation of bands in the countryside by collecting funds and encouraging Christian deserters to join.[41]

In order to get a better picture of the importance of irregular warfare for the Epirus front I refer, indicatively, to some numbers. In the villages of the Tzoumerka mountain range alone at least 21 units affiliated to the Greek cause operated that numbered 700 men, including prominent agents of the Epirote struggle[42] and veterans of the 1897 war.[43] Irregulars were not simply auxiliaries but supplemental to the army. They conducted very crucial operations by safeguarding passages and aiding the military whenever necessary. Their information networks offered a valuable advantage that made feasible to confront the experienced Muslim Albanian irregulars who knew every inch of the territory. In some occasions local ties played such an important role that determined the tide of battle. For instance, the villagers of Palaiochori in the Tzoumerka mountains after they heard the news of the capture of a Turkish garrison in the neighboring village of Michailitchi, took up arms united with

---

39 Cretan volunteers and 10,500 men of the VIII division under the command of General Sapountzaki GES, *Epitomi Istoria*, 19.

40 IAYE, 1912,34, 6, apo proxeneio Ioaninnon pros Ypourgeio Exoterikon, No 30892, 2/10/1912.

41 IAYE, 1912,34, 6, apo proxeneio Ioaninnon pros Ypourgeio Exoterikon, No 29357, 17/9/1912.

42 Such as: Gyparis, Violanis, Anagnostakis, Manousakas, Kampouris and Vavouris. GES/DIS, 1698/1000d.

43 IAYE, 1912,34, 6, apo proxeneio Prevezas pros Ypourgeio Exoterikon, No 20469, 27/9/1912.

a volunteer unit and facilitated their mission.[44] Reinforcement by armed villagers was absolutely essential not only in numerical terms but also to engage
the locals and forge a sense of a common purpose.[45] Most importantly, villages
possessed the only available supplies.[46]

At this point, it might be useful to take a closer anthropological view
at these volunteer units to obtain a better idea about their composition and
socio-cultural traits. Thomas Hutchison was an American philhellene and
along with Greek-Americans offered his services to the Great Idea. He joined
as artillery major a Garibaldian legion comprised by 2,000 men. Leader of
this force was Riciotti Garibaldi, son of the legendary Italian revolutionary
who had an adventurous spirit and arrived in Epirus to wage a guerilla war.[47]
Hutchison left a very rich memoir from his experience in the Epirus front.
Among others, he provided a very colorful image of some volunteer units he
met in the city of Preveza:

> After seeing the forts I went to the port and saw the coffee houses on the waterfront
> and around the coffee houses were bands of Cretans and mountain rebels, or the inde-
> pendent soldiers of Epirus. These rebel bands were dressed in fantastic and beautiful
> costumes {…} In the front and center each officer wore the gold crown or emblem
> of the Kingdom, showing his allegiance to the Government {…} They are not the
> desperate independent outlaws some people have pictured them {…} as a general
> rule, members of the same band were related to each other by blood or marriage. The
> officers and men had been trained to fight from youth. The lives led in the mountains
> made them very serious looking {…} The officers were the proudest men I had met in
> the Kingdom, each and every one carrying himself like a monarch, for monarch he
> really was, an independent free-lance all his days.[48]

The author's perceptions were articulated around a universe of stereotypes
ingrained by notions of masculinity. These observations also relate to the

44 GES/DIS, 1698/1004.
45 GES/DIS, 1698/1007.
46 GES/DIS, 1698/1012.
47 ÖS, HHStA, PA, XII, 387, Turkei XLV/3, aus Athen zu *Außenministerium* No 56, 7/12/
    1912. See also: Stathis Birtachas, "Ricciotti Garibaldi and the last expedition of the
    Italian Garibaldini volunteers to Greece (1912)", *Italy on the Rimland Storia militare di una
    Penisola eurasiatica* INTERMARIUM, Tomo I (Rome: Società Italiana di Storia Militare
    Nadir Media Srl, 2019), 207–222.
48 Thomas Setzer Hutchison, *An American Soldier Under the Greek Flag at Bezanie: A Thrilling
    Story of the Siege of Bezanie" by the Greek Army, in Epirus, During the War in the Balkans*
    (Nashville, Tennessee: Greek-American Publishing Company, 1913), 112–114.

concept of primary groups. Studies on the Eastern front in WWII define primary groups, as social organizations with long roots to a military tradition that anticipated from the members of a unit to share a special bond and loyalty. This special bond brings to the surface once again the issue of locality which was essential for the structure and coherence.[49]

In his colorful depiction, Hutchison attributes values that embody male virtue and honor. The first to notice is the need of the American to make a distinction between typical bandits and these "free spirits" who served higher ideals. The proof that they were not common criminals was the leaders' insignia who carried the Greek flag and showed allegiance to the national purpose. The second relates to kinship ties of the bands' members. The third is the devotion to the chief who is described as a monarch. This is the most central piece in this document implying the limits of obedience to the national cause since in the end of the day the leader was blindly followed.

An important insight testimony of this non-conventional war is additionally the report of Greek Lieutenant Vasileiou Teriakidi. Teriakidis serves as the perfect example of a broker that functioned as an intermediary between official Greece and the locals. Officers of that kind were a valuable linkage, supervised ill-disciplined volunteers, and provided intelligence. His role was very illuminative also to grasp the connection of officers with experience in counter insurgency and non-military personnel. Terikiadis enjoyed the advantage not to be considered as an outsider due to his acquaintance with the natives. He began his activities in Epirus a couple of months before the war when on July 26, 1912 he arrived to Paramithia, the capital of Chameria, so that to receive commission as a clergy man in disguise with the code name Vasileios Georgiadis. His task was to gather information for enemy movements as well as recruit, organize bands, and boost psychologically the morale of the beleaguered peasants. Having been convicted by the Ottoman authorities when his identity was unveiled, he eventually managed to escape and offered his services to the Greek Chief of Staff on the eve of the invasion of Epirus.[50] Teriakidis assumed control of a unit of 77 men and he was in overall command of three irregular formations headed by local chieftains. His mission included a series of challenging tasks assigned by the Greek High Command

---

49 See more on: Omer Bartov, *Soldiers, Nazis, and War in the Third Reich* (Oxford: Oxford University Press, 1992), 29–59.
50 AMM, Archeio Panagioti Dagkli, F.30, Ekthesis Polemikon Epichiriseon en Epiro tou Ypolochagou Vasileiou Teriakidi apo 20 Iouliou mechri telos Dekemvriou idiou etous. Arithmos 3334, Diatagi Stratou Ipirou. 13/11/1912, 1–2.

such as to instigate revolts in the Orthodox Albanian speaking villages of
Souli, arm, and recruit volunteers, and occupy strategic locations.[51]

Initially there was shared enthusiasm among the locals; and a unit comprised by 87 men led by Teriakidi took on its first mission. That was to cut
off communications between the cities of Arta and Janina by capturing the
strategic passage of Skala Paramithias. Along his way, his forces strengthened
by five other units and armed villagers numbering 270 men. A week later
this heterogeneous group managed to capture the village of Eleutherochorion
catching by surprise 40–50 redif soldiers and volunteer Chams who were celebrating the Ramadan.[52] Teriakidis' success was not coincidental. His service
in Paramithia had familiarized him with the terrain and human geography and
he was well informed about the positions of the garrisons.

However, the success of the operation was soon undermined. In many
occasions villagers including women and children were waiting for the end
of the battle to loot. After the capture of Eleutherochorion the leader of a
band named Varphis along with his supporters headed back to their villages.
Deprivation from men and supplies resulted to the recapture of Skala by the
Ottomans creating a predicament for the lieutenant. The Greek staff in an
attempt to assist Terikiadi sent Marko Deliyiannaki a Cretan chieftain with
reinforcements. Deliyiannakis was not a trained military man and as we saw
in the chapter on Bekir Aga, irregulars had often had an issue in recognizing
authority. This had inevitable side effects in the coordination of the campaign
especially when individual chieftains turned a blind eye in violations and
groups that belonged to the same side treated each other with suspiciousness.
The two men were soon involved in a blame game. Deliyiannakis was accused
not only for being idle but also for confiscating supplies and being a "tyrant"
to local communities.[53]

The case of Teriakidi was certainly not the exception. The motivations
of locals were mixed and not entirely driven by irredentist ideals. It is indeed
accurate to claim that the appeal of the Great Idea existed and the war in
some extend was colored by a religious dimension as villagers were sometimes
led by local priests in battle. Nevertheless, a pre-existing strife and a struggle over resources were equally important driving factors. Although volunteers captured some areas, they could not solidify their presence due to lack

51 AMM, Archeio Panagioti Dagkli, F.30, pp. 3–6.
52 GES/DIS, 1698/1017–1020.
53 AMM, Archeio Panagioti Dagkli, F.30, pp. 9–20.

of coordination and experience. This is something underlined in reports, of officers who demanded regular army discipline because initial enthusiasm evaporated quickly.[54] Cretan Colonel Aristotelis Korakas, an experienced leader of a scout unit, communicated a gloomy situation in that regard in late November. His task was to regroup volunteer units across Epirus but he was more than pessimistic for the success of the endeavor. According to Korakas, recruiting 400 men was the best case scenario because the vast majority of local fighters were disheartened by devastating loses and cannot be convinced to return asking for immediate dispatch of regular army units.[55] Some chieftains tried to impose disciplinary measures to prevent panicked reactions. Many inhabitants from the Zagorochoria villages evacuated to Thessaly due to the presence of Bekir. In villages in Metsovo officers were putting an effort to contain the actions of irregulars and Garibaldians. One of the initiatives was to assign the leadership of volunteers units to well respected members of native societies.[56]

In order to historicize the attitudes of these kinds of combatants, it might be useful to discuss some notions about mercenaries. According to relevant studies, the premises to be considered a fighter as mercenary are mainly three: a degree of foreignness, motivations driven by self-interest, and a transhistorical dimension.[57] At first sight, simply in terms of definition the local irregulars that fought in the Balkan Wars do not fit to this category. Yet, this comparison is not entirely irrelevant. The second premise, namely self-interest was a crucial component and it might be valid to claim that self-interest and fighting for a greater cause were not mutually exclusive but rather complementary incentives. For many fighters taking side was inevitably connected with personal goals. Put it differently, we need to identify a "mercenary mentality". Mercenary mentality means that even though these combatants can be considered neither typical mercenaries nor agents of nationalism, the fact

---

54 Another challenge was providing ammunition. From the beginning of the campaign there was shortage and the bullets for the Mannlicher rifles could only last until the end of November. The High Command in Epirus took a swift decision in collaboration with the local police, ordering the requisition of animals from the area of Arta to transport 150,000 bullets and 250,000 rifles Mannlicher and Gras. GES/DIS, 1698/1017–1018.

55 GES/DIS, 1698a/1017a.

56 GES/DIS, 1698/1000.

57 Malte Riemann, "'As Old as War Itself'? Historicizing the Universal Mercenary", *Journal of Global Security Studies*, Online Published, (February 2020): 3, https://doi.org/10.1093/jogss/ogz069.

that they were driven by self-interests attributes them a quality of this kind. A suitable example to demonstrate that was the fact that the Greek National Center offered salaries to chieftains and this practise constituted rather the rule than the exception.[58] Providing adequate funds was the only way to keep these units loyal.[59] 1,000 drachmas was allocated to bands that came from old Greece, according to some sources, but apparently this also depended on the size of each unit.[60] The receipts were stamped by chieftains implying the importance of official documents. For the National Center, in case of disciplinary behaviour it was used as a proof to remind the responsibilities to the untamed. For chieftains, it was a source legitimization that distinguished them from common bandits.

The usage of irregulars was equally crucial for the Ottomans. The invasion of the Greek army had generated for a short while a tactical convergence between Muslim chieftains and the Porte against the common Christian enemy. Within the Ottomans ranks operated Muslim Albanians sometimes spearheading the attacks. Muslim Albanians were a difficult rival to deal with since they had obtained experience in mountainous war in the constant uprisings of the late Ottoman era.[61] Yet, lack of coordination and disciplinary incidents were faced too. There was not a uniform stance among Albanianist circles regarding the organization of a guerilla campaign while conflicting visions out shadowed the Albanian agenda. The political climate was already tense due to the proclaimed Ottoman elections in August, 1912.[62] The supporters of the Liberal fraction that opposed the CUP, headed by Kâmil Pasha, had relied hopes on Great Britain expecting a rapid intervention.[63] On the other hand, many officers had linkages with the Young Turks and favoured a more active response.[64]

---

58 Around 3,000 liras was the estimate of the Greek Consulate in Janina for those salaries. IAYE, 1912, 34, 6, apo Foresti pros Ypourgeio Exoterikon, No 32637, 28/9/1912.

59 IAYE, 1912,34, 6, apo Nomarchi Kerkyras pros Ypourgeio Exoterikon, No 4005, 28/9/1912.

60 IAYE, 1912,34, 6, apo proxeneio Prevezas pros Ypourgeio Exoterikon, No 1031, 7/11/1912.

61 GES/DIS, 1698/1015.

62 ÖS, HHStA, PA, XII, Konsul Halla, Manastir an Graf Berchtold, No. 110, 17/9/1912.

63 The Liberal Entente was the Second largest political party in the Second Constitutional period and promoted an agenda that favored decentralization and greater levels of autonomy to non Muslims.

64 Hasan Kayalı, "Elections and the Electoral Process in the Ottoman Empire, 1876–1919", *International Journal of Middle East Studies* 34, no. 27 (1995): 277–278.

The existential threat that the war posed to Albanian provinces had put everything at stake. The great dilemma was whether to behave as the loyal supporter of the Porte hoping for a renewed position in the Empire or to find a modus vivendi with the Balkan states. A quick glance at the conflict of views is visible from the reaction of a group of Albanian Christian priests in the United States who issued a statement in the early stages of the war. In particular, they adopt a critical position against the Balkan states praising the role of the Ottomans who had recognized Albanian nationality and granted civil liberties. They furthermore stated their conviction that the situation is going to deteriorate by referring to several examples in which the hawkish nature of Greek and Serbian nationalism had detrimental effects on Albanianism. The concluding remark makes an appeal to Christian Albanians to unite with the Turks to defend the motherland against the predatory appetite of the Balkan League.[65] This document is thought provoking because it bears signatures of Orthodox Christian priests reflecting how relative and sometimes misleading could be the interpretation of national movements in the Balkans simply in terms of religion or nationality. It also shows how porous were the boundaries of the alliances. As we saw in cases from Thrace and Macedonia, Muslim-Christian cooperation was not a rare phenomenon. The logic of the lesser evil was a driving force behind temporary convergences that prioritized survival.[66]

On the other side of the spectrum belonged imposing figures such as Ismail Kemal bey Vlorë. Having grown up in a multicultural environment, he received education in the famous Zosimaia School in Janina the beacon of elite training in the Balkans. Kemal mastered many languages and throughout his political career oscillated between different visions of Albanianism.[67] The eruption of the Balkan Wars involved him in debates regarding the next steps of the movement. Some local notables in Manastir suggested the formation of a militia which would include Albanian deserters from Janina. Another fraction disagreed and advocated, expectedly, a defensive policy line arguing that

---

65 IAYE, 1913,14,1, apo Proxeneio Neas Yorkis pros Ypourgeio Exoterikon, No 3060, 3/10/ 1913.

66 Furthermore, it reflected certain implications related to the Albanian Diaspora rooted back in 1907 when under the auspices of the Archbishop Theofan Stilian Noli, more known as Fan Noli, the future Prime Minister of Albania, was founded a club called Besa in Boston. The main goal of this association was to spread Albanianism but it encountered difficulties because it had to compete with numerous Macedonian, Hellenic, and Vlach Christian Orthodox organizations. Clayer, *Oi Aparches tou Alvanikou Ethnikismou*, 368.

67 Ismail Kemal Bey Vlorë, *Memoirs*, trans. Stephanos Papageorgiou (Athens: Papazisis, 2017).

such a local militia would simply be too weak to withstand the Serbian assault and only succeed in provoking further Serbian aggression. Ismail Kemal confidentially informed the Austrian consul, that his plan was, either: (a) in case of a short war and a peace treaty, the remaining weaponry and ammunition would be used for the liberation/ re-conquest of parts of Albania, or: (b) in case of a prolonged war, guerilla warfare would be organized among locals in order to continuously disturb the Serbian occupation forces and gradually deprive them the control of the land.[68] Kemal's first response was in accordance with the ideas that he advocated at the turn of the century. That was the incorporation of Albania into a wider and reformed political nation of the Ottomans by having a dual loyalty: to the state and to the community. Only the rapid Ottoman collapse made him shift his opinion declaring on November 28, 1912 in Vlorë the independence of Albania.[69]

To that end it had definitely contributed the mobilization which had weakened the Ottoman security apparatus allowing to numerous raiding bands to freely operate. Unconventional warfare left a vivid imprint in Epirus. On the eve of war, many Muslim volunteers along with reserve units of the Ottoman army committed a series of atrocities against Christian populations around the cities of Vlorë and Gjirokaster.[70] Essad Pasha Toptani, an experienced CUP commander encountered difficulties in disciplinary issues and numerous incidents were reported in which his soldiers plundered and attacked villages.[71] Eqrem Bey, an important Albanian activist from Vlorë, managed to recruit 1,000 volunteers in the area south of Himarë while others villages were preparing resistance activities to the advance of the Greek army.[72] Muslim Albanian villages around the fortress of Bezanie kept a hostile position and waged a guerilla war in the midst of the siege trying to harm logistical supply.[73]

---

68 ÖS, HHStA, PA, XII, Konsulate Vlorë zu *Außenministerium*, No 8, 20/2/1913.

69 Adrian Brisku, "Renegotiating the Empire, Forging the Nation-State: The Albanian Case through the Political Economic Thought of Ismail Qemali, Fan Noli, and Luigj Gurakuqi, c. 1890–1920s". *Nationalities Papers* 48, no. 1 (2020): 165–166.

70 ÖS, HHStA, PA, XII, Konsulate Janina 11, aus Vlorë zu Außenministerium, No 43, 30/ 10/1912.

71 ÖS, HHStA, PA, XII, 386, Turkei XLV/3, aus Janina zu Außenministerium No 89, 17/11/ 1912.

72 ÖS, HHStA, PA, XII, Konsulate Janina 11, aus Vlorë zu Außenministerium, No 36, 27/ 11/1912.

73 ÖS, HHStA, PA, XII, Konsulate Janina 11, aus Janina zu Außenministerium, No 8, 3/ 1/ 1913.

Around Louros river Muslim Albanian brigands burnt down Christian set-tlements.[74] Pressures on Christian populations forced locals to ask for protec-tion whereas many left to the mountains to form militias.[75] Rumors that the authorities were arming Muslim Albanians had panicked the Greek Consul who warned that the raids had isolated villages bringing them on the verge of starvation.[76] Greek foreign minister Koromilas complained to the representa-tives of the Great Powers about brutalities of Albanian bands against Greek populations.[77]

Villages were burnt down by the retreating Ottomans so that to deprive the opponent from safe shelter, recruits, and supplies.[78] The occupants with the pretext of the locals being hostile ripped off villages. The town of Konitsa, for instance became the base of Djavit Pasha who was feeding his 8,000 troops by plundering nearby Christian villages igniting a reign of terror.[79] Not surprisingly, Christian bands were behaving in a similar fashion feeding this spiral of violence. The Greek Avant garde was comprised by irregulars who committed brutalities and confronted the Ottoman army and volunteer Muslim units.[80] Various bands were active in villages and towns throughout Zagori and Janina. Christian populations seemed to cooperate, some times out of fear, and some other out of self-interest. Guerillas and villagers commit-ted atrocities against Ottoman soldiers and unarmed Muslim populations. For example, a band led by a chieftain named Krommidas arrived in the village of Podrogjani and burned the local notable, Eyeb Pasha and all of his servants and valuable belongings. Afterwards, the bands taking advantage of the vil-lagers' despair converted protection into a racket. In a neighboring village to Podrogjani, Greek bands demanded a statement of loyalty from notables to provide protection. This statement was obviously accompanied by a series of prerogatives such as access to supplies and food. Greek regular and guerilla

74 Efimerida Estia, 14/12/1912.
75 IAYE, 1912,34, 6, apo Marouli pros Ypourgeio Exoterikon, No 30456, 27/9/1912.
76 IAYE, 1912,34, 6, apo Proxeneio Ioanninon pros Ypourgeio Exoterikon, No 30853, 30/9/1912.
77 ÖS, HHStA, PA, XII, Bericht des k. und k. Legation sekretars Bilinski aus Janina, No 92, 11/12/1912.
78 AMM, Archeio Panagioti Dagkli, F. 30, Ekthesi Pepragmenon ypo aneksartitou Miktoy apospasmatos Ant. Pyrovolikoy Antonioy Ippiti kata tin ekstrateia 1912–1913, pp. 38, 42, 49.
79 GAK, Archeio Varda, apo Sideri pros Varda, No 178, 6/2/1913.
80 ÖS, HHStA, PA, XII, Konsulate Janina 11, aus Janina zu Außenministerium, No 45, 30/1/ 1913.

fighters behaved similarly against Orthodox Christian Vlach populations.[81] Agents were sent to Vlach settlements in the area of Zagori and Konitsa to supervise the actions of potential agitators who belonged to the "romanian faction". These people closely cooperated with the police and sent detailed reports back to Athens.[82] The Vlachs, as I discussed in previous chapter, were an ethnic group "suspicious" due to activities that advocated the Romanian national movement. Control of these settlements was crucial in order to shrink the supply bases of the Ottomans and Muslim Albanians. This carrot and stick tactic was an effective method of coercion combining intimidation and assurances for protection.

Nevertheless, predatory attitudes and every day necessities were not the sole driving reasons for the escalation of violence. Equally important was the psychological factor. As Sonke Neitzel and Harald Welzer argued in their book "Soldaten", the constant exercise of violence modified combat rules extending boundaries of what can be considered permissible.[83] This framework I believe is not only suitable for the regular army but also for irregulars that were exposed to war violence. Colonel Ippitis who was transferred from Grevena reported that the battle weary irregular units were more prone to commit atrocious acts. In order to prevent these attitudes he gave orders to irregulars to camp outside urban centers while officers were responsible for security precautions. The prefect of Corfu was equally concerned by the presence of irregulars Christians and Muslims alike. Approximately 6,000 refugees and guerillas were gathered in the port of the island generating pressing issues on public safety.[84] To deal with that he suggested the immediate ban of transportation of refugees and guerillas. Particularly under threat were Albanian and Cham villages on the coastal areas while Christian and Muslim Cham notables pledged for protection.[85] Cooperation of Muslims Chams was essential for the

---

81   ÖS, HHStA, PA, XII, 386, Turkei XLV/3 aus Janina zu Außenministerium No 89, 17/11/ 1912.

82   IAYE, 1913,1 4, apo proxeneio Ioaninnon pros Ypourgeio Exoterikon, No 15973, 20/5/ 1913.

83   Sonke Neitzel-Harald Welzer, *Soldaten. On Fighting, Killing and Dying. The Secret Second World War Tapes of German POWs* (New York: Simon & Schuster, 2013), 75.

84   IAYE, 1913, 13, 10, apo Nomarchi Kerkyras pros Ypourgeio Exoterikon, No 1873, 16/1/ 1913.

85   IAYE, 1913, 13, 10, apo Nomarchi Kerkyras pros Ypourgeio Exoterikon, No 5595, 8/2/ 1913.

pacification of a contested area inhabited predominantly by non-Christians.[86] Grievances had been already expressed by local Cham populations who suffered many civilian casualties.[87] After the surrender of Paramithia on February 23, 1913 Cham notables, including Muslims, handed over weapons and promised to assist in the disarmament of villages. In return the authorities provided assurances for protection and equality. This was something directed not only to Muslims, but also to Christian units in order to instill a sense of security leading to many arrests.[88]

Inevitably, violent outbreaks were not avoided in the capital of the vilayet. Janina was a city inhabited by 22,000 people in total: 14,000 Greek Orthodox, 7,000 Muslim Albanians, and 1,000 Jews. During the siege some Albanian bands, possibly deserters, rushed into the bazaar and plundered several shops. The Greek population panicked and some crowds started a protest by declaring them: "down with our enemies", "down with Albanians", and "you are still the Turkish dog". The last characterization denoted certain perceptions referring to long standing views of Albanians as the loyal "watchdogs" of the Porte in the Western Balkans which yet overlooked recent tensions due to the suppression of Albanian revolts. The capture of the city by the Greek army was accompanied by plundering mainly by irregular groups that had infiltrated. Muslim and Jewish quarters were attacked and many people were dragged to the streets after houses searches, allegedly for weapons. Turkish and Albanian notables sought for shelter in the Austrian Consulate.[89] The entrance of the Crown Prince took place in tandem with abuses of non-Christians with the pretext to disarm suspicious locals. The city's Mosque and

---

86 ÖS, HHStA, PA, XII, 386, Turkei XLV/3, aus Janina zu Außenministerium No 89, 17/11/1912, 54–59.

87 IAYE, 1913, 13, 5, 27/5/1913.

88 Chams were targeted also because some of them collaborated with Muslim Albanian bands and in the Second Balkan War tried to reinforce the provisional Government in Vlorë by sailing to the port of Corfu leading Greek authorities to impose restrictions to sailors in the island. IAYE, 1913,14,1, apo Ioannina pros Ypourgeio Exoterikon, No 18086, 17/6/1913.

89 Greek authorities condemned the role of the Austrian Consul who was accused as being essentially the military commander visiting the front line and encouraging the Ottoman soldiers, ÖS, HHStA, PA, XII, Konsulate Janina 11, aus Delvino zu Außenministerium, 14/1/1913.

the Ottoman library were destroyed with some units of the regular army took part.[90]

After the fall of Janina, in the city of Vlorë, a provisional Albanian Government was formed. The remnants of the Ottoman army and Albanian units headed to the northern parts of the vilayet signaling the end of the first phase of the battle over Epirus.[91] The Greek army after emerging victorious was gradually transferred to Macedonia to deal with Bulgaria. Still, the war was far from over. In the spring of 1913 the so called "Northern Epirus Struggle" erupted opening a new chapter in the history of ethnic symbiosis in the region.

The Northern Epirus/Southern Albania Question

The story of Northern Epirus or Southern Albania is an omitted topic of a rather complex regional crisis. Relevant studies primarily focused on diplomatic aspects adopting a top down view neglecting any grassroot agency.[92] Some other works use nationalism as an analytical framework overlooking certain socio-economic parameters.[93] This part of the western Balkans serves as a great example to grasp how certain historical events were appropriated ex post facto into state narratives. The struggle for the northern parts of the Janina vilayet entailed typical controversies related to historical, ethnographic, and socio-economic debates with respect to the issues of ethnicity and identity. As I present, the locals in 1913, in Northern Epirus/Southern Albania did not have a uniform response and their motivations were not only driven by nationalist agendas. Likewise, the original planning of Athens included an attempt to incorporate Muslim-Albanians into the Greek state implying more inclusive forms of nationhood.

90 ÖS, HHStA, PA, XII, 385, Turkei XLV/3, Aus Bericht des Militarattaches in Athen, No 200/14, 14/2/1913.

91 ÖS, HHStA, PA, XII, Konsulate Janina 11, aus Janina zu Außenministerium, No 12, 11/3/ 1913.

92 See for example: Vasil Kondis, *Greece and Albania, 1908–1914* (Thessaloniki: Institute for Balkan Studies, 1976); Miranda Vickers, *The Albanians. A Modern History* (London: IB Tauris, 2014).

93 Stavro Skendi, *The Albanian National Awakening, 1878–1912* (Princeton: Princeton University Press, 1967); Konstantinos Vakalopoulos, *Istoria tis Ipirou* (Thessaloniki: Stamoulis, 2012).

Everything started when the Greek High Command sent the experienced officer Spyridon Spyromilios in Himarë, a coastal city 73 km south of Vlorë to prepare the ground for the invasion of the Greek army. Spyromilios was another example of a valuable agent that offered his services to the national cause. A native from the same city, he received military training in Old Greece and got his baptism of fire in the 1897 war as volunteer. Afterwards he became a gendarmerie officer and served as guerilla fighter in Macedonia with the code name "captain Bouas". Along with the Head of the Chief of Staff Panagioti Dagli, they founded the Epirote Society and partook in the Goudi Movement in 1909.[94] In October 1912 he was sent to Corfu having been assigned very important tasks. That was to organize volunteer units comprised of natives from northern Epirus and to find common ground with Muslim Albanian Beys for potential cooperation and inclusion to the Greek Kingdom. On November 3, his group which was reinforced by 200 Cretans boarded on a ship and sailed to Himarë.[95]

The complex reality that Spyromilios had to deal with included challenges and dilemmas as in other parts of Rumeli due to the outbreak of war. Vasilios Melas, a Greek officer, who witnessed the events, left some interesting recollections in that regard. According to his diary, many wealthy Muslims were not in favour of the creation of an Albanian state being afraid of heavy taxation and confiscation of properties.[96] Important figures such as the Toptanis from Durrës and the Vrionis from Fier withdrew their forces in the winter of 1912 and did not comply with the Provisional Government.[97] Some Souliot clans treated with hostility any regime change and advocated the preservation of the existing structures wanting to safeguard their prerogatives.[98]

Resistance to centralization attempts was a common phenomenon in the Balkans in the nineteenth century. The old elites that had been vital parts

---

94 The Goudi Movement (August 1909) was a military pronunciamento by the officers of the army who had formed the group called the Military League. The main demands of the League concerned the influence of the Crown Prince in the Army, the corruption of the old political elite, and the need for reforms. Eventually the attempt was successful and paved the way for the triumph of Eleutherios Venizelos in the upcoming elections signalling a new period for the history of Modern Greece. Konstantinos Tsatsos, ed., *Istoria tou Ellinikou Ethnous* (Athens: Ekdotike Athinon, 1977), 87.

95 GES, *Epitomi Istoria*, 151–152.

96 IEE, Archeio Vaseliou Mich. Mela, Diary, 29/6/1913.

97 Krisztián Csaplár-Degovics, "The Policy of the Provisional Government of Vlora between December 1912 and April 1913", *Journal of Balkan and Black Sea Studies* 2, no. 3 (2019): 99.

98 IEE, Archeio Mela, 10/7/1913.

for the struggle for national emancipation were also the forces that resisted modernization and radical changes in the socio-economic status.[99] Similar tendencies were present in the Tosk population in the city of Vlorë leading the Austrian Consul to express very critical views stating that: "The South Albanian people that until recently acclaimed patriotic credentials, during the war they seem unwilling to prove that with actions and only care about the fate of Vlorë."[100] Lack of patriotism yet might be a misleading interpretation. The different faces of locality reflected an ongoing process of negotiation in places where non solidified nationalist projects overlapped with the imperial reality.

Responses varied and depended on local dynamics and group interests. Georgios Christakis Zographos, an experienced diplomat and former foreign minister with origins from Gjirokaster who became the General Governor of Epirus in 1914, chose for this delicate job a person with local clout, a former Ottoman MP named Shourla who had ties with Muslim Beys.[101] Foreign Minister Koromilas in coordination with the Commissioning Governor of Tepeleni tried to side with some prominent Albanian Beys providing assurances for the granting of civil liberties in exchange to expel representatives that served Austrian and Italian interests.[102] Koromilas in his correspondence made it clear that in order to appease prominent notables he was willing to provide financial compensation.[103] This tactic seemed to pay off in some occasions. For instance, a Muslim priest from the district of Vlorë informed, that he was ready to return to Gjirokaster to work with Greek authorities with the premise that he would be financially assisted with the amount of 60,000 drachmas for the damages that suffered during the war, something that Koromilas agreed.[104] Another suggestion was to appoint in Muslim villages civil servants accustomed to local traditions,[105] while Greek consular

---

99 The most typical example was the assassination of the first Greek Governor, Ioanni Kapodistria in 1831 by a member of the prominent Mavromichalis family from Morea.

100 ÖS, HHStA, PA, XII, Konsulate Janina 11, aus Vlorë zu Außenministerium, No 52, 18/11/1912.

101 AMM, Archeio Dagkli, apo Geniko Dioikiti Ipirou pros Ypourgeio Exoterikon, No 138, 1/5/1913.

102 AMM, Archeio Dagkli, apo Koromila pros Archigeio Ipirou, No 8796, 1/5/1913.

103 AMM, Archeio Dagkli, apo Ypourgeio Exoterikon pros Geniko Dioikiti Ipirou, No 240, 14/5/1913.

104 AMM, Archeio Dagkli, apo Ypourgeio Exoterikon pros Geniko Dioikiti Ipirou, No 262.

105 AMM, Archeio Panagioti Dagkli, F. 33, apo Geniko Dioikiti Ipirou pros Ypourgeio Exoterikon, No 193.

authorities underlined the need to print pamphlets in Albanian language to reduce the fears of locals.[106]

The attempt to appease reactions of locals was directly related to the impact of the presence of irregular forces. Spyromilios reported that 800 people and seven prosperous villages in Himarë had been impoverished and conveyed an urgent message for supplies in order not to jeopardize local support and loose legitimization.[107] Humane behaviour constituted a key element to keep civilians disciplined. Harsh occupation, not proper alimentation, and persecutions were causes for drastic reactions from the bottom-up. Civilians after the wars, as it was the case in WWI in the Polish-Romanian border in 1918, had certain expectations regarding legal security; measures such as the continuation of requisitions after the end of hostilities was considered as a wartime practise in peace.[108] Spyromilios was concerned also from rumors that Ismail Kemal was recruiting local people for militias. The experienced officer knew that he would not be able to control the areas between Himarë, Tepelenë, and Tragjasi because Kemal's men with were well acquainted with the locals. The fears of Spyromiliou were not unfounded. Some villages despite their initial neutral benevolent to the Greek army soon raised the Albanian flag and volunteered to Kemal's militias.[109] Meanwhile, a tense situation existed in Tepelenë, when after the arrival of Isa Boletini an anti-Greek riot was organized. The appearance of Boletini exacerbated fears because he was one of the most effective commanders that the Albanian movement had at its disposal.[110]

Already activities of Albanian activists and people that did not embrace the Greek cause had worried Athens. Since the outbreak of war many Albanian reservists of the Ottoman army from the areas of Delvinë, Gjirokaster, and Vlorë refused to go to Janina.[111] Tensions were increasing also because some Muslim-Albanians were repatriating from Istanbul prompting a tighter control of travel documents into the Greek zone.[112] In spring 1913, a certain

---

106 IAYE, 1913,14,1, apo Ioannina pros Ypourgeio Exoterikon, No 16413, 25/5/1913.

107 IAYE, 1913,79,4, apo Spyromilio pros Ypourgiko Sumvoulio, 7/1/1913.

108 Elisabeth Haid, "Robbery and Murder": Conflicts at the Polish-Romanian Border in the Aftermath of the War, in: Pudłocki-Ruszała, Postwar Continuity and New Challenges in Central Europe, 227.

109 IAYE, 1912,22, 1, apo Kerkyra pros Ypourgeio Exoterikon, No 8504, 20/3/1913.

110 IAYE, 1913,14,1, apo Ioannina pros Ypourgeio Exoterikon, No 16413, 25/5/1913.

111 IAYE, 1912,34, 6, apo Spyromilio pros Ypourgeio Exoterikon, No 30780, 10/10/1912.

112 IAYE, 1913,22,5, apo Dioikitiko Epitropo Koritsas pros Ypourgeio Exoterikon, No 158, 12/6/1913.

American missionary named Kennedy was about to start touring areas under the Greek zone propagating against Athens. The Consulate of Korçë was particularly anxious not to allow Kennedy to promote the Austrian and Italian agenda due to rumors about a potential referendum.[113] Missionaries have had a long standing impact on Albanian speaking lands in the late Ottoman era. Ottoman-Albanian-Greek relations were shaped not only by a competition among the Orthodox and the Protestant Church, but also by a "nationally defined difference" which was related to a vision of some Albanian-Christian workers that envisaged a protestant independent Albania.[114]

As the clouds of the Second Balkan War were gathering, the situation was becoming even trickier. Bulgaria tried to side with Albanianists by employing anti-Greek and anti-Serbian sentiments while IMRO chieftains appeared in Epirus and Kosovo. The Greek foreign ministry suggested the formation of local militias to counterbalance a potential invasion by Albanian units.[115] Two arrested Italians, a journalist and an officer, disclosed information about the formation of four bands in Gjirokaster aimed to conduct subversive activities against the Greek military while Bulgarian bands arrived to assist Javit Pasha and the remnants of his army.[116] This seemingly tactical convergence as I discussed in previous section was the fruit of an existential fear that prevailed in Bulgarian and Albanian circles. Decisions makers in Sofia heavily relied on insurgency activities in case of an interallied war. The vilayets of Manastir and Janina were ideal in that regard. The overall plan was to set ablaze the Greek and Serbian zones of occupation in order to assist the offensive of the Bulgarian army in Macedonia. This mobility did not go unnoticed leading to a series of initiatives. Zographos urged the Greek government to allocate weapons to the local population[117] and obstruct Albanians to move in different districts.[118]

This unstable climate brought to the surface once again the need to side with local notables. There were already considerations to endorse economically

113 IAYE, 1912,34, 6, apo proxeneio Koritsas pros Ypourgeio Exoterikon, No 11246, 8/4/1913.

114 Nevila Pahumi, Constructing Difference: American Protistantism, Christian Workers, and Albanian-Greek Relations in Late Ottoman Europe, *Journal of Modern Greek Studies* 36, no. 2 (2018): 293–327.

115 IAYE, 1913,22,5, apo Dioikitiko Epitropo Koritsas pros Ypourgeio Exoterikon, No 143, 18/6/1913.

116 IAYE, 1913,14,1, apo Ioannina pros Ypourgeio Exoterikon, No 17538, 21/6/1913.

117 IAYE, 1913,14,1, apo Ioannina pros Ypourgeio Exoterikon, No 19567, 3/7/1913.

118 IAYE, 1913,14,1, apo Ioannina pros Ypourgeio Exoterikon, No 19567, 20/6/1913.

Beys to instigate revolts so that to destabilize the Albanian movement from within.[119] Zographos in particular asked a donation to be allocated to Muslims to attract Bektashi supporters[120] and went a step further by asking permission to form militias regardless of the outcome of negotiations with the Beys. The idea was to prepare the ground for a potential invasion of the Greek army and create a de facto situation for Athens to intervene.[121] Permission was soon granted by Koromila who issued orders to tighten control in Chameria due to disturbances caused by the local population.[122]

This recommendation signaled the first stages of the so called Northern Epirote Struggle which continued long after the end of the war and dominated relations between Greece and Albania for decades. On the eve of the Second Balkan War Spiromilios from his headquarters in Himarë sent a very detailed letter for the ongoing challenges and the ambiguous position of Athens. In a population that numbered 25,000, he stated, he has been struggling with 200 Cretans and a handful of volunteers to preserve order. Around 2,500 of the inhabitants perished from war while the Greek Government had sent only 40,000 drachmas and 1,700 bags of flower for feeding nearly 13,500 people. Nevertheless, his most utmost concern was related with some state officials from Corfu (who does not name) that had been creating impediments to his struggle. The island, according to Spriromilio, had become a nest for Albanianists who collaborate with local authorities asking for the surveillance of certain persons of Greek origin.[123] The key to success was to fulfill demands of Albanian Beys sooner rather than later and accelerate the appointments of officials sympathetic to the Greek cause.[124]

The emotional tone of Spiromilios denoted tensions. Operational issues were just the tip of the iceberg reflecting a deeper problem which was related to an antagonism among irredentist, official, and local networks.[125] General

119 AMM, Archeio Dagkli, apo Geniko Dioikiti Tepeleniou pros Geniko Dioikiti Ipirou, No 536, 22/6/1913.
120 IAYE, 1913,14,1, apo Ioannina pros Ypourgeio Exoterikon, No 17176, 6/6/1913.
121 AMM, Archeio Dagkli, apo Geniko Dioikiti Ipirou pros Ypourgeio Exoterikon, No 453, 14/6/1913.
122 AMM, Archeio Dagkli, apo Ypourgeio Exoterikon pros Geniko Dioikiti Ipirou, No 124, 18/6/1913.
123 AMM, Archeio Panagioti Dagkli, F. 33, apo Geniko Dioikiti Ipirou pros Ypourgeio Exoterikon, 1/6/1913.
124 AMM, Archeio Panagioti Dagkli, F. 33, apo Geniko Dioikiti Ipirou pros Ypourgeio Exoterikon, No 43158, 30/4/1913.
125 AMM, Archeio Panagioti Dagkli, F. 33, apo Kapetan Tsakra pros Archigo Geniko Epiteleiou, 7/3/1913.

Dagklis from the Chief of Staff, a person well acquainted with the latter from the Epirote Society, accused him of reviving "obsolete feudal structures" disregarding any military and political hierarchy.[126] Obviously Dagklis by using the term feudal did not imply the term *per se* but something rather different that can be interpreted in a binary way. The first is to see it as an attempt of Spiromilios to establish a regime to serve personal aspirations, as it was the appointment of local notables under his control and his suggestion to persecute officials in Corfu. Another interpretation might perceive his actions as more pragmatic considering him as the native operative who was aware of the importance to side with local networks and accommodate conflicting interests.

Spiromilios was eventually replaced to appease Italy and avoid further implications. Already the Italian press was mobilized against Greek interests and a newspaper based in Rome was reporting horrendous experience of Muslims who left Vlorë and Gjirokaster.[127] This came as a response to a detailed list of atrocities committed by Muslim Albanian irregulars provided to the Great Powers by the Greek Foreign Ministry.[128] When the war was over the Northern Epirus Struggle was about to begin. Zographos took the reins from Spiromilio and instigated a counter insurgency campaign that lasted until February, 1914 when the dispute was settled temporarily by the Protocol of Florence.

The northern Epirus/Southern Albania experience resembled socio economic fermentations similar to Western Thrace making it relevant in conclusion to draw some parallels with the Republic of Giumiurdzhina. Both attempts constituted reactions to new border demarcations and involved a variety of protagonists such as paramilitaries, state agents, and most importantly the locals. Shady actors such as Spiromilios and Suleiman Askeri shared a lot in common. Both men had local roots and received education and training elsewhere. They had also obtained valuable experience in guerilla warfare from their service in Ottoman Macedonia and Libya respectively. In the wars of 1912–3 they championed independent movements and managed to mobilize the locals in defiance of ratified peace treaties. The fact that the Northern Epirote Movement was much more enduring than the Thracian can

---

126 Panagiotis Dagklis, *Anamniseis, Eggrafa, Allilografia* (Athens, 1965), 72.

127 AMM, Archeio Dagkli, apo Ypourgeio Exoterikon pros Geniko Dioikiti Ipirou, No 872, 30/7/1913.

128 AMM, Archeio Panagioti Dagkli, apo Foresti pros Geniko Dioikiti Ipirou, No 805, 22/7/1913.

be partially explained by the weakness of the newborn Albanian state and the fractions within its leadership.

Yet, these political experiments can be considered neither as continuations of the empire, nor nation states. The movements in Epirus and Thrace incorporated people that shared a common living space and originated from a diverse religious and ethnic background. This is not to say however that a bucolic utopia materialized in these places. Tensions and violence between Muslims and Christians left their imprint and legacy intensely in the region for many years. Although the rupture of war destabilized the structures of these communities it did not dismantle them entirely. The death blow constituted the implementation of assimilation policies by Albania, Greece, Turkey, Bulgaria, and Serbia, in a process rather not effortless and time consuming.

CONCLUSIONS

The Balkan Wars inherited a notorious legacy to the states of the peninsula. As Maria Todorova argued, the term *balkanism* originated this period and generated a negative connotation which stigmatized the region for decades.[1] The human toll of the wars was also tremendous. The Carnegie Endowment for International Peace, an American nongovernmental organization, put together an international mission to observe the conduct of war. The findings of the Commission confirmed stereotypes associated with the Balkans warning Western public opinion for the horrors of modern warfare. The irony was that a year later the countries that were shocked by Balkan savagery resorted to same violent practices in a war that lasted for over four years. This report nevertheless has been utilized repeatedly by scholars, politicians, and journalists as a valid source creating a lot of misconceptions. While its importance as a historical document is undeniable, its validity as a testimony is highly doubtful. The intellectuals that edited this volume conveyed their own views which were shaped by a combination of biased perceptions and political priorities.[2] Thankfully we are long past these views and recent historiographical production has made significant steps in that regard.

1 Todorova, *Imagining the Balkans*, 3.
2 Frances Trix, "Peace-Mongering in 1913: The Carnegie International Commission of Inquiry and Its Report on the Balkan Wars", *First World War Studies* 5, no. 2 (2014): 147–162.

A second thing that has troubled relevant literature was whether the wars of 1912–3 constituted a prelude to the First World War and the beginning of an era of mass killings and genocide in the Ottoman Empire. In fact, both approaches have valid points. The military technology which was tested in the Balkan Wars was imported by major European Empires who sent military observers to record their effectiveness. On the other hand, the Balkan Wars inaugurated an era of mass violence in the wider Near East that that lasted until the signing of the Treaty of Lausanne in 1923.[3] However, these approaches are not beyond criticism. Modern technology was largely used in the Balkans but the regular armies were assisted by traditional irregular fighters. To quote King Constantine, the *romeikos* type of war infused different traditions of warfare combining old bandits with conscript armies. Moreover, by perceiving the Balkan Wars as a starting point for a regional event, meaning the bloody collapse of the Ottoman Empire, not only we adopt a teleological view of events but we also detach the causal link of Balkan Wars from the Greater War of 1912–1923.

As I suggested in the introduction, the Balkan Wars were indeed a prelude for the Great War but for rather different reasons. In other words there is continuity, but without teleology. This episode, which was an inner part of WWI in East Central Europe, was a story about imperial aftershocks, porous borderlands, rise of warlords, communal violence, and emergence of new states. The new element of the Balkan Wars regarding the conduct was that systematically regular armies assisted by irregulars were mobilized for an expansive campaign and waged a war against the local populations. While the usage of irregulars was by no means something new for the tradition in the peninsula, it was the first time that this type of warfare was combined with modern technology and the effectiveness of the state machinery leading to ethnic cleansing and deportations.

The multiple nuances of paramilitarism constitute a crucial compotent to deepen our understanding for the war decade of 1912–1923. Some historians rightfully argued that paramilitarism in East Central Europe and the Balkans did not share same roots. While for East Central Europe it was a phenomenon associated with WWI and the challenges of demobilization, for the Balkans represented a deeply embedded tradition cultivated in a specific

3 Murat ÖNSOY- Ayşe Ömür ATMACA, "The Shaping of the Young Turk Ideology in the Balkan Trauma and Its Reflection on the CUP Policy towards the Ottoman Middle East", *SUTAD, Bahar*, 39 (2016): 71–87.

socio-economic framework.[4] Despite their different origins, however, the para-militaries of the Greater War were still part and parcel of the same story. The comitadjis, chetniks, and scouts of the Balkans started the wars in 1912 while their "peers" took the baton and continued after the armistice in 1918. While the Balkan states after 1913 managed partially to restrain irregular activities for a short period and monopolize violence, this problem surfaced once again when the peninsula was involved to the Great War. Thus, in order to scrutinize the transnational dimension of paramilitarism and enrich views that perceived this issue as a regional peculiarity, I suggest to examine that as an inherently connected phenomenon with imperial borderlands. Paramilitary violence in Eastern Europe was characterized by a combination of pragmatism, possession of arms, and a sense of superiority and it was no different for the Balkan case.[5] This phenomenon, in the different political setting of the interwar, provided opportunities to many political actors and contributed to the rise of authoritarianism and totalitarianism.

On the other hand, the Balkan Wars alone could not have initiated a process of ethnic cleansing and genocide in Anatolia. The collapse of the Ottoman Empire was not inevitable or self-evident in 1913. It was WWI and its long duration that accelerated dangerous dynamics and transferred violent practices from the Balkans to Asia Minor's mainland. The traumatic memories of the refugees from Rumeli indisputably played an important role for the radicalization from the bottom up, but this element only cannot tell us the whole story. This culture of violence was also linked with practices that the Ottoman state had been exercising against its ethnic-groups since the late Hamidian era. The challenges of mobilization and the power vacuum that had been created by the war in certain parts of the empire intensified the breach between local societies who victimized each other in a struggle for survival.[6] In that sense, the Balkans resembled Anatolia as a micrograph. Regular Ottoman army units aided by numerous paramilitaries clashed with rival bands, the Russian army, and refugees in a Hobbesian type of war. However, these events were primarily sparked by spasmodic reactions of the CUP due to the participation of the empire in a global conflict.

---

4 John Paul Newman, "The Origins, Attributes, and Legacies of Paramilitary Violence in the Balkans", in War in Peace: Paramilitary Violence in Europe After the Great War, ed. Robert Gerwarth and John Horne (Oxford: Oxford University Press, 2012), 145–146.

5 Böhler, Civil War in Central Europe, 146.

6 I use this concept from: Hans-Lukas Kieser, "From 'Patriotism' to Mass Murder: Dr. Mehmed Reşid (1873–1919)," in A Question of Genocide, ed. Naimark, 126–148.

Similarly no one could have ever predicted the levels of violence in East-Central Europe in WWI. While violent practices against civilians occurred in the Western front I assert that there was a crucial difference. The German army waged a war against non-combatants in Belgium driven mainly by practical necessities and an obsession from the Franco-Prussian War detonating an action-reaction process. One the other hand, the shared borderlands of the Tsarist, the Hapsburg, and the German Empires followed different paths. In the aftermath of war the western borders of the former German Empire did not face paramilitarism and state defiance. It was actually within the former imperial zones that took place what historian Robert Gerwarth called as the Central European counter-revolution.[7]

This point leads to the next and most crucial conclusion of this book. As I presented, by and large, the occupation policies of the Balkan states did not significantly differ from those implemented by the continental empires in East-Central Europe. Deportations, forced assimilation, and economic exploitation were applied massively during the Great War.[8] Yet, regional variations existed even within the same territory. Therefore, the suggestion is to think of the dynamics of violence as the product of an equation. In that case, the denominator is the applied state policies and the numerator is the diverse historical backgrounds.

An alternative way to tackle with violence as a combination of the historical background and the dynamics of the occupation could be shown by the events that transpired in different areas in the Balkans throughout the war. As we came across, the locals by no means remained passive and were involved in numerous ways. From the Northern Epirote Movement to the insurgency of Bekir, and from the Tikves uprising to the Republic of Giumiurdzhina segments of the native population assisted attempts that opposed new occupation regimes and ratified peace treaties. What is important to keep in mind is that these political experiments were not exceptional. British officials suggested analogous solutions for Balkan Muslims after 1913, while after the end of WWI places in the Middle East took similar initiatives as a reaction to the mandates. Perhaps a transnational approach of these movements might be

---

7 Robert Gerwarth, "The Central European Counter-Revolution: Paramilitary Violence in Germany, Austria and Hungary after the Great War", *Past & Present* 200, no. 1 (August 2008): 175–209.

8 Terry Martin, "The Origins of Soviet Ethnic Cleansing", *Journal of Modern History* 70, no. 4 (2018): 818.

able to shed some new light to a forgotten link of the transition from Empires to nation states and broaden our scope of analysis.[9]

Parts of Macedonia and Thrace, on the other hand, became zones of ethnic cleansing. The occupation and interaction with the locals combined with a troubled past sparked fatal dynamics. The Bulgarian army upon retreat targeted enemy aliens. The Greek and the Serbian followed suit. The Ottomans behaved similarly when they evacuated Macedonia and recaptured Eastern Thrace. The Greek, Serbian, and Ottoman reaction in the Second Balkan War was linked to state policies but also driven by revenge motivations from incidents that took place during the undeclared war. For Bulgaria there was an additional factor connected to the fear of encirclement. Many contemporaries considered this country as the "Prussia of the Balkans" due to its military strength. In that sense a given parallel existed with imperial Germany because both countries since unification had been preoccupied with the existential fear of being isolated. This scenario materialized in the summer of 1913 for Bulgaria prompting a violent reaction that fed a vicious cycle.

A different view of the same issue from the bottom up presents the connection of ethnic cleansing with inner-communal violence. Violence between communities was a by-product of war and ethnic cleansing, composed by two crucial elements. The first concerned prewar relations and the second was the opportunities and challenges of war. Although these notions of violence cannot be described strictly as a civil war because it involved different ethnoreligious groups, the assumption yet is not irrelevant. Hundreds of villages in Rumeli inhabited by Muslims and Christians of various doctrines had developed intimate relations. These relations, whether hostile or friendly, quite often were motivators determining certain behaviours during the war. Political scientist Stathis Kalyvas maintains that one of the reasons that render civil wars more violent is that they provide opportunities for indirect participation and violence sometimes could be: "a reflection and not a transgression of neighborliness."[10] Hence, so as to understand deeper the mechanisms of inner communal violence, we need to identify in some occasions dynamics of a civil strife. Otherwise it is impossible to explain this type violence in mixed areas. Bekir's village is a perfect example in that regard: a place populated by Greek speaking Muslims and Christians that inflicted violent to each other, detonated by war and recent symbiotic memories. The same goes for villages that

---

9 Emily Greble, *Muslims and the Making of Modern Europe*, 81.
10 Kalyvas, *The Logic of Violence*, 14, 332.

switched from the Patriarchate to the Exarchy and vice versa. There is already literature discussing this issue in the context of the late Ottoman Macedonia and WWI and I suggest to incorporate this problematic to the Balkan Wars.[11]

Last but not least, I shall conclude by arguing that the Balkan Wars of 1912–3, despite their tremendous levels of violence, did not have a genocidal intent. Forced assimilation was part of the agenda and in many occasions the civil and military authorities deliberately targeted certain groups on the grounds of ethnicity and religion. Yet, the Greek state actively pursued the assistance of Muslims in Southern Albania and Macedonia, while Bulgarians cooperated with Muslim Albanians in the Serbian zone of occupation. Likewise Serbians equipped Muslim militias to confront the IMRO in the summer of 1913. The ultimate goal of the belligerents was to displace populations that were considered hostile and not to physically annihilate them. Civilians that evacuated swiftly avoided the wrath of the Balkan armies and paramilitaries, while thousands of people survived the war in new borders becoming an object of negotiation in bilateral agreements for population exchange.[12]

On the other hand, ethnic cleansing practices characterized these wars. Destruction of enemy villages, intimidation, murdering of civilians as well as resettlement of refugees went hand in hand with other forms of violence related to the conduct of war. This laboratory in turn created new "technologies of violence" and a knowhow that would be applied later on against "foreigners". The interwar period and the establishment of Treaties for minority protection by the League of Nations shifted the dynamics. The once ethnicgroups of the empire were converted into national minorities and were placed at the epicenter of a new form of rivalry between the Balkan states. Still, the homogenizing attempts were only partially successful in the aftermath. The presence of concrete ethno-religious minorities was intense until 1923 and even afterwards.

That was the ending point of these wars and this was one of the main reasons that drove my attempt to integrate this story into the Greater War. What started as a regional affair in 1912 was gradually transformed by the colossal wave of WWI. The Great War, in which the Balkans belonged, became a testing ground for state practices that could not have been exercised in

11 Tasos Kostopoulos, «La guerre civile macédonienne de 1903–1908 et ses représentations dans l'historiographie nationale grecque », *Cahiers balkaniques*, 38–39 (2011): 213–226.

12 Alexander Pallis, "Racial Migrations in the Balkans during the Years 1912–1924." *The Geographical Journal* 66, no. 4 (1925): 315–31.

peacetime.[13] Without this precondition probably the Balkan conflicts would have been limited within the confines of the Ottoman Empire. Nevertheless, history went to the opposite direction and sealed the fate of old Empires that dominated East Central Europe and paved the way for new nation states. The main difference of these newborn political entities with the Balkan counter-parts was that the latter preceded imperial collapse while the former came into being because of it. Ultimately, these different historical trajectories converged in 1923 and generated the fragile geopolitical landscape of the interwar years.

---

13 Theodora Dragostinova, "Continuity vs. Radical Break: National Homogenization Campaigns in the Greek-Bulgarian Borderlands before and after the Balkan Wars", *Journal of Genocide Research* 18, no. 4 (2016): 414.

BIBLIOGRAPHY

Archives

Greece

- Elliniko Istoriko kai Logotechniko Archeio, Greek Historical and Literally Archive.
- Gennadios Vivliothiki Archeio, American School of Classical Studies, Athens.
- Genika Archeia tou Kratous: Archeio Tsondou Varda, Central State Archives.
- Geniko Epiteleio Stratou/Dieuthinsi Istorias Stratou, Army History Directory.
- Istoriko Archeio Ypourgeiou Exoterikon, Historical Archive of the Ministry of Foreign Affairs.
- ~~Istoriko Archeio Mouseiou Benaki, Historical Archive of Benaki~~ Museum.
- Istoriki kai Ethnologiki Etaireia, Historical and Ethnological Society.

Bulgaria

- Central State Archive (Tsentralen Dûrzhaven Arhiv), Sofia.
- Central Military Archive (Tsentralen Voenen Arhiv), Veliko Tûrnovo.

- National Library Sofia.
- Naoutsen Archiv, Balgarskata Akademiya na Naoukite, Bulgarian Academy of Sciences.

Austria

- Österreichisches Haus-Hof und Staatsarchiv (ÖS, HHStA).

The United Kingdom

- The National Archives (Kew), Foreign Office.

Primary Published and Secondary Sources

Aarbake, Vemund. "The Report of Petâr Chaulev to Prime Minister Vasil Radoslavov about the Situation in Western Thrace in February 1914." *Balkan Studies* 49 (2014).

———. *Ethnic Rivalry and the Quest for Macedonia, 1870–1913.* Boulder: Eastern European Monographs, 2003.

Adanir, Fikret. Die Makedonische Frage. Ihre Entstehung und Entwicklung bis 1908. Wiesbaden: Franz Steiner Verlag, 1979.

Adjemian, Boris et Mikaël Nichanian. "*Rethinking* the "Hamidian massacres": the issue of the precedent." *Études arméniennes contemporaines* 10 (2018).

Agelopoulos, Georgios. "Perceptions, Construction, and Definition of Greek National Identity in Late Nineteenth–Early Twentieth Century Macedonia." *Balkan Studies*, 36(2).

Ahmad, Feroz. *The Young Turks: The Committee of Union and Progress in Turkish Politics, 1908–1914.* Oxford: Clarendon Press, 1969.

Anastasopoulos, Nikolaos, *I Listeia sto Elliniko Kratos. Mesa 19ou aiona—arches 20ou.* Athens: Estia, 2018.

Anastasopoulos, Vasileios, *Bizani, 1913–1913.* Athens: Gnomon, 2012.

Anscombe, Frederick. "The Balkan Revolutionary Age." *The Journal of Modern History* 84, no. 3 (2012).

Army History Directorate, GES/DIS. *Epitomi Istoria ton Valkanikon Polemon.* Athens: GES, 1987.

Arslan, Ali. "Greek-Vlach konflict in Macedonia." *Études balkaniques* no. 2 (2003).

———. "The Vlach Issue During the Late Ottoman Period and the Emergence of the Vlach Community (Millet)." *Études balkaniques,* 4.

Bakalov, Georgi, Christo Matanov, Plamen Mitev, Ivan Iltsev, and Roumiana Marinova. *Istoria tis Boulgarias,* Translated by Georgios Christidis. Thessaloniki: Epikentro, 2015.

Balamaci, Nickolas. "Can the Vlachs Write Their Own History?" *Journal of Hellenic Diaspora* 17, no. 1 (1991).

Balcells, Laia. "Rivalry and Revenge: Violence against Civilians in Conventional Civil Wars." *International Studies Quarterly*, 54 (2010).

Balkelis, Tomas. *War, Revolution, and Nation-Making in Lithuania, 1914–1923*. Oxford: Oxford University Press: 2018.

Baltsiotis, Lambros. "The Muslim Chams of Northwestern Greece." *European Journal of Turkish Studies* [Online], 12 (2011).

Bartov, Omer. *Soldiers, Nazis, and War in the Third Reich*. Oxford: Oxford University Press, 1992.

Bartov, Omer and Eric D. Weitz, eds. *Shatterzone of Empires: Coexistence and Violence in the German, Habsburg, Russian and Ottoman Borderlands*. Bloominghton: Indiana University Press, 2013.

Bataković, Dušan T. "A Balkan-Style French Revolution? The Serbian Uprising in European Perspective." *Balkanica*, XXXVI (2005).

———. "Serbia, the Serbo-Albanian Conflict and the First Balkan War." *Balkanica* (2014): 45.

Bayraktar, Uğur. "Reconsidering Local versus Central: Empire, Notables, and Employment in Ottoman Albania and Kurdistan, 1835–1878." *International Journal of Middle East Studies* 52, no. 4 (2020).

Bechev, Dimitar. *Historical Dictionary of the Republic of Macedonia*. Maryland: Scarecrow Press, 2009.

Bego, Fabio. "Beyond the Albanian–Slav Divide: Political Cooperation and National Identities in the Balkans at the Turn of the Twentieth Century." *East European Politics and Societies*, 34, no. 1 (2020).

Bergholz, Max, "Sudden Nationhood: The Microdynamics of Intercommunal Relations in Bosnia Herzegovina after World War II." *The American Historical Review* 118, no. 3 (June 2013).

———. *Violence as a Generative Force: Identity, Nationalism, and Memory in a Balkan Community*. Ithaca, NY: Cornell University Press, 2016.

Bernard, Cheryl. "Rape as Terror: The Case of Bosnia." *Terrorism and Political Violence* 6, no. 1 (1994).

Biondich, Mark. *The Balkans: Revolution, War, and Political Violence Since 1878*. Oxford: Oxford University Press, 2011.

Bischof, Gynter, ed. *Austrian Foreign Policy in Historical Context*. UK: Transaction, 2006.

Bjelajac, Mile. "The Austro-Hungarian Creation of a 'humanitarian' Pretext for the Planned Invasion of Serbia in 1912–1913: Facts and Counter-Facts", *Balcanica*, no. 50 (2019).

Blumi Isa. "Teaching Loyalty in the Late Ottoman Balkans: Educational Reform in the Vilayets of Manastir and Yanya, 1878–1912." *Comparative Studies of South Asia, Africa and the Middle East* 21, no. 1 (2001).

———. "Contesting the Edges of the Ottoman Empire: Rethinking Ethnic and Sectarian Boundaries in the Malësore, 1878–1912." *International Journal of Middle East Studies* 35 (2003).

———. *Reinstating the Ottomans*. London: Palgrave, 2011.

Böhler, Jochen. *Civil War in Central Europe, 1918–1921: The Reconstruction of Poland*. Oxford: Oxford University Press, 2018.

Böhler, Jochen, Wlodzimierz Borodziej and Joachim von Puttkamer, eds. *Legacies of Violence: Eastern Europe's First World War.* Oldenburg: Degruyter, 2014.

Bouhey, Vivien. "*Anarchist Terrorism in Fin-de-Siècle France and its Borderlands.*" Oxford Handbooks Online (February 2014), accesed October 2020.

Boyar, Ebru, *Ottomans, Turks and the Balkans: Empire Lost, Relations Altered.* London: I.B. Tauris, 2007.

Brailsford, Henry Noël. *Macedonia: Its Races and Their Future.* Metheun, 1906.

Bramsen, Isabel. How Violence Breeds Violence: Micro-Dynamics and Reciprocity of Violent Interaction in the Arab Uprisings. *International Journal of Conflict and Violence* 11, (2017).

Bridge, Roy. *From Sadowa to Sarajevo, The Foreign Policy of Austia-Hungary.* London: Routledge, 1972.

Brisku, Adrian. "Renegotiating the Empire, Forging the Nation-State: The Albanian Case through the Political Economic Thought of Ismail Qemali, Fan Noli, and Luigj Gurakuqi, c. 1890–1920s." *Nationalities Papers* 48, no. 1 (2020).

Brooks, Julian. *Managing Macedonia: British Statecraft, Intervention, and 'Proto-peacekeeping' in Ottoman Macedonia, 1902–1905.* Unpublished PhD Thesis, Simon Fraser University, 2014.

Brown, Keith. *Loyal Unto Death: Trust and Terror in Revolutionary Macedonia.* Bloomington: Indiana University Press, 2013.

Brunnbauer, Ulf. "Families and Mountains in the Balkans." *The History of the Family* 7, no. 3 (2002).

Buschoten, Riki Van. *Anapoda Chronia: Syllogiki Mnimi kai Istoria sto Ziaka Grevenon.* Athens: Prethron, 1997.

Campos, Michelle. *Ottoman Brothers. Muslims, Christians, and Jews in Early Twentieth-Century Palestine.* Stanford: Stanford University Press, 2010.

Carabott, Philip, ed. *Greek Society in the Making, 1863–1913: Realities, Symbols and Visions.* Brookfield, Vt.: Variorum, 1997.

Carmichael, Cathie. *Ethnic Cleansing in the Balkans. Nationalism and the Destruction of Tradition.* London: Routledge, 2003.

Cassavetti, Demetrius-John. *Hellas and the Balkan Wars.* London: Fisher, 1914.

Cetinkaya, Dogan. "Atrocity, Propaganda and the Nationalization of the Masses in the Ottoman Empire during the Balkan Wars (1912–13)." *International Journal of Middle East Studies,* 46 (2014).

———. *The Young Turks and the Boycott Movement: Nationalism, Protest and the Working Classes in the Formation of Modern Turkey.* London and New York: I.B. Tauris, 2014.

Cevik, Zeki. "The Policies that Bulgarian Government Implemented on the Turkish Population during the Balkan Wars." In *Recent Advances in Social Sciences,* edited by Recep Efe, Irina Koleva, and Münir Öztürk. Cambridge: Cambridge Scholars Publishing, 2019.

Charters, Erica, Eve Rosenhaft, and Hannah Smith, eds. *Civilians and War in Europe 1618–1815.* Liverpool: Liverpool University Press, 2012.

Chatzopoulos, Dimitrios. *Oi Garivaldinoi sti Machi tou Driskou.* Athens: Fexis, 1914.

Chekalarov, Vasil. *Dnevnik, 1901–1903.* Sofia: Sineva, 2001.

Chokova, Polina. "The Activities of Nevrokop Bishopric in the Period of the Wars 1912–1919." *Istoritseski Pregled,* 1–2.

Christodoulou, Christos. *Oi Treis Tafes tou Chasan Tachsin Pasa*. Thessaloniki: Epikentro, 2012.

Clark, Christopher. *The Sleepwalkers: How Europe Went to War in 1914*. London: Penguin, 2013.

Clayer. *Nathalie, Oi Aparches tou Albanikou Ethnikismou trsnl. Andreas Sideris*. Ioannina: Isnaphi, 2009.

Clayer, Nathalie, Hannes Grandits, and Robert Pichler, eds. *Conflicting Loyalties in the Balkans. The Great Powers, the Ottoman Empire and Nation Building*. London: IB Tauris, 2011.

———. ", Religious Pluralism in the Balkans in the Late Ottoman Era." In *Imperial Lineage and legacies in the Eastern Mediterranean*, edited by Rhoads Murphey, 105–107. London: Routledge, 2017.

Cohen, Deborah and Maura O'Connor, eds. *Comparison and History: Europe in Cross-National Perspective*. New York–London: Routledge, 2004.

Cohen, Julia Phillips. *Becoming Ottomans: Sephardi Jews and Imperial Citizenship in the Modern Era*. Oxford: Oxford University Press, 2014.

Crampton, Richard J. *A Concise History of Bulgaria*. Cambridge: Cambridge University Press, 2005.

Dabove, Juan Pablo. "Paramilitarism and Banditry." *The Global South* 12, no. 2 (2018).

Dakin, Douglas. *The Greek Struggle in Macedonia*, 1897–1913. Thessaloniki: Institute for Balkan Studies, 1966.

———. *I Enopoiesi tis Elladas*, 1770–1923. Translated by Xanthopoulos Athanasios. Athens: Morfotiko Idruma Ethnikis Trapezis, 2012.

Daskalov, Roumen. *The Making of a Nation in the Balkans: Historiography of the Bulgarian Revival*. Budapest and New York: Central European University Press, 2005.

Davaris, Nikolaos. *Imerologio Stratiotou Dimitriou Davari*. Athens, 2003.

Dedijer, Vladimir. *The Road to Sarajevo*. London: Macgibon, 1966.

Degovics, Krisztián Csaplár. "The Policy of the Provisional Government of Vlora between December 1912 and April 1913." *Journal of Balkan and Black Sea Studies* 2, no. 3 (2019).

Demeter, Gabor. "The Behavior of Bulgaria towards Albania in 1912–1913." Proceedings, 26–27, November, 2012, Tirana (100 years of Albanian Independence).

Deringil, Selim. *Conversion and Apostasy in the Late Ottoman Empire* (Cambridge: Cambringe Univeristy Press, 2012).

Despot, Igor. *The Balkan Wars in the Eyes of the Warring Parties: Perceptions* and Interpretations. Bloomingtthon: IUniverse, 2012.

Dimevski, Slavko. *Makedonskoto Nacionalno Osvoboditelno Dvizhenie i Egzarhiyata (1893–1912)*. Skopje: Kultura, 1963.

Dimitrakopoulos, Anastasios. *O A Valkanikos Polemos mesa apo ta Archeia tis Istorikis Ypiresias tou Gallikou Nautikou*. Peireas: Nautiko Mouseio Ellados, 1996.

Dimitrov, Bozhidar. *Istinskata Istoriya na Balkanskata Voyna*. Sofia: 168 Tsasa, 2007.

Divani, Lena. *Ellada kai Meionotites: to Sistima Diethnous Prostasias tis Koinonias ton Ethnon*. Athens: Kastaniotis, 1999.

———. *I Edaphiki Oloklirosi tis Elladas*. Athens: Livanis, 2000.

Djordjevic, Dimitrije, Stephen Fischer-Galati. *The Balkan Revolutionary Tradition*. New York: Columbia University Press, 1981.

Dochev, Ivan. *Saga za Balkanskata voina. Dnevnik na sveshtenik*, ed. Lizbet Lyubenova. Sofia: Iztok-Zapad, 2012.

Dogiamas, Konstantinos. *Oi Makedonomachoi Adelfoi Dogiama*. Thessaloniki: University Studio Press, 2009.

Doumanis, Nicholas. *Before the Nation: Muslim Christian Coexistence and Its Destruction in late Ottoman Anatolia*. Oxford: Oxford University Press, 2013.

———. "Peasants into Nationals: Violence, War, and the Making of Turks and Greeks, 1912–1922." In *Totalitarian Dictatorship: New Histories*, edited by Baltieri D, Edele M, and Finaldi G. London: Routledge, 2014.

Doxiadis, Evdoxios. *State, Nationalism and the Jewish Communities of Modern Greece*. London: Bloomsbury, 2018.

Dragostinova, Theodora. *Between Two Motherlands. Nationality and Emigration among the Greeks of Bulgaria, 1900–1949*. Ithaca, NY: Cornell University Press, 2011.

———Yana Hashamova, eds. *Beyond the Moscue, Church the State. Alternative Narratives of the Nation in the Balkans*. Budapest: CEU Press, 2016.

———. "Continuity vs. Radical Break: National Homogenization Campaigns in the Greek-Bulgarian Borderlands before and after the Balkan Wars." *Journal of Genocide Research* 18, no. 4 (2016).

Duijzings, Ger. *Religion and the Politics of Identity in Kosovo*. New York: Columbia University Press, 2001.

Dumbalakov, Mikhail Atanasov. *Prez plamŭtsitie na zhivota i revoliutsiiata*. Sofia: Xydoznik, 1937.

Dwyer, Philip G. "'It Still Makes Me Shudder': Memories of Massacres and Atrocities during the Revolutionary and Napoleonic Wars." *War in History* 16, no. 4 (2009).

Ekmekcioglu, Lerna. "A Climate for Abduction, a Climate for Redemption: The Politics of Inclusion during and after the Armenian Genocide." *Comparative Studies in Society and History* 55, no. 3 (2013).

Eldarov, Svetlozar. *Varhovniyat Makedono-Odrinski Komitet i Makedono-Odrinskata Organizatciya v Balgariya*. Sofia: Ivray, 2003.

Elsie, Robert, Bejtullah D. Destani, and Rudina Jasini, eds. *The Cham Albanians of Greece. A Documentary History*. London: IB Tauris, 2013.

Embiricos, Léonidas. «Kilkis 1913: territoire, population et violence en Macédoine ». *European Journal of Turkish Studies* [Online] 12 (2011), Online since 21 May 2012.

Eminov, Ali. "Social Construction of Identities: Pomaks in Bulgaria." *Journal on Ethnopolitics and Minority Issues* 6, no. 2 (2007).

Erickson, Edward J. "From Kirkilisse to the Great Offensive Turkish Operational Encirclement Planning, 1912–22", *Middle Eastern Studies*, Vol. 40, No. 1 (2004).

Erickson, Edward J. and Mesut Uyar. *A Military History of the Ottomans: From Osman to Ataturk*. Praeger, 2009.

Esmer, Tolga U. "Economies of Violence. Banditry and Governance in the Ottoman Empire around 1800." *Past and Present*, 224 (2014).

Fahmy, Khaled. *All the Pasha's Men. Mehmed Ali, His Army and the Making of Modern Egypt*. Cambridge: Cambridge University Press, 1997.

Featherstone, Kevin, Dimitris Papadimitriou, Argyris Mamarelis, and Georgios Niarchos, eds. *The Last Ottomans: The Muslim Minority of Greece, 1940–1949*. London: Palgrave Macmillan, 2011.

Ferrara, Antonio, and Niccolò Pianciola. "The Dark Side of Connectedness: Forced Migrations and Mass Violence between the Late Tsarist and Ottoman Empires (1853–1920)." *Historical Research* 92, no. 257 (2019).

Fortna, Benjamin. *The Circassian: A Life of Eşref Bey, Late Ottoman Insurgent and Special Agent.* London: Hurst, 2017.

Frevert, Ute. *Europeanizing German History*. Eighteenth Annual Lecture of the GHI, November 18, 2004.

Friedman, Jim Hlavac-Victor. *On Macedonian Matters: From the Partition and Annexation of Macedonia in 1913 to the Present. A Collection of Essays on Language, Culture and History.* Munchen: Verlag Otto Sagner, 2015.

Gandev, Hristo. *Problemi na Bălgarsko văzrazhdane*. Sofia: BAN, 1976.

Gatrell, Peter, and Liubov Zhvanko, eds. *Europe on the Move: Refugees in the Era of the Great War*. Manchester: Manchester University Press, 2017.

Gawrych, George Walter. *The Crescent and the Eagle: Ottoman Rule, Islam and the Albanians, 1874–1913*. London: IB Tauris, 2006.

Gelber, N. M., D. Florentin, Adolf Friedmann and G. F. Török. "An Attempt to Internationalize Salonika, 1912–1913." *Jewish Social Studies* 17, no. 2 (1955).

Genov, Georgi. *Sa protivata na Balgarite ot Belomorska Makedonija Srešću Grackoto igo 1912–1916*. Sofia: Veritas et Pneuma, 1998.

Georgiev, Georgi N. The *Bulgarian National Liberation Movement in Macedonia (1893–1912)*. *Macedonian Review*, no. 17: 2.

———. "Backround and Planning of Bulgarian Albanian Uprising of 1913." In *100 Years from the Ohrid Debar Uprising*. Sofia, 2014.

Georgiev, Velichko and Staiko Trifonov, eds. *Pokrûstvaneto na bûlgarite Mohamedani, 1912–1913: Dokumenti*. Sofia: Academichno Izdatelstvo "MarinDrinov", 1995.

Geppert, William-Dominic and William Mulligan, eds. *The Wars Before the Great War*. Cambridge: Cambridge University Press, 2015.

Gerhard Haupt, Heinz and Jürgen Kocka, eds. *Comparative and Transnational History, Central European Approaches and New Perspectives*. New York, Oxford: Berghahn Books, 2009.

Gerlach, Christian. "Extremely Violent Societies: An Alternative to the Concept of Genocide." *Journal of Genocide Research* 8, no. 4 (2006).

Gerwarth, Robert. *The Vanquished: Why the First World War Failed to End, 1917–1923*. London: Penguin, 2016.

Gerwarth, Robert and John Horne, eds. *War in Peace: Paramilitary Violence in Europe After the Great War*. Oxford University Press, Oxford, 2012.

———. "Vectors of Violence: Paramilitarism in Europe after the Great War, 1917–1923." *The Journal of Modern History* 83, no. 3 (2011).

———. "The Central European Counter-Revolution: Paramilitary Violence in Germany, Austria and Hungary after the Great War." *Past & Present* 200, no. 1 (2008).

GES/DIS. *O Ellinikos Stratos kata tous Valkanikous Polemous*, Vol. I, Appendix. Athens, 1932.

Giannoulopoulos, Giannis. *I Eugenis mas Tiphlosis. Exoteriki Politiki kai Ethnika Themata apo tin Itta tou 1897 eos ti Mikrasiatiki Katastrophi*. Athens: Vivliorama, 2003.

Gingeras, Ryan *Sorrowful Sorrows*. Oxford: Oxford University Press, 2009.

———.. "Beyond Istanbul's 'Laz Underworld': Ottoman Paramilitarism and the Rise of Turkish Organized Crime, 1908–1950." *Contemporary European History* 19, no. 3 (2010).

———. "'Scores Dead in Smerdesh': Communal Violence and International Intrigue in Ottoman Macedonia." *Balkanistika* 25 (2012).

———. "The Internal Macedonian Revolutionary Organization: 'Oriental' Terrorism Counterinsurgency, and the End of the Ottoman Empire." In *The Oxford Handbook of the History of Terrorism*, edited by Carola Dietze and Claudia Verhoeven. Feb. 2014, https://doi.org/10.1093/oxfordhb/9780199858569.013.019.

———. *The Fall of the Sultanate: The Great War and the End of the Ottoman Empire 1908–1922*. Oxford: Oxford University Press, 2016.

Ginio, Eyal. "Mobilizing the Ottoman Nation during the Balkan Wars (1912–1913): Awakening from the Ottoman Dream." *War in History* 12, no. 2 (2005).

———. "Enduring the Shift from an Empire to Nation-State: The Case of the Jewish Community of Kavala during the First Balkan War." In *Jewish Communities between East and West*, edited by Anna Mahera and Leda Papastefanaki. Ioannina: Isnafi, 2016.

———. *The Ottoman Culture of Defeat*. Oxford: Oxford University Press, 2016.

Giza, Anthony. *Balkanskite Darzbavi i Makedonskiya Vapros*. Sofia: Macedonian Scientific Institute, 2001.

Glavinas, Giannis. "Oi Vallaades tou Voiou Kozanis 1912–1924 mesa apo tis ektheseis toy ypodoiekiti tis Eparxias." *Valkanika Symmeikta*, 12–13 (2001–2002).

———. *Oi Mousoulmanikoi Plithismoi stin Ellada*. Thessaloniki: Stamoulis, 2013.

Glenny, Misha. *The Balkans, 1804–2012: Nationalism, War and the Great Powers*. London: Penguin, 2001.

Golbasi, Edip. "The 1895–1896 Armenian Massacres in the Ottoman Eastern Provinces: A Prelude to Extermination or a Revolutionary Provocation?" *Papers of the Strassler Center for Holocaust and Genocide Studies* 25 (2015).

Gotzev, Dimitar. *Ideyata za Avtonomiya Kato Taktika v Programite na Natsionalnoosvoboditelnoto Dvizhenie V Makedoniya i Odrinsko 1893–1941*. Sofia: Universitetsko izdatelstvo "Sv. Kliment Ohridski", 1983.

Gounaris, Basil "Preachers of God and Martyrs of the Nation. The Politics of Murder in Ottoman Macedonia in the Early Twentieth Century." *Balkanologie* IX, no. 1–2 (2005): 31.

———. *Ta Valkania ton Ellinon. Apo to Diafotismo eos ton A' Pagkosmio Polemo*. Thessaloniki: Epikentro, 2007.

Greble, Emily. *Muslims and the Making of Modern Europe*. Oxford: Oxford University Press, 2021.

Grigor Suny, Ronald, Fatma Müge Göçek, and Norman M. Naimark, eds. *A Question of Genocide: Armenians and Turks at the End of the Ottoman Empire*. Oxford: Oxford University Press, 2011.

Gumz, Jonathan E. *The Resurrection and Collapse of Empire in Habsburg Serbia, 1914–1918*. Cambridge: Cambridge University Press, 2010.

Hasicalihoglu, Mehmet. *Die Jungtürken und die Mazedonische Frage (1890–1918)*. Munich: R. Oldenbourg, 2003.

———. "The Young Turk Revolution and the Negotiaton for the Solution of the Macedonian Question." *Turcica* 36, no. 4 (2004): 168–170.

Hagen, Mark von. *War in a European Borderland: Occupations and Occupation Plans in Galicia and Ukraine, 1914–1918*. University of Washington Press, 2007.

Haid, Elisabeth. "Galicia: A Bulwark against Russia? Propaganda and Violence in a Border Region During the First World War." *European Review of History: Revue européenne d'histoire* 24, no. 2 (2017).

Hakki Oztan, Ramazan. "Tools of Revolution: Global Military Surplus, Arms Dealers, and Smugglers in the Late Ottoman Balkans, 1878–1908." *Past & Present*, 237 (November 2017).

———. "Point of No Return? Prospects of Empire after the Ottoman Defeat in the Balkan Wars (1912–13)." *International Journal of Middle East Studies* 50, no. 1 (2018).

Hall, Richard C. *The Balkan Wars: Prelude to the First World War*. London: Routledge, 2000

———. "The Next War: The Influence of the Russo-Japanese War in Southeastern Europe and the Balkan Wars of 1912–1913." *The Journal of Slavic Military Studies* 17 (2004): 3.

———. *The Modern Balkans: A History*. London: Reaktion Books, 2011.

Hanioğlu, Şükrü. *Preparation for a Revolution: The Young Turks, 1902–1908*. New York: Oxford University Press, 2001.

Hasluck, Frederick W. *Christianity and Islam under the Sultans*. Oxford: Oxford Clarendon Press, 1929.

Hasluck, Margaret M. "The Basil-Cake of the Greek New Year." *Folklore* 38, no. 2 (1927).

Hayden, R. M., Erdemir, A., Tanyeri-Erdemir, T., Walker, T. D., Rangachari, D., Aguilar-Moreno, M., López-Hurtado, E., and Bakić-Hayden, M. *Antagonistic Tolerance: Competitive Sharing of Religious Sites and Spaces*. 1st ed. London: Routledge, 2016.

Heraclides, Alexis and Ada Dialla. *Humanitarian Intervention in the Long Nineteenth Century: Setting the Precedent*. Manchester: Manchester University Press, 2016.

Hewitson, Mark. "Princes' Wars, Wars of the People, or Total War? Mass Armies and the Question of a Military Revolution in Germany, 1792–1815." *War in History* 20, no. 4 (2013).

Hilmi Ozkan, Selim. "Arms Smuggling across Ottoman Borders in the Second Half of the Nineteenth Century." *Journal of Balkan and Near Eastern Studies* 18, no. 3 (2016).

Hobsbawm, Eric. *Bandits*. New York: Pantheon Books, 1981.

Hughes Mathew, Philpott W. J., eds. *Palgrave Advances in Modern Military History*. London: Palgrave Macmillan, 2006.

Hutchison, Thomas Setzer. *An American Soldier Under the Greek Flag at Bezanie: A Thrilling Story of the Siege of Bezanie' by the Greek Army, in Epirus, During the War in the Balkans*. Nashville, Tennessee: Greek-American Publishing Company, 1913.

Indos, Christos. *Valkanikoi Polemoi, 1912–1913. Ta Gegonota stin Periochi tou Dimou Paionias*. Thessaloniki: Kyriakidis, 2012.

Idrima Meleton tou Chersonisou tou Aimou. *O Makedonikos Agonas Apomnimoneumata*. Thessaloniki, 1984.

Ilchev, Ivan. *My Country-Right or Wrong! The Propaganda of the Balkan Countries in Europe and the US in 1821–1923* [in Greek]. Salonika: Epikentro Publications, 2011.

Jelavich, Barbara. *History of the Balkans*. Cambridge: Cambridge University Press, 1983.

Jentzsch, Corinna, Stathis N Kalyvas, and Livia Isabella Schubiger. "Militias in Civil War." *Journal of Conflict Resolution* 56, no. 5 (2015).

Kaliakatsos, Michalis. "Ion Dragoumis and 'Machiavelli': Armed Struggle, Propaganda, and Hellenization in Macedonia and Thrace, (1903–1908)." *Journal of Modern Greek Studies* 31, no. 1 (2013).

Kalinderis, Michalis. "Sumvoli eis tin Meleti tou Thematos ton Vallaadon." *Etaireia Makedonikon Spoudon* (1977).

Kalyvas, Stathis. *The Logic of Violence in Civil War*. Cambridge: Cambridge University Press, 2007.

Kann, Robert. *A History of the Habsburg Monarchy*. California: University of California Press, 1980.

Karakasidou Anastasia. *Fields of Wheat, Hills of Blood: Passages to Nationhood in Greek Macedonia, 1870–1990*. University of Chicago Press, 1997.

———. "Affections of a Greek Hero: Pavlos Melas and Heroic Representations in Greece." In *Balkan Identities: Nation and Memory*, edited by Maria Todorova. New York: NYU Press, 2004.

Karavas, Spyros. *Mistika kai Paramithia apo tin Istoria tis Makedonias*. Athens: Vivliorama, 2014.

Karavia Flora, Thaleia. *Endiposeis apo ton Polemo tou 1912–1913*. Athens: Idrima gia ton Koinovouleutismo kai tin Demokratia, 2012.

Karavitis, Ioannis. *O Valkanotourkikos Polemos*. Athens: Petsivas, 2001.

Karayanev, Atanas. Poslednite dni na Balgarskata targovska gimnaziya i zatochenie na o. Trikeri. Spomenat se sahranyava v Tsarkovno-istoricheskiya arhiven institut s inv. № 10847.

Katsiadakis, Helena. "The Balkan War's Experience: Undestanding the Enemy." In *War in the Balkans*, edited by Pettifer Buchanan.

Kauchev, Naoum. "Notes on Some Trends in Serbian and Greek Historiography of the First Balkan War." *Etudes Balkaniques*, 2 (2013).

Kayali, Hasan. "Elections and the Electoral Process in the Ottoman Empire, 1876–1919". *International Journal of Middle East Studies* 34, no. 27 (1995).

Kechriotis, Vangelis. "The Modernization of the Empire and Community Privileges. Greek Orthodox Responses to Young Turk Policies." In *The State and the Subaltern*, edited by Touraj Atabaki, 69–70. London: IB Tauris, 2007.

Kelaidi, Stavrou. *I Drasi ton Ethelondikon Somaton Kriton en Makedonia*. Athens, 1913.

Ketsemanian, Varak. "The Hunchakian Revolutionary Party and the Assassination Attempts Against Patriarch Khoren Ashekian and Maksudzade Simon Bey in 1894." *International Journal of Middle East Studies* 50, no. 4 (2018).

Kienzler, Hanna and Sula-Raxhimi. "Collective Memories and Legacies of Political Violence in the Balkans." *Nationalities Papers* 47, no. 2 (2019).

Kieser, Hans Lukas, Kerem Oktem, and Maurous Reinkowski, eds. *World War I and the End of the Ottomans. From the Balkan Wars to the Armenian Genocide*. London: IB Tauris, 2015.

Kitromilides, Paschalis M. "'Imagined Communities' and the Origins of the National Question in the Balkans." *European History Quarterly* 19, no. 2 (1989).

———. *Religion and Politics in the Orthodox World: The Ecumenical Patriarchate and the Challenges of Modernity*. London: Routledge, 2019.

Klein, Janet. *The Margins of Empire. Kurdish Militias in the Ottoman Tribal Zone*. Stanford: Stanford University Press, 2011.

Kolerovic, Ksenija. *The Vlachs and the Serbian Primary School (1878–1914): An Example of Serbian Nation-Building*. Unpublished PhD Thesis, University of Manchester, 2015.

Koliopoulos, John S. "*Brigands with a Cause: Brigandage and Irredentism in Modern Greece 1821–1912*." Oxford: Oxford University Press, 1987.

———. "Brigandage and Irredentism in Modern Greece." *European History Quarterly* 19, no. 2 (1989).

Konortas, Paraskevas Benjamin C. Fortna, Stefanos Katsikas, and Dimitris Kamouzis, eds. *State-Nationalisms in the Ottoman Empire, Greece and Turkey: Orthodox and Muslims*. London: Routledge, 2012.

Konstantinova, Yura. "Followers of the Patriarchate and Slavic Speakings at the End of the Nineteenth and the Beginning of Twentieth Century." *Études Balkaniques* 3.

———. "The Race for Salonica." *Études balkaniques* 49, no. 2 (2013).

———. *Balgari i Gartsi v Borba za Osmanskoto Nasledstvo*. Sofia: Faber, 2014.

Kontogiorgi, Elizabeth, *Population Exchange in Greek Macedonia: The Rural Settlement of Refugees 1922–1930*. Oxford: Oxford Historical Monographs, Clarendon Press, 2006.

Kosev, Cyril, *100 Godinata ot Podviga na Balgarite v Valkanskata Voina* (Sofia: Voenno izdatelstvo, 1986).

Kostopoloulos, Tasos. *Polemos kai Ethnokatharsi. I xechasmeni plevra mias dekaetous eksormisis*. Athens: Vivliorama, 2008.

———. « La guerre civile macédonienne de 1903–1908 et ses représentations dans l'historiographie nationale grecque ». *Cahiers Balkaniques*, 38–39 (2011).

———. "*Land to the Tiller*. On the Neglected Agrarian Component of the Macedonian Revolutionary Movement, 1893–1912." *Turkish Historical Review*, 7 (2016).

Kotzagiorgis, Phokion. "Conversion to Islam in Ottoman Rural Societies: The Cases of Vallahades and Pomaks." In *Ottoman Rural Societies and Economies*, edited by Elias Kolovos, 133–135. Crete University Press: Rethymno, 2015.

Koutsoukos, Vasilis. *Apo tin Autokratoria sto Ethnos Kratos. Opseis tis Chorikis Ensomatosis tis Thrakis*. University of Crete: Unpublished PhD Thesis, 2012.

Kovachev, Stiliyan. *Zapiski na Generala ot Pehotata*. Sofia: 1992.

Kramer, Alan. *Dynamic of Destruction. Culture and Mass Killing in the First World War*. Oxford: Oxford University Press, 2007.

Kuehn, Thomas. *Empire, Islam, and Politics of Difference. Ottoman Rule in Yemen, 1849–1919*. Leiden: Brill, 2011.

Kühn Thomas, ed. "Borderlands of the Ottoman Empire in the Nineteenth and Early Twentieth Centuies." *The MIT Electronic Journal of Middle East Studies*, 3 (Spring 2003).

Kurt, Ümit. "Theatres of Violence on the Ottoman Periphery: Exploring the Local Roots of Genocidal Policies in Antep." *Journal of Genocide Research* 20, no. 3 (2018).

Leustean, Lucian N., ed. *Orthodox Christianity and Nationalism in Nineteenth-Century Southeastern Europe*. Fordham University Press: New York, 2014.

Liakos, Antonis. *O Ellinikos Eikostos Aionas*. Athens: Polis, 2019.

Lieberman, Benjamin. *Terrible Fate: Ethnic Cleansing in the Making of Modern Europe*. Maryland: Rowman and Littlefield, 2013.

Liulevicius, Vejas. *War Land on the Eastern Front: Culture, National Identity, and German Occupation in World War I*. Cambridge: Cambridge University Press, 2000.

Livanios, Dimitris. "Conquering the Souls: Nationalism and Greek Guerrilla Warfare in Ottoman Macedonia, 1904–1908." *Byzantine and Modern Greek Studies* 23 (1999).

Lohr, Eric. *Nationalizing the Russian Empire: The Campaign against Enemy Aliens during World War I*. Cambridge MA: Harvard University Press, 2003.

Lubanska, Magdalen. *Muslims and Christians in the Bulgarian Rhodopes. Studies on Religious (Anti) Syncretism*. Berlin, Boston: De Gruyter, 2015.

Majstorovic, Darko. "The 1913 Ottoman Military Campaign in Eastern Thrace: A Prelude to Genocide?" *Journal of Genocide Research* 21, no. 1 (2018).

Malecevic, Sinisa. *The Rise of Organized Brutality: A Historical Sociology of Violence*. Cambridge: Cambridge University Press, 2017.

Mann, Michael. *The Dark Side of Democracy: Explaining Ethnic Cleansing*. Cambridge: Cambridge University Press, 2005.

Marco-Mercedes Rodrigo, Joce. "Irregular War. Local Community and Intimate Violence in Spain (1939–1952). *European History Quarterly* 49, no. 2 (2019).

Markov, Georgi. *Bûlgarskoto Krushenie 1913*. Sofia: Bûlgarska Akademiya na Naukite, 1991.

Martin, Terry. "The Origins of Soviet Ethnic Cleansing." *Journal of Modern History* 70, no. 4 (2018).

Mayerhofer, Lisa. Making Friends And Foes: Occupiers and Occupied, in First World War Romania, 1916–1918." In *New Perspectives in First World War Studies. Series*, edited by Heather Jones, Jennifer O'Brien, Hristoph Schmidt-Supprian. Leiden: Brill, 2008.

Mazarakis, Ioannis. *Ta Ethelondika Somata ton Proskopon kata tous Valkanikous Polemous, 1912–1913*. Vol. 2. Athens: Deltion tis Istorikis kai Ethologikis Etaireias, 1989.

Mazarakis, Konstantinos Ainian. *Apo to Makedoniko Agona stous Valkanikous Polemous*. Athens: Ethniko Istoriko Mouseio, 2016.

Mazower, Mark. *The Balkans. A Short History*. New York: Modern Library, 2000.

———. "Review Essay Violence and the State in the Twentieth Century." *The American Historical Review* 107, no. 4 (2002): 1162.

———. *Salonica, City of Ghosts: Christians, Muslims and Jews 1430–1950*. London: Harper Perennial, 2004.

Megas, Giannis. *Oi Varkarides tis Thessalonikis. I Anarchiki Voulgariki omada kai oi Vombistikes Energeies tou 1903*. Athens: Troxalia, 1994.

Melas, Spyros. *I Epanastasi tou 1909*. Athens: To Vima Vivliothiki, 2009.

———. *Oi Polemoi tou 1912–1913*. Athens: Vlassis, 1972.

Methodieva, Milena B. *Between Empire and Nation. Muslim Reform in the Balkans*. California: Stanfrod University Press, 2020.

Michailidis, Iakovos-Konstantinos Papanikolaou. *Aphanois Gigeneis Makedonomachoi*. Thessaloniki: Etaireia Makedonikon Spoydon, 2008.

Mick, Hristoph. "Legality, Ethnicity and Violence in Austrian Galicia, 1890–1920." *European Review of History: Revue européenne d'histoire* 26, no. 5 (2019).

Miletic, Lyubomir. *Turkish Atrocities Committed against Thracian Bulgarians*. Sofia: Sofia Press, 1987.

Minov, Nikola. "The Vlachs and the IMRO." *Macedonian Historical Review*, УДК 94, 497.7:135.1.

Mishkova, Diana, ed. *We, the People: Politics of National Peculiarity in Southeastern Europe*. New York: Central European University Press, 2009.

Mojzes, Paul. *Balkan Genocides: Holocaust and Ethnic Cleansing in the Twentieth Century*. Maryland: Rowman & Littlefield Publishers, 2015.

Molho, Rena. *Oi Evraioi tis Thessalonikis. Mia idiaiteri koinotita*. Athens: Patakis, 2014.

Motta, Giuseppe. "The Fight for Balkan Latinity. The Vlachs until WWI." *Mediteranean Journal Social Sciences* 2, no. 3 (2011).

Mylonas, Georgios. *I Drasis ton Andartikon Somaton en Makedonia kata ton Ellinotourkiko Polemo*. Volos: Thessalia, 1913.

Mylonas, Harris. "Nation Building Policies in the Balkans: An Ottoman or Manufactured Legacy." *Nations and Nationalism*, 25, no. 3 (2019).

Myuhtar-May, Fatme. *Identity, Nationalism, and Cultural Heritage under Siege*. Leiden: Brill, 2014.

Naimark, Norman. *Fires of Hatred, Ethnic Cleansing in Twentieth-Century Europe*. Harvard: Harvard University Press, 2002.

Neitzel, Sonke and Harald Welzer. *Soldaten. On Fighting, Killing and Dying. The Secret Second World War Tapes of German POWs*. New York: Simon & Schuster, 2013.

Neuburger, Mary. Pomak Borderlands: Muslims on the Edge of Nations. *Nationalities Papers* 28, no. 1 (2000).

———. *The Orient Within*. Ithaka and London: Cornell University Press, 2004.

———. *Balkan Smoke: Tobacco and the Making of Modern Bulgaria*. Ithaca; London: Cornell University Press, 2013.

Nikolov, Stoyan. "Sadbata na Balgarite v Solun predi i po Vreme na Valkanskite Voini (1912–1913)." *Makedonski Pregled Makedonski Pregled*, 2 (2008).

Nikopoulos, Vangelis. *Grevena 1912–1940 Photographika Dokoumenta kai Tekmiria*.

Önsoy, Murat – Ayşe Ömür Atmaca. "The Shaping of the Young Turk Ideology in the Balkan Trauma and its Reflection on the CUP Policy towards the Ottoman Middle East." *SUTAD*, *Bahar*, 39 (2016).

Özbek, Nadir. "Policing the Countryside. Gendarmes of the Late Nineteenth Century Ottoman Empire." *International Journal of Middle East Studies* 40, no. 1 (2008).

Özdoğan, Mehmet. "Eastern Thrace: The Contact Zone Between Anatolia and the Balkans." In *The Oxford Handbook of Ancient Anatolia*, edited by Gregory McMahon-Sharon Steadman. Online Publication Date: Nov. 2012.

Pahumi, Nevila. "Constructing Difference: American Protestantism, Christian Workers, and Albanian-Greek Relations in Late Ottoman Europe." *Journal of Modern Greek Studies* 36, no. 2 (2018).

Pallis, Alexander. "Racial Migrations in the Balkans during the Years 1912–1924." *The Geographical Journal* 66, no. 4 (1925).

Pammakedonikos Syllogos. *Makedoniko Imerologio*. Athens: 1909.

Papadimitriou, Apostolos. *Selides Istorias ton Grevenon*. Grevena: Tsiartsianis, 2016.

Papadimitriou, Ioannis. *O Ethnomartys Mitropolitis Aimilianos*. Athens, 2011.

Papafloratos, Ioannis S. "The Italian Policy in Epirus (1861–1918)." *Balkan Studies*, 50 (2015).

Papageorgis, Kostis. *Ta Kapakia*. Athens: Kastaniotis (2009).

Papaioanou, Stefan. *Balkan Wars between the Lines. Violence and Civilians in Macedonia 1912–18*. Unpublished PhD Thesis, University of Maryland, 2012.

Pappas, Vasileios. *O Chalkidiotis Makedonomaxos Kapetan Giaglis. I Drasi tou Iroikou Enoplou Somatos tou sti Chalikidiki, Nigrita Serron kai Agio Oros*. Ierissos Chalkidikis, 2011.

Paraskevopoulos, Leonidas. *Valkanikoi Polemoi, 1912–1912. Epistoles pros ti Sizigo tou Koula*. Athens: Kastaniotis, 1998.

Peçe, Ugur. "The Conscription of Greek Ottomans into the Sultan's Army, 1908–1912." *International Journal of Middle East Studies* 52, no. 3 (2020).

Perry, Duncan M. *The Politics of Terror: The Macedonian Liberation Movements: 1893–1903*. Durham, N.C.: Duke University Press, 1988.

Pettifer, James and Tom Buchanan, eds. *War in the Balkans: Conflict and Diplomacy before World War I*. London: IB Tauris, 2016.

Petrov, Bisser-Svetlozar Eldarov. "Institutionalizing Memory: 100 Years Balkan War Studies in Bulgaria." *Etudes Balkaniques*, 2 (2013).

Philliou, Christine. *Biography of an Empire. Governing Ottomans in an Age of Revolution*. Berkeley: University of California Press, 2011.

Pippidi, Alina Mungiu and Van Meurs, eds. *Ottomans into Europeans: State and Institution Building in Southeastern Europe*. Hurst, London, 2010.

Ploumidis, Spyros, Nuances of Irredentism: The Epirote Society of Athens (1906–1912). *The Historical Review/La Revue Historique*, 8, 2012.

Popek, Krzysztof. "'A Body Without a Head'. The Elite of the Muslim Minority in the Bulgarian Lands at the Turn of the Twentieth Century." *Balcanica Posnaniensia. Acta et studia* (Poznań), t. 25 (2018).

———. "De-Ottomanisation of Land. Muslim Migrations and Ownership in the Bulgarian Countryside after 1878." *Zeszyty Naukowe Towarzystwa Doktorantów UJ Nauki Społeczne*, NR 24, no. 1 (2019).

Psilos, Christopher. *The Young Turk Revolution and the Macedonian Question*. Unpublished PhD Thesis, Leeds University, 2000.

Pudłocki, Tomasz and Kamil Ruszała, eds. *Postwar Continuity and New Challenges in Central Europe, 1918–1923: The War That Never Ended*. London: Routledge, 2021.

Raktivan, Constantinos. *Egrafa kai Simeioseis Apo ti Doiikisi tis Makedonias*. Thessaloniki, 1951.

Reynolds, Michael A. *Shattering Empires. The Clash and Collapse of the Ottoman and Russian Empires*. Cambridge: Cambridge University Press, 2011.

Riemann, Malte. "'As Old as War Itself?' Historicizing the Universal Mercenary." *Journal of Global Security Studies, Online Published*, February 2020, https://doi.org/10.1093/jogss/ogz069.

Ristovski, Blazhe. *Istoriya na Makedosnkata Natziya*. Skopje: MANU, 1999.

Robert, Elsie. *Historical Dictionary of Albanian History*. London: Tauris, 2012.

Rogan, Eugene. *I Ptosi ton Othomanon*. Translated by. Eleni Asteriou. Athens: Alexandreia, 2015.

Roussos, Nikolaos. "Charilaos Trikoupis and the Serbo-Greek Alliance of 1867." *Balkan Studies* 12, no. 1 (1971).

Rutar, Sabine and Katrin Boeckh, eds. *The Balkan Wars from Contemporary Perception to Historic Memory*. London: Palgrave, 2017.

———. *The Wars of Yesterday. The Balkan Wars and the Emergence of Modern Military Conflict, 1912–1913. Experience, Perception, Remembrance*. New York: Bergham Books, 2018.

Safi, Polat. "History in the Trench: The Ottoman Special Organization – Teşkilat-ı Mahsusa." *Middle Eastern Studies*, 48 (2012).

Sanborn, Joshua. "The Genesis of Russian Warlordism: Violence and Governance during the First World War and the Civil War." *Contemporary European History* 19, no. 3 (2010).

———. *Imperial Apocalypse. The Great War and the Destruction of the Russian Empire*. Oxford: Oxford University Press, 2014.

Šarenac, Danilo. "The Forgotten Losses. Serbian Casualties from the Balkan Wars 1913–1913." *Analele Universității Ovidius din Constanța-Seria Istorie*, no. 10–11 (2013).

Scheer, Tamara. "Denunciation and the Decline of the Habsburg Home Front During the First World War." *European Review of History: Revue européenne d'histoire*, 24 (2017).

Schick, Irvin Cemil, and Amila Buturovic, eds. *Women in the Ottoman Balkans: Gender, Culture and History*. London; New York: I.B. Tauris, 2007.

Schoenberg, Philip Ernest. "The Evolution of Transport in Turkey (Eastern Thrace and Asia minor) under Ottoman Rule, 1856–1918." *Middle Eastern Studies*, 13, no. 3 (1977).

Schwartz, Michael. "IV. Modernisierung durch Vertreibung: Der Balkan als europäischer Lernort für ethnische, Säuberungen." In *Ethnische „Säuberungen" in der Moderne*. Berlin, Boston: De Gruyter, 2013.

Scott, James C. *Weapons of the Weak: Everyday Forms of Peasant Resistance*. New Haven: Yale University Press, 1985.

Shopov, Atanas. Dnevnik, *Diplomaticheski Raporti i Pisma* [A *Diary, Diplomatic Reports, and Letters*], edited by Iliya Paskov. Sofia: Maked. nauchen inst, 1995.

Silyanov, Hristo. *Ot Vitosha do Gramos*. Sofia Izdanie na Kosturskoto blagotvoritelno bratstvo, 1920.

Skendi, Stavro. Crypto-Christianity in the Balkan Area under the Ottomans. *Slavic Review*, 2 (1967).

Skopetea, Elli. *To Protypo Vasileio kai i Megali Idea. Opseis tou Ethnikou Provlimatos stin Ellada*. Athens: Polytypo, 1988.

Sofoulis, Manolis. *Imerologio apo tous Valkanikous Polemous*. Athens: Grigoris, 2007.

Sotirović, Vladislav. *Serbia, Montenegro and the Albanian Question, 1878–1912: A Greater Albania between Balkan Nationalism & European Imperialism*. Saarbrucken: Lambert Academic Publishing, 2015.

Sphetas, Spiridon. "To Istoriko Plaisio ton Ellinoroumanikon Scheseon." *Makedonika* 33, no. 1 (2002).

———. *Ellino-Voulgarikes Anataraxeis 1881–1908. Anamesa ste Ritoriki tis Dimerous Synergasias kais tin Praktiki ton Ethnikon Andagonismon.* Thessaloniki: Epikentro, 2008.

Stainov, Gencho. *Pisma ot Odrin, 1912–1913. Pisma i snimki ot Balkanskata i Mezhdusayuznicheskata voini, nyakoi ot koito nepublikuvani dosega,* edited by Radina Nancheva. Sofia: Izd. atelie Ab, 2009.

Stamatopoulos, Dimitris, ed. *Balkan Nationalism(s) and the Ottoman Empire.* Vol. II. Istanbul: ISIS Press, 2015.

Stamenova, Svetlana. "The Specifics of Balkan Ethnic Identity Construction: Ethnicisation of Localities." *National Identities* 19, no. 3 (2017).

Stavrianos, Lefteris. *Balkan Federation. A History of the Movement toward Balkan Unity in Modern Times.* Northampton: Smith College, 1944.

Steed, Henry. *The Habsburg Monarchy.* London: Constable, 1914.

Stefanidis, Ioannis, Stathis Kalyvas, and Vasilis Gounaris, eds. *Anorthodoxoi Polemoi. Makedonia, Emphylios, Kypros.* Athens: Patakis, 2013.

Stoneman, Mark. "The Bavarian Army and French Civilians in the War of 1870–1871: A Cultural Interpretation." *War in History* 8, no. 3 (2001).

Stoyanoff, Stoyan. "Balgaromohamedanski Vapros po Vreme na Balkanskata Voina." In *80 Godini ot Valkansikte Voini.* Sofia, 1995.

Strezova, Aleka. "Bulgarian Commercial Agencies or Consulates in the Ottoman Empire Foundation, Development, Influence and Personnel (1896–1912)." *Historical Review*, 3.

Svirčević, Miroslav. "The New Territories of Serbia after the Balkan Wars of 1912–1913. The Establishment of the First Local Authorities." *Balcanica*, 44 (2013).

Svolopoulos, Konstantinos. *Elliniki Exoteriki Politiki, 1900–45* (Athens: Estia, 2008).

Tanvir Wasti, Syed. "The 1912–13 Balkan Wars and the Siege of Edirne." *Middle Eastern Studies* 40, no. 4 (2004).

Tasić, Dmitar. "Repeating Phenomenon: Balkan Wars and Irregulars." In *Les guerres balkaniques (1912–1913): Conflits, enjeux, memories,* edited by Catherine Horel. Bruxelles Peter Lang, 2014.

———. *Paramilitarism in the Balkans: Yugoslavia, Bulgaria, and Albania, 1917–1924.* Oxford: Oxford University Press, 2020.

Ther, Philipp. *The Dark Side of Nation State: Ethnic Cleansing in Modern Europe.* New York and Oxford: Berghahn Books, 2014.

Todorova, Maria. *Imagining the Balkans.* Oxford: Oxford University Press, 2009.

Trifonov, Staiko. *Trakiiā: Administrativna Uredba, Politicheski i Stopanski Zhivot, 1912–1915.* Trakiiskia Fondatsia Kapitan Petko Voivoda, 1992.

Trix, Frances. "Peace-Mongering in 1913: The Carnegie International Commission of Inquiry and Its Report on the Balkan Wars." *First World War Studies* 5, no. 2 (2014).

Trotski, Leon. *Ta Valkania kai oi Valkanikoi Polemoi.* Translated by Paraskevas Matalas. Athens: Themelio, 1993.

Tsourkas, Konstantinos and Stilpon Kuriakidis. "Tragoudia Valaadon." *Makedonika*, 2 (2017).

Turan, Ömer. "Pomaks, Their Past and Present." *Journal of Muslim Minority Affairs*, 19, no. 1 (1999).

Tutuncu, Mehmed. "Grebeneli Bekir Fikri Bey Albay Thomson'a Karşi 1914 Avlonya Olayı [Grebeneli Bekir Fikri Bey against Colonel Thomson: The Case of Vlorë 1914]". *Düşünce ve Tarih* 3, no. 31: 40, 42.

Tzanakaris, Vasilis. *O Kokkinos Soultanos. O Avdul Chamit kai i Agnosti Thessaloniki.* Thessaloniki: Metaixmio, 2011.

Uğur Ümit Üngör. "Mass Violence against Civilians During the Balkan Wars." In *The Wars before the Great War*, edited by Geppert and Mulligan.

———. *The Making of Modern Turkey: Nation and State in Eastern Anatolia, 1913–50.* Oxford: Oxford University Press, 2011.

———. "Rethinking the Violence of Pacification: State Formation and Bandits in Turkey, 1914–1937." *Comparative Studies in Society and History* 54, no. 4 (2012).

———. *Paramilitarism: Mass Violence in the Shadow of the State.* Oxford: Oxford University Press, 2020.

Vakalopoulos, Apostolos. *Istoria tis Makedonias, 1354–1833.* Institute for Balkan Studies: Thessaloniki, 1973.

———. *Istoria tis Meizonos Thrakis. Apo ton Othomanokratia mechri tis Meres mas.* Athena: Stamoulis, 2004.

Valkov, Martin. *The Internal Macedonian-Adrianople. Revolutionary Organization and the Idea for Autonomy for Macedonia, Adrianople and Thrace, 1893–1912.* Masters' Thesis, Budapest: Central European University, 2010.

Varvounis, Manolis. Historical and Ethnological Influences on the Traditional Civilization of Pomaks of the Greek Thrace. *Balcanica*, 34 (2003).

Vovchenko, Denis. *Containing Balkan Nationalism: Imperial Russia and Ottoman Christians, 1856–1914.* New York: Oxford University Press, 2016.

Vučetić, Biljana. "Some Considerations on the Emergence of the Serbian Chetnik Movement in Macedonia during the Last Period of Ottoman Rule." *Istoriski Zapiski Godina* LXXXVIII, no. 3–4 (2015).

Watson, Katherine D., ed. *Assaulting the Past: Violence and Civilization in Historical Context.* Newcastle: Cambridge Scholars Publishing, 2007.

Westerhoff, Christian. "'A kind of Siberia': German Labour and Occupation Policies in Poland and Lithuania during the First World War." *First World War Studies* 4, no. 1 (2013).

Wilkinson, Henry Robert. Maps and Politics: A Review of the Ethnographic Cartography of Macedonia. Liverpool: Liverpool University Press, 1951.

Wimmer, Andreas, Richard J. Goldstone, Donald L. Horowitz, Conrad J. Schetter, and Ulrike Joras. *Facing Ethnic Conflicts: Toward a New Realism.* Lanham: Rowman & Littlefield, 2004.

Winnifrith, Tom. *The Vlachs. The History of a Balkan People.* New York: St. Martin's. 1987.

Winter, Jay, ed. *The Cambridge History of the First World War*, 3 Vol. I. Cambridge University Press: Cambridge, 2013.

Winter, Jay. *The Day the Great War Ended, 24 July 1923: The Civilianization of War.* Oxford: Oxford University Press, 2022.

Yavuz Hakan and Hakan Erdagöz. "The Tragedy of the Ottomans: Muslims in the Balkans and Armenians in Anatolia." *Journal of Muslim Minority Affairs* 39, no. 3 (2019).

Yavuz Hakan and Isa Blumi, eds. *War and Nationalism The Balkan Wars, 1912–1913, and Their Sociopolitical Implications.* Utah: University of Utah Press, 2013.

Yavuz, M. Hakan and Ahmad, Feroz, eds. *War and Collapse. World War I and the Ottoman State.* Salt Lake City 2016: The University of Utah Press.

Yiğit, Yücel. The Teşkilat-ı-Mahsusa and World War I. *Middle East Critique* 23, no. 2 (2014).

Yosmaoğlu, Ipek. *Blood Ties: Religion, Violence and the Politics of Nationhood in Ottoman Macedonia.* Ithaca, NY: Cornell University Press, 2014.

Zelepos, Ioannis. "Redefining the 'Great Idea': The Impact of the Macedonian proxy war1904–1908 on the Formation of Athanasios Souliotis-Nikolaides 'Oriental Ideal'." *Neograeca Bohemica*, 15 (2015).

Zürcher, Erik Jan. "The Young Turks – Children of the Borderlands?" *International Journal of Turkish Studies* 9, no. 1–2 (2003).

———. "Macedonians in Anatolia: The Importance of the Macedonian Roots of the Unionists for their Policies in Anatolia after 1914." *Middle Eastern Studies* 50, no. 6 (2014).

———. "The Young Turk Revolution: Comparisons and Connections." *Middle Eastern Studies* (2019).

South-East European History

Mihai Dragnea, *Series Editor*

This series is published in conjunction with the Balkan History Association (BHA) and comprises original, high-quality disciplinary and interdisciplinary comparative study of South-East Europe from ancient to contemporary times. It welcomes submissions in various formats, including monographs, edited volumes, conference proceedings, and short form publications between 30,000 to 50,000 words (Peter Lang Prompts) on various sub-disciplines of history—political, cultural, military, economic, urban, literary, oral, or the history of science communication—art history, history of religions and archaeology.

Proposals should be sent to the series editor:

Mihai Dragnea (University of South-Eastern Norway)
mihaidragnea2018@gmail.com

To order books in this series, please contact our Customer Service Department:

peterlang@presswarehouse.com (within the U.S.)
orders@peterlang.com (outside the U.S.)

Or browse online by series at:

https://www.peterlang.com/series/seeh